Voice Secrets

Music Secrets for the Advanced Musician

Music Secrets for the Advanced Musician is designed for instrumentalists, singers, conductors, composers, and other instructors and professionals in music seeking a quick set of pointers to improve their work as performers and creators of music. Easy to use and intended for the advanced musician, contributions to **Music Secrets** fill a niche for those who have moved far beyond what beginners and intermediate practitioners need. It is the perfect resource for teaching students what they need to know in order to take that next step forward and for reinforcing a set of best practices among advanced and professional musicians.

Clarinet Secrets: 52 Performance Strategies for the Advanced Clarinetist, 2nd edition, by Michele Gingras, 2006

Saxophone Secrets: 60 Performance Strategies for the Advanced Saxophonist, by Tracy Lee Heavner, 2013

Oboe Secrets: 75 Performance Strategies for the Advanced Oboist and English Horn Player, by Jacqueline Leclair, 2013

Drum Kit Secrets: 52 Performance Strategies for the Advanced Drummer, by Matt Dean, 2014

Violin Secrets: 101 Strategies for the Advanced Violinist, by Jo Nardolillo, 2015

Voice Secrets: 100 Performance Strategies for the Advanced Singer, by Matthew Hoch and Linda Lister, 2016

Voice Secrets

100 Performance Strategies for the Advanced Singer

Matthew Hoch
Linda Lister

ROWMAN & LITTLEFIELD
Lanham • Boulder • New York • London

Published by Rowman & Littlefield
A wholly owned subsidiary of The Rowman & Littlefield Publishing Group, Inc.
4501 Forbes Boulevard, Suite 200, Lanham, Maryland 20706
www.rowman.com

Unit A, Whitacre Mews, 26-34 Stannary Street, London SE11 4AB

Copyright © 2016 by Matthew Hoch and Linda Lister

All images courtesy of the authors unless otherwise noted.

All rights reserved. No part of this book may be reproduced in any form or by any electronic or mechanical means, including information storage and retrieval systems, without written permission from the publisher, except by a reviewer who may quote passages in a review.

British Library Cataloguing in Publication Information Available

Library of Congress Cataloging-in-Publication Data

Names: Hoch, Matthew, 1975– | Lister, Linda.
Title: Voice secrets : 100 performance strategies for the advanced singer / Matthew Hoch, Linda Lister.
Description: Lanham, Maryland : Rowman & Littlefield, 2016. | Includes bibliographical references and index.
Identifiers: LCCN 2016009921 (print) | LCCN 2016011077 (ebook) | ISBN 9781442250253 (pbk. : alk. paper) | ISBN 9781442250260 (electronic)
Subjects: LCSH: Singing–Instruction and study. | Singing–Vocational guidance.
Classification: LCC MT820 .H7 2016 (print) | LCC MT820 (ebook) | DDC 783/.043–dc23 LC record available at http://lccn.loc.gov/2016009921

∞™ The paper used in this publication meets the minimum requirements of American National Standard for Information Sciences—Permanence of Paper for Printed Library Materials, ANSI/NISO Z39.48-1992.

Printed in the United States of America

To our students, past and present.

Contents

Foreword	xi
Preface	xiii
Acknowledgments	xv

1 Vocal Technique — 1
  Secret 1: Stand Up Straight! Posture and Alignment Awareness — 1
  Secret 2: Lean on Me—*Appoggio* and Breath Management — 5
  Secret 3: Wax On, Wax Off—Onset and Release — 7
  Secret 4: Ring and Rumble—Resonance — 8
  Secret 5: Riffs and Runs—Flexibility — 10
  Secret 6: Understand Registration—"Head" versus "Chest" Voice — 12
  Secret 7: Be Smooth—*Sempre Legato* — 16
  Secret 8: "Place" the Voice—What Does That Actually Mean? — 18
  Secret 9: Warm Up Enough (but Not Too Much) — 20
  Secret 10: Know What's Really Happening—Fact versus Fiction — 22
  Secret 11: Find Your *Fach*—Your Sound and Psyche — 23
  Secret 12: Shake It! Musings on Vibrato — 25
  Secret 13: Always Sing on Your Interest, Never Your Capital — 27
  Secret 14: Try and Trust—Finding the Right Teacher — 28

2 Musicianship — 31
  Secret 15: Connect to the Page—Score Study — 31
  Secret 16: Prioritize Rhythm—the Essence of Musicianship — 33
  Secret 17: Master Intervals and Scale Degrees — 35
  Secret 18: Intimately Know the Piano Accompaniment — 38
  Secret 19: Study the Orchestration—There Won't Be Trumpets
    (or Will There?) — 40
  Secret 20: Singing in Style—Cultural Context and Historical Traditions — 42

3 Vocal Health — 45

Secret 21: *Libiamo!* Water and Hydration — 45
Secret 22: Develop a Healthy Speaking Voice—Pitch and Breath — 47
Secret 23: Use Straw Phonation (and Other SOVT Exercises) — 49
Secret 24: Food as Fuel Not Fad—Diet Matters — 51
Secret 25: Exercise—Your Body Is Your Instrument — 52
Secret 26: Avoid Vocally Abusive (Loud) Environments—Can You Hear Me Now? — 53
Secret 27: Ahem! Avoid Clearing Your Throat—Try *Ujjayi* Breathing Instead — 55
Secret 28: Phlegm Is Not Your Friend (Coping Strategies) — 56
Secret 29: Combat Acid Reflux Disease (GERD and LPRD) — 57
Secret 30: Manage Your Medications—Balancing RX and OTC with TLC — 59
Secret 31: Embracing Bodywork—Yes, Everyone Is Doing Yoga — 61
Secret 32: How to Work with Metal in Your Mouth—the Joy of Braces — 63

4 Practice Strategies — 65

Secret 33: Regarding Vowels—the Rooms in Which Singers Live — 65
Secret 34: Regarding Consonants—the Doors That Propel Singers from Room to Room — 68
Secret 35: Be an Active Participant—Go to Your Lesson with a Plan — 70
Secret 36: Mirror, Mirror on the Wall—Using the Mirror as a Practice Tool — 72
Secret 37: Train Your Tongue—Freeing Codependent Articulators — 74
Secret 38: Johnny One Note—from Monotone to Legato — 75
Secret 39: Don't Listen to Yourself! (or Should You?) — 76
Secret 40: Use a Metronome—They Aren't Just for Instrumentalists — 78
Secret 41: Your Focus Needs More Focus—Practice Mindfulness — 80
Secret 42: Whose Line Is It Anyway? Tips for Memorization — 82
Secret 43: Get out of Your Head and into Your Body—Let's Get Physical — 84
Secret 44: Listen Intelligently to Great Recordings — 86
Secret 45: Viewer Be Wary—the Pleasures and Perils of YouTube — 88
Secret 46: Record Yourself—I Look and Sound like That? — 90
Secret 47: Do You Hear What I See? Using Spectrographic Analysis (VoceVista) — 92
Secret 48: Be Gleeful! Remember That You Love to Sing! (Just like the Kids on *Glee*!) — 95

5	**Language and Diction**	**97**
	Secret 49: Singing in English—American versus British Diction	97
	Secret 50: Embrace IPA—Singing in Foreign Languages	99
	Secret 51: *Si canta come si parla*—Singing in Italian	101
	Secret 52: *Singet nicht in Trauertönen*—Singing in German	103
	Secret 53: *Savoir faire*—Singing in French	105
	Secret 54: *Canto ergo sum*—Singing in Latin	107
	Secret 55: *Si puedes hablar, puedes cantar*—Singing in Spanish	109
	Secret 56: *Век живи́—век учи́сь*—Singing in Russian	111
	Secret 57: Explore Languages That Are Off the Beaten Path	113
	Secret 58: Know Your Translation Inside and Out	115
6	**Singing Classical Genres (and Singing Them Well)**	**117**
	Secret 59: Go beyond the Twenty-Four Hits—Using Italian *Arie Antiche* as Your Foundation	117
	Secret 60: Brits and Yanks—English and American Song	119
	Secret 61: *Lieder* of the Pack—German Art Song	121
	Secret 62: A Pretty Girl Is like a *Mélodie*—French Art Song	123
	Secret 63: Go beyond the Big Four—Art Songs in Other Languages	125
	Secret 64: Handling Recitative—Singing Oratorio	127
	Secret 65: *Vissi d'arte*—Singing Opera	129
	Secret 66: Utopia Unlimited—the Joys of Light Opera	132
	Secret 67: Collaborate with Other Musicians through Chamber Music	136
	Secret 68: Be HIP—Exploring Early Music	138
	Secret 69: Extend Your Technique—the World of Avant-Garde Music	140
	Secret 70: Approach Choral Music in a Healthy Way	142
7	**Singing CCM (Nonclassical) Styles**	**145**
	Secret 71: Understand Differences between Classical and CCM Styles	145
	Secret 72: Belting, Body Type, and Ballet—Musical Theatre	147
	Secret 73: Know Your Mic and Your Niche—Rock and Pop Music	149
	Secret 74: Be an Instrument of Inspiration—Gospel	151
	Secret 75: Standards, Structure, and Scatting—Jazz	153
	Secret 76: Share Your Struggles and Celebrations—Country Music	155
	Secret 77: Conquer the World—Global Music Styles	157
	Secret 78: Tag Along—Barbershop Harmony	159
	Secret 79: Be Cognizant of the Raw Facts of the Industry	161
8	**Stage Presence**	**163**
	Secret 80: Meditation Not Medication—Combating Performance Anxiety	163

Secret 81:	Sing from the Heart—Why Do You Sing?	165
Secret 82:	Gesticulate! Overcoming Fear of Gestures	167
Secret 83:	Express Yourself (Facially)—Somewhere between Botox and Overacting	169
Secret 84:	Open Up and Write It Down—Taking Stage Direction	171
Secret 85:	Interact with Your Partners Onstage—Safety and Chemistry	173

9 Business Tips — 175

Secret 86:	Don't Be a Diva—You're Not That Important	175
Secret 87:	Always Be Prepared (and Never Be Late)	177
Secret 88:	Cultivate an Important Relationship—Getting Along with Your Voice Teacher	179
Secret 89:	Be a Gracious Collaborator—Getting Along with Your Accompanist	181
Secret 90:	Serve the Production Not Yourself—Getting Along with Your Opera Director	183
Secret 91:	Watch and Follow—Getting Along with Conductors	185
Secret 92:	Find Your (Short-Term) Fit—Auditioning for Summer Programs	187
Secret 93:	Yes, You May Need Another Degree—Auditioning for Graduate School	189
Secret 94:	Competing without Defeating Yourself—Auditioning for Voice Competitions	191
Secret 95:	Represent Yourself Well on Paper—Spelling and Spacing Matter	193
Secret 96:	Have Good Communication Skills—Proofreading and Professionalism	195
Secret 97:	Manage Your Finances—How Not to Be a Starving Singer	197
Secret 98:	Professional Choral Singing Can Be Rewarding	200
Secret 99:	Stay in Touch with Your Art Form through Teaching	202
Secret 100:	Be Resourceful—Use Every Tool at Your Disposal	204

Epilogue	207
Anthologies	209
Professional Organizations for Singers	213
Bibliography	219
Index	253
About the Authors	263

Foreword

Have you ever wondered how Renée Fleming could spin those immaculate high notes so effortlessly or how Anna Netrebko can make you believe without question that she *is* Violetta, Mimì, or Juliette when she's onstage? Perhaps you've marveled at Nathan Lane's impeccable comic timing or fallen in love with Kristin Chenoweth's vocal pizazz and charming stage presence. Sure, all these performers were born with the "goods," but quite a bit of blood, sweat, and tears was expended on the long road to the top. But what exactly does that road look like? How do we even get directions?

In Matthew Hoch and Linda Lister's *Voice Secrets: 100 Performance Strategies for the Advanced Singer*, you might just find that map. Here are one hundred pearls of wisdom describing everything from essential singing languages, breath support, musical styles, and student/teacher decorum to microphone technique and auditions. Best of all, it's succinct and easy to understand.

I first came across Linda's work in the excellent book *Yoga for Singers*, in which she describes ways in which this universal exercise can benefit the body specifically for singing. This theme continues in chapters dedicated to overall health, including diet, hydration, exercise, and, of course, psychological balance. Our bodies are our instruments, aren't they? Why not learn how *Ujjayi* breath can help clear your throat or how meditation might be just what you need to center your mind before auditions? If you've ever heard a singer talk about singing in the "masque" or using *appoggio* to support their sound, *Voice Secrets* uncovers this mystery, along with myriad other technical hills and mountains most successful singers have had to climb. Some tenors were born with killer high Cs, but most have had to work very hard to perfect that all-important money note. But despite how beautiful that note may be, it means nothing if you are a lazy student or a bad colleague. Check out secrets 85 and 86 if you feel a little big for your britches. This being the digital age, I was happily surprised to read about crowdfunding and YouTube!

Linda and Matthew have kept things refreshingly modern in this manual, which is essential for anyone hoping to break into a business that is quite different than it was even a decade or two ago. There's so much that goes into building a singer, creating a career for yourself or your students, and eventually sustaining this career. The materials available are almost overwhelming, and while we are so lucky to have access to so much, it's refreshing to find one source that provides an overview of everything.

Nicole Cabell
2005 Cardiff Singer of the World

Preface

Throughout much of its history, the art of singing and voice teaching has been somewhat mysterious. Perhaps this is in part because of the "invisibility" of the instrument: one cannot "see" the voice functioning the same way one can view keys on the piano or fingerings on the clarinet. There is also an attitude, among some, that singing is a "God-given" ability; one can only marginally improve within a predestined aptitude. While it is certainly true that natural talent plays a significant role in great singing, nature is only half of the story. There are many components in addition to natural ability that make up the training of the complete singer. What is the "secret" to singing well?

Voice Secrets attempts to untangle the mystique of singing by breaking down some of its most essential elements. In fact, most of these bits of wisdom are not "secrets" at all. Rather, they are simply elements of advice that the advanced singer should digest and consider in order to sing at the next level. Attempts were made to delineate topics as cleanly as possible, but in the interconnected world of singing, some overlap between chapters was unavoidable. The singer or voice teacher is encouraged to use this book however he or she sees fit, either flipping from section to section as needed or indulging in a cover-to-cover reading.

Because we are both products of classical conservatory training and have been teaching classical voice at the college level for a combined four decades, there is inherently a classical bias to many of the entries in this book. Although the classically trained performer and teacher is the primary target audience for this book and series, efforts were made to acknowledge other styles as well, hence an entire chapter devoted to contemporary commercial music (CCM) singing. In the ever-expanding world of vocal music, we viewed engaging in a discussion of nonclassical styles as essential information for twenty-first-century singers to consider.

This book—part of the Rowman and Littlefield Music Secrets for the Advanced Musician series—emphasizes breadth over depth and inclusiveness instead of a narrow focus. This philosophy required us to address a host of diverse topics as briefly and succinctly as possible. Any one of these topics could have been, and perhaps *should have* been, written about at much greater length than there was room for here. It was with great restraint that we ultimately had to stop writing or resist the urge to include one last point. We are reminded of the poet Paul Valéry's quote regarding his own work: "Poems are never finished—just abandoned." Readers desiring to know more about a given topic are strongly encouraged to consult the comprehensive and categorized bibliography located at the end of this book.

We hope that you enjoy reading *Voice Secrets* as much as we enjoyed writing it.

Acknowledgments

Many people were involved in the creation of this book, and we would like to express gratitude toward several individuals in particular. First, we would like to thank the staff at Rowman & Littlefield, including Natalie Mandziuk, Bennett Graff, Monica Savaglia, and the entire editing and production team for the opportunity to contribute to this series and for their help throughout the entire process. We would also like to thank Nicole Cabell, 2005 Cardiff Singer of the World, for her willingness to write the foreword. In addition, Linda would like to thank Alicia Micco for her assistance with chapter titles and especially Nate Bynum for his love and support throughout the process. Matt is indebted to his wife, Theresa, for her tolerance of his many academic projects—some of which tend to get prioritized over assorted family matters. Last, but not least, we would like to thank all of our mentors, colleagues, and students for everything they have taught us about the art of singing—this book would not have been possible without you!

Note: Like most pedagogical publications, much of the material in this book is indebted to other scholarly resources. All printed books consulted are listed in the comprehensive bibliography in the end of this book. When quotations are taken from a specific scholarly work, footnotes are provided. When a technique was absorbed empirically from a specific teacher or experience, that person or organization is credited within the text. Lastly, several definitions within chapters are adaptations and augmentations of research undertaken three years ago for A Dictionary for the Modern Singer; *earlier prototypes may be found in that resource.*

CHAPTER 1

Vocal Technique

SECRET 1: STAND UP STRAIGHT! POSTURE AND ALIGNMENT AWARENESS

Your mother was right, or mostly right, when she told you "Stand up straight!" Our spine is not actually straight—it actually has a natural S curve—but it is important for singers to align their spine and stack their joints without rigidity (see figure 1.1). Your body is your instrument, and it is hard to breathe well with a collapsed sternum and rib cage or to sing well with the head or neck out of alignment, possibly affecting laryngeal position.

Pedagogue Giovanni Battista Lamperti first wrote about the ideal of "noble" posture in his book of maxims entitled *Vocal Wisdom*. He pictured a soldier at ease but alert and aligned. I like to picture a king or queen with the regal posture of an elevated sternum and with the head synchronized with the spine to keep one's crown from falling.

Technique

To achieve alignment of your spine, neck, and head, try this yoga technique, which uses gravity to help rather than hinder good posture. Bend at the waist to let your upper body hang over your legs in a standing forward bend (see figure 1.2). Let your arms hang freely as they reach toward the ground, or you can clasp opposite elbows. This is called a "rag doll" pose (see figure 1.3). Keep a slight bend in the knees so that you don't strain your hamstrings, and do exercise caution if you have blood pressure issues or are prone to fainting. Enjoy the stretch as gravity lengthens your spine in this upside-down position.

Then slowly roll up, one vertebra at a time, stacking each on top of the next until you arrive to an upright position. This is called a "mountain" pose. Finally, do a slow *relevé*, rising onto the balls of your feet. If you are aligned, then you should be able to remain balanced for a second or two.

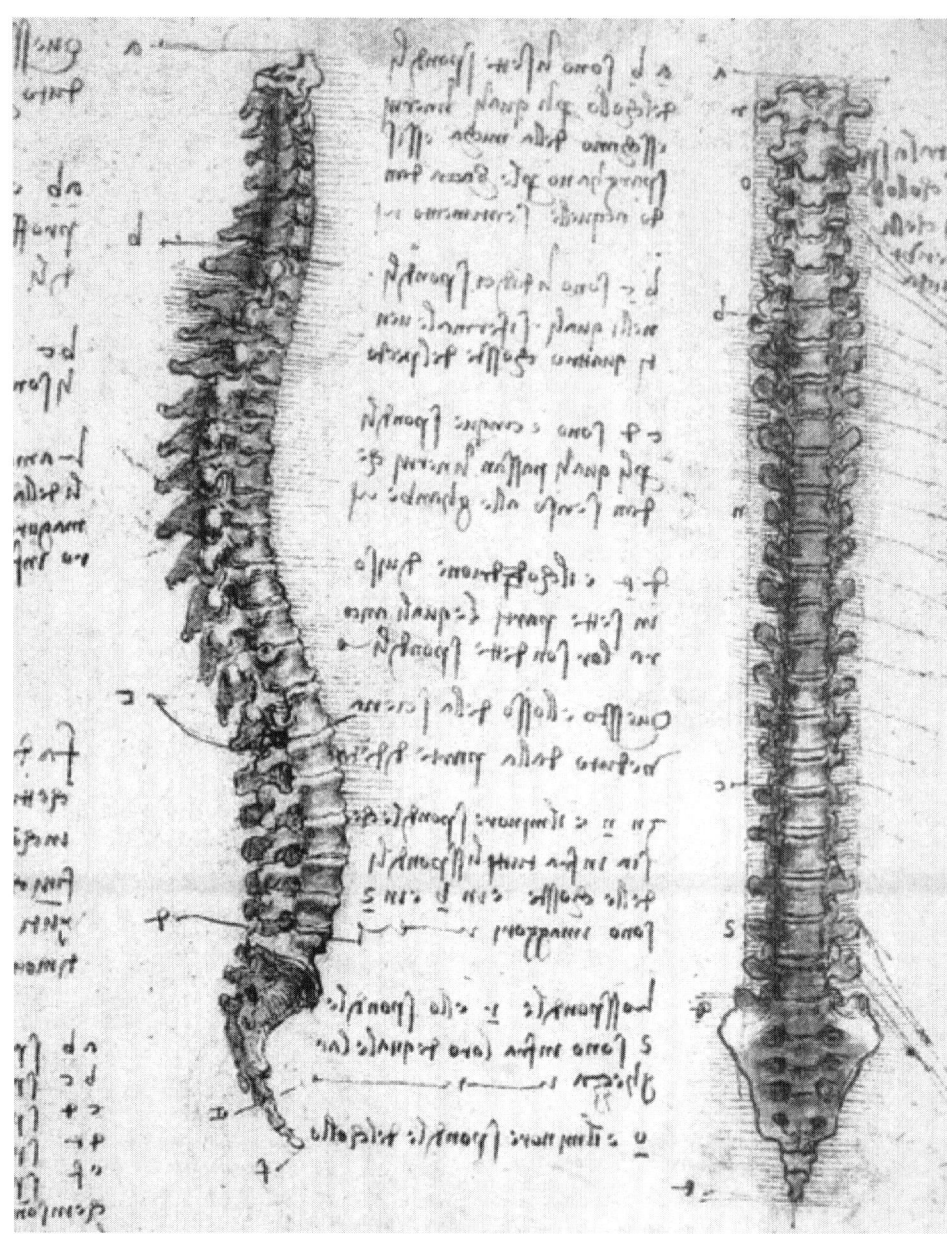

Figure 1.1. Leonardo da Vinci's Rendition of the Spine

Figure 1.2. Forward Bend

Figure 1.3. Rag Doll Pose

Benefit

By avoiding an arched sway back or a rounded spine, you can find optimal postural alignment. Healthy posture helps to facilitate efficient breath management, stable laryngeal positioning, and a confident presence onstage. You'll be a winning, singing soldier at ease (not at war) with your own posture.

SECRET 2: LEAN ON ME—*APPOGGIO* AND BREATH MANAGEMENT

Good breathing technique is one of the key elements of good vocal technique. Without efficient breath management, a singer might not have the breath control to sing the extended runs of Handel's *Messiah* or a Mariah Carey song. While there are many schools of thought on breathing technique, the bel canto concept of *appoggio* is widely accepted among singing teachers. The term comes from the Italian verb *appoggiare*, which means to lean or support. *Appoggio* involves *la lotta vocale* (or "the vocal contest"), in which you try to sustain the exhalation of air as the diaphragm ascends.

Often singers will hear somewhat meaningless maxims such as "support more" (an unclear and nonspecific instruction) and "sing from your diaphragm" (the diaphragm is actually an involuntary muscle of inhalation, not exhalation). While these phrases are not helpful in and of themselves, you can work to maintain your inspiratory posture and slow the diaphragm's ascent, thereby "leaning" and lengthening your expiratory process. At the end of the day, words mean less than specific physical strategies for achieving good *appoggio*.

Technique

To help extend your inhalation and keep air flow even during exhalation, try a yoga breath-control technique called the *kala* breath. Start your inhalation with what is often called a "low breath," feeling expansion below the navel as the lungs expand, the diaphragm descends, and the abdominals release. Inhale for four beats and then exhale on a hiss for four beats, establishing an even flow to the breath cycle. Repeat several times. Be sure that your hiss stays consistent; if it were being measured on a graph, it should have a steady line instead of one that has peaks and valleys. You want to resist not assist the exhalation. Then try what I call the "double *kala*" breath, where your exhalation will be twice as long as your inhalation. So if you inhale for four beats, you would exhale on a hiss for eight beats. To build kinesthetic awareness, you could practice this technique in a few different positions, such as the following:

1. Lie on your back with your knees bent, the soles of your feet on the floor, and a book on your lower abdominals, just below the navel.
2. Flatten the top of a music stand into a horizontal position and stand with it touching your lower abdominals, just below the navel.

Benefit

The *kala* and "double *kala*" breathing technique helps singers gain greater breath control by sustaining and lengthening their exhalation. This will help in sustaining the long phrases of composers such as Johannes Brahms and Richard Strauss. In "the vocal contest" (*la lotta vocale*), you will lose the battle every time, but at least you'll know you fought the good fight with *appoggio*!

SECRET 3: WAX ON, WAX OFF—ONSET AND RELEASE

Onset and release are essential elements of phonation. Just like a gymnast needs a clean mount and dismount or a skater needs a synchronized entry and landing to a jump, a singer needs a coordinated onset to bring the vocal folds together to phonate and a coordinated release to part the glottis. Singers need to find a happy medium, avoiding a harsh glottal attack (where the glottis is closed before you phonate) as well as a breathy onset (where the breath activates the folds with an audible aspirant *h*). As Richard Miller describes in *The Structure of Singing*, the goal is a balanced onset, neither glottal nor breathy, and a balanced release, neither soft nor hard. Singers also need to avoid a so-called operatic release (with an abrupt, audible grunt preceding the release), a breathy post-phonation exhalation (the singing should be the exhalation), or an imprecise, sliding descent off the pitch (akin to a Bob Dylan–esque portamento).

Technique

Onsets and releases involve practicing the adduction and abduction of the vocal folds, bringing them together (adducting) and taking them away from each other (abducting). Onset vocalises are a great way to start your practice session. Start simply in the middle of your range by singing [i] on the same note three times. Breathe in between each note so that you practice the complete cycle of onset and release three times. The inhalation for the next note becomes the release of the previous note and preparation for the next repetition of the note. Keep the process simple and streamlined, like Mr. Miyagi's "wax on, wax off" mantra from the popular 1984 movie *The Karate Kid*: adduct, abduct; phonate, inhale; onset, release.

Benefit

A consistent, well-controlled coordination of onset and release is the foundation of healthy vocal technique. A ballet dancer begins daily barre work with *pliés* in preparation for leaps, or *jetés*. Similarly, a singer can benefit from developing control of the phonatory process, thus strengthening this essential building block of singing.

SECRET 4: RING AND RUMBLE—RESONANCE

Resonance is a way of enhancing the tone quality of your voice. In the classical realm, resonance is also an important part of helping your voice project without amplification. The ideal is a balance of light and dark in the tone. The Italian bel canto school borrowed the visual art term *chiaroscuro* to describe this timbral ideal of a sound with both clarity and depth. In musical theatre, awareness of resonance can help you alter your tone quality to portray vocally distinctive types of characters, such as the nasal Adelaide in *Guys and Dolls* or rich-voiced Mufasa in *The Lion King* (voiced on-screen by the king of resonance, James Earl Jones).

Technique

To explore forward "placement" (see Secret 8)—or a bright sound associated with the Italian term "*squillo*" ("ping" or "ring")—try humming. With vibrant portamento, slide up and down the fifth from tonic to dominant on the velar nasal "eng" [ɛŋ]. Focus on maintaining a frontal sensation of the hum in the face or "masque." Or try a descending syllabic five-note pattern (from fifth to tonic) on a combination of nasal consonants—[n], [m], or [ŋ]—or labiodental fricatives—[v] or [f]—and bright vowels such as [æ], [e], or [i]. One such combination vocalise could be [vi-ve-v*a*-ve-vi] (see figure 1.4).

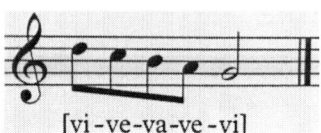

Figure 1.4.   Fricative Vocalise

To bring more depth and roundness to your tone, employ labial or "lip" vowels such as [o] and [u]. Bringing the lips forward lengthens the vocal tract (the distance from lips to larynx) and encourages a richer and darker tone quality. Begin with an open-throated, yawn-like inhalation, then round the lips into open [ɔ], closed [o], or closed [u] before descending once again from fifth to tonic on a five-note pattern. If your lips start to shake, do a lip trill (imagine you are imitating a horse) to release the tension.

Benefit

Cultivating both bright and dark qualities (*chiaroscuro*) in your voice helps to keep your sound in a healthy balance, like the complementary forces of yin and yang. Besides enhancing the quality of your tone, good resonance also helps increase the intensity of your voice, so that you can be your own "woofer" and "tweeter" and project your voice without a microphone. Furthermore, awareness of how to create different types of sounds gives you a wider color palette from which to create and define diverse characters and qualities befitting the role or genre you are singing.

SECRET 5: RIFFS AND RUNS—FLEXIBILITY

Not everyone will run a marathon or race the Tour de France, but everyone can benefit from aerobic exercise. Similarly, not all singers will have to negotiate the fiendish fioritura of Zerbinetta's aria or the complicated riffs of an Aretha Franklin–inspired gospel arrangement. Still, every singer should include some agility training in his or her practice. Just as an athlete's body is optimized by a balanced program of aerobic, strength, and flexibility training, a singer's instrument can maintain healthy balance and secure technique by working to improve strength and stamina (via sostenuto singing) as well as flexibility (through coloratura).

Technique

Practice singing florid music. If you like the baroque era, there are plenty of coloratura songs and arias, from Purcell's "I'll Sail upon the Dog Star" to Handel's "Oh Had I Jubal's Lyre" (from the oratorio *Joshua*). Or you may prefer the limpid lines of Wolfgang Amadeus Mozart—"Zeffiretti lusinghieri" from *Idomeneo*—or the grandiose runs of Gioachino Rossini. (Listen to the performers Cecilia Bartoli and Juan Diego Florez.)

To get you started, here is a basic vocalise that can be helpful in developing good flexibility in the singing voice: Starting on the fifth, descend and ascend back up to the fifth stepwise on eighth notes. Then descend the fifth on triplets with an upper neighbor-tone pattern before running up and down the fifth on sixteenth notes to finish (see also figure 1.5).

Figure 1.5. Agility Exercise

For more complex melismas, try the Marchesi vocal method, which is still widely available in print and used by many singing teachers. Mathilde Marchesi was a nineteenth-century singer and singing teacher who trained under the famous voice pedagogue Manuel Garcia II. She became a famous teacher herself, with star pupils such as Nellie Melba and Emma Calvé. Epitomizing the bel canto era in which she lived, her method employed scales of gradually increasing speed and range, akin to the virtuosic (and sometimes dreaded) piano exercises of Charles-Louis Hanon. In addition to Marchesi, other well-known vocal methods for developing flexibility include those by Nicola Vaccai, Giuseppe Concone, and Heinrich Panofka.

Benefit

Coloratura isn't just for coloratura sopranos! Melismatic singing keeps the voice nimble, especially as one matures. Runs can help a basso profondo whose voice is slowing down or can keep an alto's vibrato from getting too wide. For inspiration, enjoy Ella Fitzgerald's spry scatting in her iconic 1960 Berlin live version of "How High the Moon." Or listen to Barbara Cook, who in her late eighties still performed live cabaret shows sixty years after premiering Leonard Bernstein's coloratura showpiece from *Candide*, "Glitter and Be Gay." I once heard modern jazz diva Dianne Reeves live, and I was surprised to hear her sing a few lines from the Bach *Magnificat* in between her sets. Her example of versatility and flexibility proves that an agile voice is a healthy voice, regardless of the genre one sings.

SECRET 6: UNDERSTAND REGISTRATION—"HEAD" VERSUS "CHEST" VOICE

Registration can be a controversial issue among voice teachers. How many registers are there? One? Two? Three? Four? Once a colleague of mine (who was and still is a very fine singer) even went as far as to insist that the very best singers had no registers at all . . . they just sang! He probably knew that he was engaging in hyperbole with this comment, but it is illustrative of the wide variety of discourse that surrounds any discussion of registers.

One of the main reasons that singers and voice teachers argue about registration is that there is not yet a unified terminology among voice pedagogues. In addition, when terminology is used, it is often not fact based in nature. For example, the terms "head voice" and "chest voice" are used ubiquitously, even though both registers are the result of laryngeal activity—nothing vocal is literally occurring in either the chest or head when singers shift between these two registers.

This short discussion will outline and attempt to define some of the most commonly used terminology regularly encountered in discussions of vocal registration in an attempt to clarify this potentially confusing issue.[1]

Terminology

Head (or head voice): The common name for a CT (cricothyroid)–dominant (mode 2) register in singing. Also sometimes referred to as "*voce di testa*," "loft register," or "light mechanism." Although head is not the natural register of human speech, it is the preferred register for female voices in classical genres of singing.

Chest (or chest voice): The common name for a TA (thyroarytenoid)–dominant (mode 1) register in singing. Also sometimes referred to as "*voce di petto*," "ring register," "modal register," "heavy mechanism," or "belt." As chest is the natural register of human speech, it is often the preferred register in theatrical genres of singing and popular music.

Mixed register: Refers to a balance of TA/mode 1 and CT/mode 2 registration in singing. While the vocal folds are ultimately more engaged in one mode (register) than the other, modification of the acoustic space in the *zona di passaggio* can give the singer the feeling—and the listener the perception—of a third ("mixed") register. The mixed register concept is controversial among voice pedagogues, many of whom do not acknowledge it as a true register. The term is most frequently encountered when discussing the middle range of the singer and in reference to the transition that occurs between chest (TA/mode 1) and head (CT/mode 2) voice. In this sense, "mixed register" refers to the gradual and subtle shifting between registers to eliminate abruptness and give the illusion of a smooth and seamless tone quality throughout the range of the singer. Also called "coordinated register."

"Operatic" head voice: A kind of vowel modification—or cover—that male classical singers use in their higher range. Operatic head voice is TA dominant and part of the coordinated or mixed register. The label is misleading: operatic head voice is not a new register, nor is it head voice in any way (i.e., falsetto, a CT-dominant sound, or mode 2 register). It is simply the selection of warmer, darker vowels to conform to the classical aesthetic of an even register and good tone quality.

Belt: A frequently encountered term that can refer to a style, a register, and a technique used by singers who perform in nonclassical styles. Because "belt" can mean so many things, it is often a confusing term to discuss and difficult to define precisely. Indeed, "belt" can serve as a noun (indicating the register or the technique), an adjective (describing the tone quality or sound), or a verb (describing what the singer is doing). Perhaps no other word in singing is as multifarious. Most singing teachers would agree that "belt" is most frequently associated with the female chest voice (or the TA-dominant or mode 1 register). As classical female singers largely avoid this register, the belt sound emerged as a distinctly different, refreshing commercial sound in the late 1920s, when Ethel Merman did much to popularize the new technique. While women are most frequently cited in discussions involving belting, men can belt as well. Since men (with the exception of countertenors) sing in their chest voices already, their belt may sound less distinctive than the female belt. Male belting usually involves brighter, spread vowels in the higher register with the complete absence of cover or operatic head voice.

Belt-mix: A term frequently used by contemporary commercial music (CCM) and musical theatre pedagogues to refer to a female, TA-dominant "pop" sound but often with a range extension on top. While a true belt might be delivered in 100 percent chest voice—and at a lower range and tessitura—a female who uses a belt-mix is often capable of singing in a higher range, employing cricothyroid activity in combination with brighter vowel choices.

Falsetto: Another name for head voice. Although "falsetto" can be used to describe any CT-dominant/mode 2 production—either male or female—it is almost exclusively used among voice professionals to describe the male head voice, which generally is not used by men in classical singing. The big exception to this practice is the countertenor, who develops his falsetto (or head voice) similarly to the way that female classical singers do. Some voice pedagogues and voice scientists make a distinction between head voice and falsetto, citing more thyroarytenoid activity—or "mix"—in the head voice; in this definition of falsetto, the thyroarytenoid muscle is completely unengaged.

Mix: A CCM term used to describe a register that is somewhere in between head (CT) and chest (TA) voice. Some schools of CCM pedagogy—such as Somatic Voicework—describe two different kinds of mix: head mix and chest mix. While mixing certainly occurs in classical music (see mixed register), the term is used with more frequency among CCM singers and teachers, particularly in the musical theatre genre, where mix often becomes necessary when singing high in the female belt range. The term "mix" is also used in combination with other words to subjectively describe various timbres and styles; examples include hybrid terms like "belt-mix," "pop-mix," "rock-mix," and others. The terminology, while used with frequency in musical theatre listings, is not at all standardized.

***Passaggio*:** Literally meaning "passage" in Italian, the *passaggio* is a pivotal point in the vocal register where the singer must begin vowel modification in order to give the impression of a seamless tone quality throughout his or her vocal range. It is generally agreed that both men and women have two *passaggio* points, labeled the "*primo passaggio*" (first *passaggio*) and the "*secondo passaggio*" (second *passaggio*). In women, the *primo passaggio* usually occurs between C4 and A4, and the *secondo passaggio* between E5 and A5. In men, the *primo passaggio* usually occurs between F3 and C4, and the *secondo passaggio* between C4 and A4 (the same location as the female *primo passaggio*). The location of specific *passaggio* points within these parameters varies from singer to singer, and the specific pitch level at which these transitions occur is one of several determining factors (along with color and tessitura comfort level) in establishing one's voice type (or *Fach*). *Passaggio* points are also related to the finer nuances of registration. For instance, the location between the two *passaggio* points (in both female and male voices) is often considered to be the mixed register, regardless of the principal registration, which is determined at the laryngeal level. In female classical singers, the pitches located above the *secondo passaggio* are usually produced in a pure head voice (CT voice). Male classical singers usually employ vowel modification above their *secondo passaggio* to achieve the desired warmth and tone quality; they sometimes call this new "register" "operatic head voice."

Glottal fry: Phonation at the lowest pitches of the voice, either male or female, it produces an imprecise phonation reminiscent of clicking. Minimal airflow is needed to produce glottal fry. It is sometimes used as a therapeutic technique; also called "pulse" or "mode 0 register."

Flageolet register: This is the highest vocal range in the female voice, usually only occurring at the pitch of C6 or higher. While technically an extreme end of the CT register (and not a truly unique register in and of itself), the flageolet register resembles the CT register in function, though more acute and extreme. In flageolet register, only the edges of the vocal folds are approximated, and there is high subglottic pressure and considerable longitudinal tension in the vocal ligaments. Only a small portion of the opera and art song repertory requires frequent use of the flageolet register, though it should be accessed and practiced with regularity by all classical sopranos. Some CCM singers, such as Mariah Carey, also use flageolet register. It is also called "flute," "whistle," or "mode 3 register."

Benefit

Understanding the most often encountered terminology related to registration will facilitate discussion and help to eliminate confusion when discussing this important issue in singing.

SECRET 7: BE SMOOTH—*SEMPRE LEGATO*

The concept of legato is a hallmark of classical vocal technique and one of the cornerstones of the Italian bel canto singing tradition. Legato—which literally means "bound" in Italian—describes a seamless, well-supported, and resonant vocal line. Singing legato is a technique, and while some singers seem to have a "natural" legato with minimal effort, the vast majority of us must work diligently to cultivate good legato through efficient voice use, excellent language skills, and good breath management (see Secret 2).

Achieving good legato also requires us to confront and debunk certain myths about legato. The biggest myth that is regularly encountered is that consonants are somehow the enemy of legato. While consonants can present some challenges (see Secret 34), they should never be regarded as "the enemy." In fact, consonants can be very friendly to legato as long as the singer knows how to handle them. Since every language has consonants, it is the singer's responsibility to learn how to sing consonants to the benefit—not detriment—of legato.

Technique

1. Try vocalizing your song or aria on a semi-occluded vocal tract (SOVT) exercise (see Secret 23). Straw phonation is ideal for maximizing the efficiency of phonation. During this exercise, be mindful of your breath. Is it consistent, smooth, and even? Is vibrato present throughout? Make sure that you are maintaining good posture (see Secret 1) and *appoggio* (see Secret 2) throughout this exercise.
2. Alternate between singing passages on SOVT exercises and singing the same passage on an open vowel. Maintain the same flow and efficiency on the vowels as you achieved during the SOVT exercise. The feeling of ease should remain the same.
3. Sing the piece on just vowels, preserving the legato achieved in the two exercises listed above.
4. Finally—and only after spending some time with these first three steps—add consonants, using them to the benefit of the legato line. Voiced consonants should all be pitched, and unvoiced consonants should be as short as possible, never interfering with breath flow. A good visual image is a thrown rock skipping quickly along the water. As Oren Brown used to say: "Vowels are the rooms in which singers live. Consonants are the doorways that propel you from room to room."
5. Listen to great performers who exemplify seamless legato (see Secret 44). Form a mental concept of what great legato should be and strive toward that

model. Imagine how your own voice would sound with ideal legato—never imitate someone else's voice.

Benefit

Legato is an ideal toward which all classical singers strive. A well-produced legato is aesthetically appealing and can be applied to any language. Because of its long association with classical resonance in general—and opera specifically—legato is a concept that is less valued and discussed in CCM circles. Good legato, however, does encourage ease of production and good breath connection, which can be valuable when applied to any style.

SECRET 8: "PLACE" THE VOICE—WHAT DOES THAT ACTUALLY MEAN?

One concept that is used almost universally among singers is that of "placing" the voice. This term, however, is often unclear. What does "placing" the voice really mean?

The problem with using the verb "place"—in all of its forms—is that the word implies an actual location. Where (physically) are you putting the voice? On the roof of the mouth? On the back of your bottom front teeth? Are you singing through your forehead or "third eye"? In your chest? (Those last two are especially absurd, since no one has a third eye and the vocal folds are housed by the laryngeal cartilages in the neck, but believe it or not we have heard instructions like these on many occasions.) Thus, telling a student to "place" the voice is problematic for two reasons:

First, singing is an acoustic phenomenon involving the breath, the entire vocal tract (from the glottis to the lips), and the room or space into which the singer is resonating. In a sense, all of these factors are part of the singer's voice production. The voice is not a physical object. The instruction can't really be followed because a single place cannot be isolated. All of these components listed are a part of singing.

Second, when singers describe "placing" the voice in a certain way, they are often alluding to a feeling. "Place the voice higher—do you feel the vibration in your cheekbones?" Well, one singer might indeed feel vibration there, but another singer might not, even though he or she may be singing equally well. Sensation is very subjective and will vary from singer to singer. While it is fair game to ask a student to remember a feeling when you objectively determine that they are singing well, it is another matter completely to tell them how something should feel.

Technique

Instead of telling a student to "place" his or her voice in a certain way, try a simple vowel modification instead. For example, if the sound is dull and not resonant enough, say, "Instead of singing a dark American [ɑ], try a brighter Italian [a] on this note when you are in this register." If you are using the concept of "placing" to solve a resonance or tone-quality issue, try experimenting with specific vowel adjustments instead (see Secret 33).

Or perhaps the issue is not resonance but a sense that a student is singing with too much jaw and tongue tension (or with too high of a laryngeal position). Instead of asking the student to "place your voice higher, out of the jaw and throat," try confronting the issue directly and in a more fact-based way (see Secret 10): "I am noticing some compensatory jaw and tongue tension. Try singing that passage again, on a neutral vowel sound, while releasing your jaw and gently massaging your masseter muscles." Chances are this direct approach will achieve better results and make more sense to the student.

Benefit

When singers talk about "placing" the voice, they are probably talking about something else. Think about the problem and the goal and try a more specific, descriptive, and fact-based way to resolve the issue.

SECRET 9: WARM UP ENOUGH (BUT NOT TOO MUCH)

Singing warm-ups are universally practiced by both singers and voice teachers. The exact purpose of warming up, however, is often unclear. Is its primary function a physical or psychological one? Is a warm-up geared toward skill acquisition? If so, which skills in particular? Can the right warm-up help to manage fatigue and thus prevent injury? And how long should a warm-up be?

Historically, warm-ups have been geared primarily toward skill acquisition for classical bel canto repertoire. This is particularly true of the methodologists of the International Italian School: Vaccai, Panofka, Marchesi, Concone, and others. The modern singing teacher, however, must move beyond this paradigm. Twenty-first-century singers often engage in musical theatre and CCM styles, and the classical world is also more diverse than ever before. Singing Puccini is not the same as singing Bach, Sondheim, or rock.

Modern science has also provided evidence that informs the singing warm-up in ways that move beyond skill acquisition. Fatigue management is another vital component that historically has not been covered in the standard voice pedagogy literature and is currently being explored and studied. While there is much that we are still learning about warming up, the following techniques can be useful in making your warm-up more efficient.

Technique

1. Use the warm-up time to get focused (see Secret 41). Your warm-up routine should be an opportunity to prepare mentally for singing and performing. Turn off all distractions, such as cell phones and iPads. Closing your eyes while you vocalize may also help to focus on the task at hand.
2. Begin with SOVT exercises such as lip trills, humming, and straw phonation (see Secret 23). These exercises promote vocal efficiency and are the perfect way to "run in" your voice before proceeding to more complex exercises on open vowels. Start in the middle of your voice before singing in the extremes of your range.
3. Warm up enough but not too much. While it is important to make sure that your voice is physically primed and ready to sing, a common mistake that singers make—especially young singers—is to warm up too much, thus fatiguing the voice immediately before you need it. Don't leave your voice in the practice room!
4. Vary your warm-up routine. Since most traditional vocalises are skill-acquisition based, warm-ups should be selected based on the repertoire you are about to sing. Another common mistake that singers make is to al-

ways use the same warm-up routine regardless of what they are preparing themselves to sing. A mindful warm-up should always be goal oriented.

5. Allow a period of rest in between the vocal warm-up and your actual performance. Never move directly from the practice room to your lesson or audition. Allow fifteen minutes to a half an hour to quietly focus and hydrate. Use this time to think about your music, text, and expressive intentions. This "buffer" time will help to ensure a better performance.

Benefit

A focused vocal warm-up prepares a singer physically, mentally, and psychologically for singing. Skill-acquisition warm-ups will prepare you for the repertoire you are about to sing, and a carefully timed, mindful warm-up will maximize the opportunity for an excellent performance.

SECRET 10: KNOW WHAT'S REALLY HAPPENING—FACT VERSUS FICTION

The art of singing has persisted for centuries. Over the past several decades, however, there has been an explosion of research in voice science, some of which has been applied to the art of singing. As a result, modern singers and voice teachers have a much better understanding of how the voice works than we did one hundred years ago. While modern science has proven many instincts of eighteenth- and nineteenth-century pedagogues correct (their ideas having been preserved in important treatises), some historical maxims should be reevaluated in light of newer, fact-based approaches to singing.

Technique

Find ways to describe vocal phenomena that describe what is really happening and, thus, what you really mean! For example, "Sing from your diaphragm." This is heard frequently. However, it doesn't make any literal sense. The diaphragm is a muscle of inhalation, and singing almost virtually occurs on the exhalation, never when one inhales. A variation on this phrase, "breathe from your diaphragm," is also somewhat pointless, as all breathing (regardless of quality, technique, or whether one is singing, speaking, or not phonating at all) engages the diaphragm on the inhalation. The only time the diaphragm stops working is in the event of death.

What singers and teachers really mean when they say "sing from the diaphragm" is probably "take a low, relaxed breath to encourage good *appoggio* on the exhalation" (see Secret 2).

There are many other familiar maxims that don't express reality, such as "breathe through your nose because it raises the soft palate" (the soft palate cannot be engaged when one breathes through his or her nose) or "sing through your third eye" (no one literally has a third eye). All such sayings should be reevaluated in light of current voice science and pedagogical knowledge.

Benefit

Not all imagery is necessarily bad—voice teachers and singers have used non-fact-based mantras for centuries. But truthful maxims that are accurate and descriptive can prove to be even more fruitful and universal. Fact-based pedagogy allows one to maximize one's vocal technique and realize his or her fullest potential.

SECRET 11: FIND YOUR *FACH*—YOUR SOUND AND PSYCHE

Like the lyric from the Michael W. Smith song, we all want to find our "place in this world." Voice classification is a means of finding your niche and figuring out what repertoire best suits your voice. The German word "*Fach*"—pronounced [fax]—means compartment or pigeonhole. The *Fach* system has been used throughout German opera houses as a way to help define what roles are appropriate for a singer. Still, some defy *Fach*: Anna Netrebko sings everything from Norina to Lady Macbeth, and Aretha Franklin filled in for an ailing Luciano Pavarotti to sing "Nessun dorma" for the 1998 Grammy Awards. While pop music doesn't have the same operatic labels, you still need to figure out where you might fit best. Are you a pop country singer (Faith Hill, Taylor Swift), classical crossover crooner (Andrea Bocelli, Josh Groban), or pop falsettist (Michael Jackson, Justin Timberlake)? Your *Fach* can change throughout your life, just as your voice changes and matures. While younger singers shouldn't obsess about defining themselves too soon, it is helpful to use voice classification to guide not just choral part assignment but also solo song selection.

Technique

Try to determine these four elements that contribute to determining your *Fach*:

1. Range: What is your comfortable singing range from lowest note to highest note?
2. Tessitura: What is the most comfortable part of your range to sustain for a long period of time (i.e., low, middle, upper middle, high)?
3. Quality or timbre: What words do people use to describe what your voice sounds like (bright/dark, light/heavy, limpid, metallic, mellow, shimmering, warm, dusky)?
4. Personality type: What is your energy or personality like onstage (hyper/calm, vulnerable/powerful, earnest, mysterious, quirky, romantic, heroic)?

While range is important in voice classification, it is also important to determine what tessitura you can easily sustain, what the color and quality of your voice evoke, and what your stage persona implies. For instance, a lyric baritone may be able to hit a high C, but that doesn't necessarily mean that he should be singing tenor instead if his tessitura, timbre, and personality indicate otherwise. You may find yourself to be *Zwischenfach*, or between *Fach*, thus defying classification (like Cecilia Bartoli or Björk), and that's okay, but ask your voice teacher. Also be sure to check out several resources in the bibliography of this book that are devoted to *Fach*.

Benefit

Fach is especially helpful in casting. For better or worse, if you can be categorized, it's easier for people to determine what roles or repertoire fit you. *Fach* can help you be cast or help you book a gig because it makes it clear that you fit the "compartment" or character description, be it bird-like lyric coloratura soprano, bumbling basso buffo, charismatic pop baritenor, or sultry alto chanteuse.

SECRET 12: SHAKE IT! MUSINGS ON VIBRATO

Perhaps nothing in singing is more unique from singer to singer than vibrato. Vibrato can be controversial: people have widely different opinions on what describes a "tasteful" vibrato for a given style. Vibrato is also somewhat mysterious. Even now, during the second decade of the twenty-first century, there is still considerable debate about vibrato and whether it is something that can be taught at all. As a result, many teachers approach vibrato indirectly, believing that it is something that simply "happens" when students sing with good breath management (see Secret 2) and resonance (see Secret 4). A systematic pedagogy for teaching vibrato has yet to emerge.

Following is a brief discussion about vibrato based on current use of terminology and consensus among prominent voice pedagogues.

Facts and Thoughts about Vibrato

1. Voice scientists believe that vibrato is the result of neurological impulses that occur when singers balance their power source (breath) with proper coordination of the source (vocal folds) and resonator (vocal tract). While vibrato cannot be controlled directly, it can be influenced via changes in the breath pressure as well as manipulations of the vocal tract.
2. Vibrato and the vibration of the vocal folds are separate phenomena. These vibrations function independently of one another. When one pauses and thinks about this, it is common sense: a mezzo-soprano singing an A4 may have a vibrato rate of six cycles per second (cps) even though her vocal folds are vibrating at a rate of 440 Hz—a big difference! We have learned, however, that these multiple simultaneous oscillations can be a confusing concept for singers new to the art form.
3. Voice pedagogues typically cite two variables with respect to vibrato: rate (referring to the number of vibrato cycles per second) and extent (referring to the degree of pitch fluctuation above and below the pitch being sung). In classical singing, a desirable average rate is considered to be 6–7 cps. If the rate is too slow (fewer than 5.5 cps), the singer is said to have a "wobble," and if the rate is too fast (exceeding 7.5 cps), the singer is said to have a "tremolo"; both are pejorative terms. Extents, however, tend to vary widely.
4. In the world of singing, there is still a myth that is perpetuated from time to time that vibrato is "natural" and therefore is something that a singer cannot control. This is mostly nonsense. If it were true that vibrato is something that cannot be controlled, a freshman singing straight tone would never be able to cultivate an even vibrato by his or her senior year. Also, when choral directors

ask for a final cadence to be straight tone, most choirs can respond and do this upon command. (Whether they have the technique to sing straight tone in a healthy way is another matter.)

5. Some pedagogues argue—rather convincingly—that there is no such thing as straight-tone singing; what we perceive as straight tone actually still has fluctuation, but the extent of pitch variation is so minimal that it is practically imperceptible. If this is true, then vibrato is something that is always present within our oscillatory singing instrument and not something that simply can be turned on and off. That means that singing with a "straight tone" really means that we are controlling the extent of our ever-present vibrato.

6. Vibrato is an essential element of style. In the baroque era, vibrato was considered to be an ornament that was to be used for expressive purposes. Cultivating a vibrato for a specific style is by and large something that singers can (and must) train toward, although some singers do naturally gravitate toward certain styles and find some types of music physically easier and thus more "natural" to sing within the limitations of their instrument. A singer who sings Verdi and Wagner is not likely to be the same person who sings Monteverdi and Schütz. That being said, sometimes there is a wide variation among vibrato rates and extents among singers, even within the same style and repertoire. Vibrato is a specific hallmark of solo classical singing—opera (see Secret 65), oratorio (see Secret 64), and art song (see Secrets 60–63)—but it occurs in many other styles as well, including musical theatre (see Secret 72), country (see Secret 76), gospel (see Secret 74), and many styles of world music (see Secret 77). Other styles, such as jazz (see Secret 75) and barbershop (see Secret 78), may have little or no vibrato.

Benefit

One cannot be a singer without some understanding of vibrato. Absorbing some of the facts above is a first step toward unraveling some of the mysteries surrounding vibrato and unlocking its many "secrets."

SECRET 13: ALWAYS SING ON YOUR INTEREST, NEVER YOUR CAPITAL

"Always sing on your interest, never your capital." No one knows the precise origin of this saying, though it was popularized by the great soprano Leontyne Price, who said that it was passed along to her by one of her teachers. This oral tradition of passing down knowledge from one generation to another is typical in the world of singing. Throughout most of its history, the discipline of voice pedagogy was passed down from teacher to pupil through a sort of master-apprentice system. Voice teachers would pass down a series of maxims to their students, who would internalize them and then pass them along to the next generation. Although many of these words of wisdom were formulated before the "fact-based" (scientific) era of voice pedagogy, a great number of these old-school bel canto sayings still ring true and are helpful reminders to singers. This kind of advice forms the backbone of the International Italian School of singing, a concept still embraced by the majority of singing teachers.

Technique

The phrase "always sing in your interest, never your capital," is an analogy that compares good singing with good financial advice. If you are lucky enough to be very wealthy (which most of us, unfortunately, are not), you would only ever spend your interest, never your capital. Not drawing upon your capital would ensure that you would never become poorer and always would have security via money in the bank. In other words, a solid technique is money in the bank!

This maxim suggests a strong parallel between financial well-being and good vocal technique. "Singing on your interest" means singing in a healthy way that will not tire the mechanism (i.e., your capital) and result in fatigue. Although there are many aspects of vocal technique, we have most often heard this advice when a singer begins to "push"—working too hard at the laryngeal level and not trusting the breath and "flow" of the voice. It is helpful for singers to remember that a resonant voice is a free voice. It's not about working "harder," and the feeling of physically working harder almost never works and results in a pushed, less resonant voice. Rather, think freedom. Connect to your breath. Find an easier way to do things. Always sing on you interest, never your capital.

Benefit

This historic maxim, and many others, can preserve the bloom in your voice and promote healthy, robust singing. For other words of wisdom—many of which hold up very well, even in the fact-based era of voice pedagogy—pick up a copy of *Vocal Wisdom: Maxims of Giovanni Battista Lamperti.*

SECRET 14: TRY AND TRUST—FINDING THE RIGHT TEACHER

Finding the right voice teacher can be as challenging as finding the right therapist or hair stylist. Your voice teacher should not be your therapist (or, probably, your hair stylist), but you do need to figure out what might be right for you. Are you looking for a mentor or motivator? A hands-on Svengali or a laid-back Dalai Lama? Do you want a "diva/divo" teacher who will have amazing stories to share and perhaps some industry connections as well? Or do you want an empirical instructor to analyze your sound and give you feedback? Do you prefer a teacher who sings a lot during your lesson so you can model your sound after theirs, or do you prefer someone who avoids vocal modeling? Are you in need of nurturing or needling? Ask yourself these questions and ponder the possibilities.

Technique

Determine your learning style. Think about what teaching method seems to work best for you in your voice lessons.

1. Imagery, visceral sensation? Consider a holistic teacher.
2. Physiological, technical information? Consider a mechanistic teacher.
3. A combination of imagery and physiology? Consider a teacher who combines both.

Some voice students thrive on knowing how the intercostal muscles work or seeing a spectrum analysis of their sound via VoceVista (see Secret 47). Other students won't be able to sing any better with this knowledge and instead will improve vocally by picturing a specific image that aids in alignment or guides their ear to a new tonal ideal. As one might expect, a holistic teacher would often be a good fit for someone who is right-brained (imagine romantic Rachmaninoff with his outpouring of lyricism) while a mechanistic teacher would fit with someone who is left-brained (imagine logical Lassus and his modal counterpoint). But sometimes it is better to study with a voice teacher who will pull you out of your comfort zone and make you think (or feel) differently about how you sing. Many teachers combine these complementary styles in their lessons, so it's not as if you have to make a strict choice between vocology and ideology.

Benefit

Once you have investigated your learning style, research prospective teachers by checking out their website or NATS/AATS directory, where they might include their teaching philosophy. Ask around—word of mouth is the second-best way to find the right teacher. The best way is to take a sample or preliminary lesson to see if you two are a good fit. Keep your mind and heart (and throat) open during your initial lesson and you will be able to see if the teacher is right for you. Switching studios after you have been assigned to a teacher is often possible (and should be a professional choice, not a personal affront), but sometimes it can be awkward and lead to ruffled feathers or bruised egos. So try to find the right fit first.

NOTE

1. This list of terminology borrows heavily from Matthew Hoch's book, *A Dictionary for the Modern Singer* (Lanham, MD: Rowman & Littlefield, 2014).

CHAPTER 2

Musicianship

Note: Advanced singers with secure musicianship may wish to skip over some of the basic musicianship topics in chapter 2 of this book. It is our belief, however, that many students of singing will benefit from the advice included in these six sections, particularly those students who do not enter their studies with the benefit of an extensive instrumental background.

SECRET 15: CONNECT TO THE PAGE—SCORE STUDY

Music does not exist on the page. Music only comes alive when a performer interprets it and a listener connects to it. The composer, however, does give the singer many written clues via the score, so careful score study is important when preparing songs and arias. Much of the traditional canon of vocal repertoire was written in an era that precedes recorded sound, so the written score becomes a blueprint—the only method of communicating with the composer. Being an interpretive artist is an imaginative endeavor and a great responsibility, and one should always seek to honor the composer's intentions.

Technique

Obtain the best edition of the score possible. This is especially important in the era of free online resources, such as the International Music Score Library Project (IMSLP). While some public-domain resources are reliable, many are fraught with errors and misprints that have long been corrected by more modern editions. If possible, seek out a scholarly urtext edition, such as those published by Bärenreiter or Peters. Obviously, these higher-end scores can be expensive but are well worth it if the singer is in a financial position to acquire them. If you are performing an opera or oratorio role, the conductor will likely communicate which score to purchase, as he or she will want everyone to "be on the same page" (literally) during rehearsals.

When first rehearsing the music, work your way through the score *at a piano* and *with a pencil*. The vocal line should be played in rhythm and with a metronome (see Secret 40). Problem spots should be notated and all measures numbered. Often opera and oratorio scores consist of multiple simultaneous vocal lines; when this occurs, many singers choose to highlight their part in order to avoid confusion. If the text is in a foreign language, International Phonetic Alphabet (IPA) transcription should also be a part of score preparation (see Secret 50). Any text should be rehearsed by itself and in rhythm before singing it on pitch.

After the part is learned independently—and only then—consult up to five high-quality recordings of the work by reputable artists. You should always follow along with the score, noting interpretative decisions while keeping an open mind about how a particular artist's interpretation might be different. It is very important never to become too attached to one artist or recording; singers will inevitably internalize some idiosyncrasies of the performer, and your singing should never sound derivative.

Benefit

Being able to digest a score with accuracy is paramount. Voice teachers, coaches, and directors grow very impatient with singers who do not have the study skills or musicianship necessary to learn scores on their own. The industry no longer tolerates singers who do not arrive at lessons, coachings, and rehearsals fully prepared.

SECRET 16: PRIORITIZE RHYTHM—THE ESSENCE OF MUSICIANSHIP

The great British pianist Gerald Moore said of the legendary German baritone Dietrich Fischer-Dieskau, one of the greatest singers of the twentieth century and the most recorded singer of all time:

> It is not enough to say that his voice is wonderful, that he has an incredible technique which enables him to do what he will; it is not enough that his enunciation is flawless, with perfect marriage of word and tone. If I had to put my finger on the key to Fischer-Dieskau's supremacy, setting him apart from every other singer, I would say, in one word, *rhythm*. That is the life-blood of music, and he is the master of it.[1]

Rhythm is indeed "the life-blood of music," and to truly own a piece of music rhythmically is to do far more than execute the notation on the page. Rhythm must also be felt on a deep, structural level. For this reason, singers must address both the micro and macro aspects of rhythm. The micro aspects include the notated rhythms themselves, and the macro aspects include the metric (and hypermetric) organizational structures of the piece. Temporal shifts between sections and within sections must also be considered.

Technique

Unlike instrumentalists, singers almost always sing texts. Since composers usually start with words before setting the text, it is a good idea to master the text before attempting to sing it in rhythm or on pitch. Texts should be spoken in an expressive, declamatory fashion that identifies with the character of the language and the meter of the poetry.

After the text is "under the tongue" in a fluid way, you should then speak the text according to the rhythm assigned by the composer. This internalizes the rhythm on the micro level. Special attention should be paid to the length of pickups—composers like Schumann are notorious for "mixing things up" on seemingly strophic songs—as well as breaths; if the composer has not inserted rests between vocal phrases, then measure and mark your own breaths by shortening the note sung prior to the breath. A metronome can be helpful during this part of the process (see Secret 40).

To address the macro level of rhythm internalization, conducting the meter can be very helpful. Conducting is far more helpful than "tapping a steady beat" (a more commonly heard recommendation) because tapping alone does not draw special attention to the downbeat the way that a conducting pattern does. Very fast songs may be easier to conduct according to the hypermeter of the piece. Poulenc's "Voyage à Paris" and "Marc Chagall" are examples of lively songs in

3/8 meter that are best felt in hypermeter rather than in a fast one or (ridiculously fast) three.

Benefit

Conductors, musical directors, singing teachers, and competition judges can instantly identify strong musicians largely on the rhythmic integrity of the performance. Mastery of rhythm truly separates the women from the girls, the men from the boys, and the true artists from the amateurs.

SECRET 17: MASTER INTERVALS AND SCALE DEGREES

It is amazing to think that Western music—whether tonal or post-tonal—consists of only twelve chromatic pitches. These twelve notes are then organized into countless configurations by the composer, forming an infinite number of sonorities and expressive possibilities. This section will deal with some thoughts on interpreting pitches during score study through a discussion of intervals and scale degrees.

Technique

Pitches exist within two basic contexts: melodic and harmonic. The melodic context is the most obvious; it is the vocal line—or melody—that you sing. In this sense, intervals occur horizontally. During score study, you should note whether your part is moving diatonically (stepwise within the key), chromatically (by half-step motion), or by leap (intervals greater than a whole step). In the latter situation, you should make note of difficult intervals in the score via standard theoretical notation (P4, m6, +2, etc.).

The most commonly used method for deciphering the intervals of a melodic line is the solfège system. Solfège is the practice of using "solmization" syllables—such as do, re, mi, fa, sol, la, and ti—to represent pitches. Although these syllables were forever engrained in popular culture via the song "Do-Re-Mi" in Rodgers and Hammerstein's *The Sound of Music*, their original source is actually a medieval Latin hymn called "Ut Queant Laxis" (see figure 2.1):

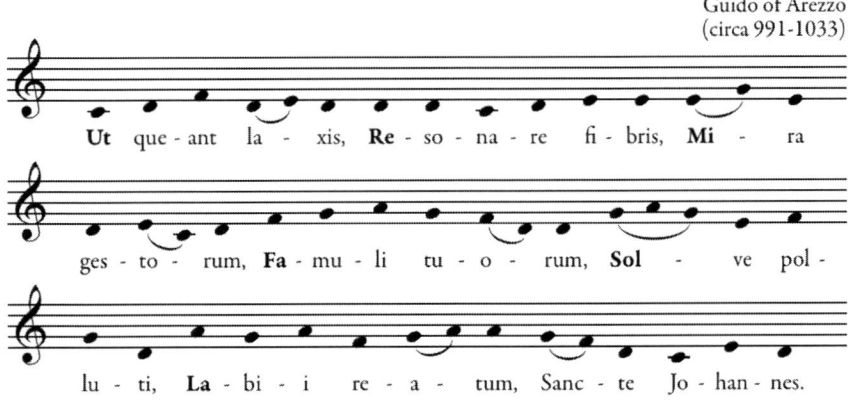

Translation:
So that your servants may, with loosened voices, resound the wonders of your deeds, clean the guilt from our stained lips, O Saint John.

Figure 2.1. "Ut Queant Laxis." *Creative Commons (CC BY-SA 3.0)*

A medieval music theorist named Guido d'Arezzo assigned initial syllables from this hymn and began using them for pedagogical purposes when teaching singers to sight-read music. Hence the famous "Guidonian Hand" (see figure 2.2).

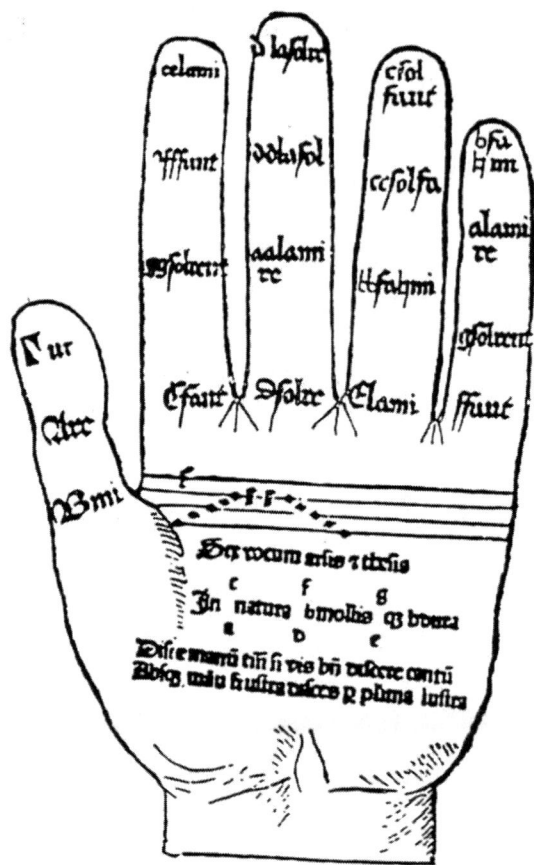

Figure 2.2. "Guidonian Hand"

Most American universities make use of a "moveable do" solfège system that is, in essence, a way of keeping track of scale degrees within a piece: do = scale degree 1, re = scale degree 2, and so on. This system also allows for pitches outside of the diatonic scale via another set of chromatic syllables: di, ri, fi, si, li (ascending) and te, le, me, and ra (descending). Due to this symbiotic relationship with actual scale degrees, some singers prefer to use numbers instead of solfège syllables as their principal means of deciphering intervals, but this method becomes a bit problematic when dealing with chromatic inflections.

Another consideration for pitch is its *harmonic* context: how the singer's pitch fits within the other pitches of the chord (e.g., the notes played in the piano accompaniment). It is a good idea to make note of whether you are singing the root, third, or fifth of a chord or whether the note sung is a non-chord tone, such as a suspension or appoggiatura. This kind of analysis is very important when thoroughly preparing your vocal line.

Benefit

Having a strategic method of studying melodic and harmonic content within a song or aria is essential for the thorough preparation of a score. The ability to hear specific intervals becomes even more important in the complex scores of late romantic, post-tonal, and modern repertoires. Being able to hear advanced intervallic content is a mark of mature musicianship.

SECRET 18: INTIMATELY KNOW THE PIANO ACCOMPANIMENT

The piano part is full of clues; look for them! The prelude, the postlude, the interludes—they are your world of the moment, your surrounding atmosphere; often they are you, your feelings, the subtext behind the words you sing.[2]

One of the biggest mistakes that inexperienced singers make is to focus exclusively on their vocal line, thus ignoring the piano accompaniment. The piano accompaniment is especially important in art song, which is the primary genre that student singers perform. The finest art song composers—such as Franz Schubert, Robert Schumann, Gabriel Fauré, and Claude Debussy—wrote piano parts that are not merely an accompaniment. Rather, they are idiomatic musical parts that share an equal partnership with the vocal line. The pianist tells the story just as much as the singer does.

Even when learning orchestrated genres such as opera, oratorio, and musical theatre, the singer will usually learn his or her part from a vocal score with a piano reduction. In these situations, the piano accompaniment must still be treated with great respect. Many of the composer's intentions can be gleaned from studying the accompaniment.

Technique

As stated before, it is beneficial to every singer to have some basic piano proficiency. This skill is valuable not only for being able to teach yourself the score (and avoid frustrating your teacher or vocal coach) but also for getting to know the score. Devote part of your practice session to playing through the piano accompaniment.

This serves two purposes. First, on a practical level, you will learn what to expect when your collaborator arrives: what the piano part sounds like, how long interludes are, and so forth. You should also determine how you are going to find the initial pitches of your vocal phrases or prepare yourself to sing a certain note against a dissonant accompaniment. This is especially important in more complex late romantic and modern repertoires. A Hugo Wolf or Claude Debussy song, for instance, will not make much sense if one studies the vocal line by itself.

Second, and perhaps more important for an artistic performance, learning the piano part alongside your vocal line will help you discover the poetic narrative. Ask yourself questions such as "Why did the composer set this word on a Ger+6 chord?" or "What is the meaning of this piano postlude?" Oftentimes, the song only reveals itself after all of its respective components are thoroughly studied and absorbed.

Benefit

Singers who only study their vocal line tend to be underprepared when rehearsing with their collaborative pianist. In addition, studying the piano accompaniment will yield clues to the expressive intentions behind the composer's setting of the text.

SECRET 19: STUDY THE ORCHESTRATION—THERE WON'T BE TRUMPETS (OR WILL THERE?)

Advanced and professional soloists will at some point have the opportunity to sing with orchestral accompaniment. This can be a thrilling experience, as an entire world of repertoire opens itself to the singer. Operatic roles, oratorio and concert repertoire, and the sumptuous orchestral songs of Gustav Mahler, Maurice Ravel, and Joaquín Rodrigo are just several examples of the magnificent marriage of the solo voice with orchestral accompaniment.

Most singers are used to practicing from piano-vocal scores, but reading an orchestral score is a completely different animal. Most instruments are assigned their own staff, which can be disorienting for the singer who is used to seeing a "reduction" of his or her accompaniment on a single grand staff in a vocal score.

Knowing the orchestration also requires the singer to understand various clefs. Sopranos and mezzos, for instance, are used to dealing only with treble clef, whereas baritones and basses seldom have to read anything but bass clef. Orchestral scores not only have both of these but also alto (and sometimes tenor) clefs as well! Viola parts, for instance, are written in alto clef. Most voice majors complain when confronted with alto clefs in ear-training class, but their practical use becomes apparent when singers have their first encounter with an orchestral score.

Technique

Find an orchestral study score and . . . study it! Listening to several reputable recordings while conducting the score is helpful as well. Make note of potential pitfalls and challenges and mark these spots accordingly.

Ultimately, singers almost always rehearse and perform from their standard vocal scores, so markings should then be transferred to the score that you will bring to rehearsals. Solo instrumental passages should be marked so that you know which instrument you will hear after the shift from piano to orchestral rehearsals. A careful study of the score will eliminate any surprise in terms of which instrument is playing which part of the accompaniment. A singer who has marked his or her score appropriately will do much to help the rehearsal process go smoothly.

Finally, even though orchestra-accompanied repertoire is often performed "on book" (although never in opera, unless it is a concert performance), it is still a good idea to have the piece as memorized as possible so that you can watch the conductor at all times. Nothing will frustrate a conductor more than the impression that the singer is not "connected" to him or her during a rehearsal or performance (see Secret 91).

Benefit

In order to sing well under the baton of an orchestral conductor, a singer must be thoroughly prepared, and the process is quite different than preparing for piano-accompanied recitals. The strategies above will help to ensure that the process goes smoothly. Pleased conductors are likely to invite singers back for future performances. The world of repertoire for voice and orchestra is a rich one, and these opportunities should be savored by every singer.

SECRET 20: SINGING IN STYLE—CULTURAL CONTEXT AND HISTORICAL TRADITIONS

Susan Sontag said that "style is everything." Style is perhaps the most important single element that one must consider as a musician. Since the human voice is capable of an almost-infinite variety of colors and nuances, style is perhaps even more complex for singers than for instrumentalists.

Singers tend to have good friendships with fellow singers, so most of us have had the experience of singing "out of style" for comic relief in informal social situations: for example, a pop song sung operatically or a standard aria sung with a country twang. The fact that we find these scenarios humorous illustrates how essential it is to sing in the correct style.

Mastery of style can be a complex endeavor that requires much time and study. As a result, many singers become specialists in certain styles. While a regional performer might be able to get away with singing both Handel and Puccini, top international specialists will probably not have reputations for singing both of these composers equally well, as the styles (and voices) listeners expect are completely different. Singing in style is a highly cultivated art.

Technique

When singers and voice teachers refer to "technique," they are usually referring to some aspect of voice production. There is, however, a certain technique to singing in style. Even within the realm of classical music, repertoire from different eras, regions, and composers often calls for extremely different stylistic approaches.

Careful listening is always the first step to singing in style. Singers need to gain a firm aural understanding of what the musical goals are for a particular genre, language, or era. While live performances are always best, the modern singer has more access to high-quality recordings than at any other time in the history of singing. Take advantage of this extensive (and ever-expanding) discography!

Next, and most important, the singer must *practice* the specific skills required by a given style. Singing Bach coloratura is a completely different endeavor than singing Bellini legato, and many of the skills needed to sing one composer well will not necessarily translate to another style. Building new skills through a disciplined practice routine takes time, so if you are approaching a new style, allow at least four to six weeks to get a new composer or work "in your voice." Ultimately, most singers will find that they have a knack for one style but not another, although the young singer should explore a wide variety of repertoire before finding his or her ultimate niche.

For a detailed discussion of singing style across various eras, one of the best books written on the topic is Martha Elliott's *Singing in Style: A Guide to Vocal Performance Practices*. All singers should read this book, especially classical singers interested in performing early music styles.

If you are a contemporary commercial music (CCM) performer or pedagogue, style becomes perhaps an even more important issue, as vocal style is one of the main elements that distinguishes rock from country or R&B from gospel. In addition to careful listening, many workshops under the direction of professional specialists are now available for singers and teachers interested in exploring a new style. Teachers interesting in teaching these styles, however, should not attempt to do so unless they have practiced and gained some experience singing in the styles themselves. Every genre requires dedicated practice on the specific skills it requires. (See chapter 7 for a more comprehensive overview of CCM styles.)

Benefit

Singing in correct style is quintessentially important to any singer and is sometimes a more subtle endeavor than it may seem to be at first. Singers should invest considerable time in researching performance practice when approaching a new style or piece of music. Research may consist of reading musicological resources, careful listening, and coaching with specialists. Ultimately, a singer must thoroughly practice the skills required by the specific style in question. The result will be a more expressive performance in the spirit of what the composer intended.

NOTES

1. Hans Adolf Neunzig, *Dietrich Fischer-Dieskau: A Biography*, trans. Kenneth S. Whitton (Portland, OR: Amadeus Press, 1998), 112.
2. Beaumont Glass, *Richard Strauss' Complete Song Texts* (Mt. Morris, NY: Leyerle, 2004), xiv.

CHAPTER 3

Vocal Health

SECRET 21: *LIBIAMO!* WATER AND HYDRATION

As the saying goes, "pee pale, sing clear." Hydration is essential for good vocal health, so most singers know they need to drink enough water. Although a voice teacher once told me "Maria Callas never had a water bottle," water bottles are now a universal accessory for singers. Hopefully your water bottle is reusable and BPA (bisphenol A) free to be better both for the environment and your own health. These days there are many types of water from which to choose: distilled water, filtered water, electrolyte water, alkaline water, coconut water, fruit-infused water, seltzer, SmartWater, and so on. (It is surprising that no one has marketed Sing-Water!) But you don't need a fancy brand; you just need to drink enough water to maintain your own healthy fluid balance.

Technique

When you drink water, it doesn't actually touch your vocal folds. (If it does, you cough.) The water you drink must first be absorbed into the bloodstream before it can reach other parts of the body. Therefore, you want to maintain consistent hydration. If you feel thirsty, you are already dehydrated. The familiar daily recommendation for water intake has been six to eight eight-ounce glasses of water, meaning forty-eight to sixty-four fluid ounces a day. To determine your recommended daily intake of water, try using this newer formula:

Your weight in pounds _____ × ⅔ (or .666) = _____ fluid ounces of water that you should drink daily. You may want to add eight to twelve ounces if you exercise heavily that day or if you are singing in a desert climate (to fight "Vegas throat") or at a high altitude (Santa Fe Opera). You can count juices toward your fluid intake. Tea and coffee can also count as long as your caffeine intake stays below 300 mg, after which there may be a negative diuretic effect. If you are practicing Bikram yoga (at 105°F and 40 percent humidity), be very careful to monitor your fluid levels and prevent dehydration.

Benefit

Staying hydrated helps thin mucus and phlegm. Hydration helps to keep your mucous membranes moist, boosting your ability to fight off a cold. Also, even mild dehydration causes fatigue, which can affect your ability to perform at your best. It is possible to overhydrate, but it is unlikely unless you partake in a dangerous hazing/ritual water-drinking contest. So keep your voice sounding clear and your energy feeling high. *Libiamo!*

SECRET 22: DEVELOP A HEALTHY SPEAKING VOICE— PITCH AND BREATH

In the film *He's Just Not That into You*, Drew Barrymore asks, "My voice doesn't match my face?" The implication was that her adorable and appealing face didn't match the gargling, gruff vocal fry of her speech. It is especially odd in an operetta or musical when characters' singing and speaking voices don't have the same quality. For instance, soprano ingénue Laurey in *Oklahoma!* should not sound like sultry Lauren Bacall, and Jean Valjean in *Les Misérables* shouldn't sound like comedian Gilbert Gottfried. Your speaking voice should be similar in timbre and pitch to your singing voice, not just for the audience's sake but for your own vocal health.

Technique

1. Find your optimal pitch range. Record yourself speaking, both informally chatting and more formally reading something aloud. Then listen to the recording, since many of us don't have an accurate perception of our own speaking voice because we are busy speaking, not listening (see Secret 39). Then ask yourself a few questions. Is there some pitch variety to your speech or is it monotone? Is your voice clearly audible or is the pitch too low to project well? Is your voice too high-pitched and, as a result, strident or piercing? Unless he is a falsettist like Michael Jackson, a male singer will speak primarily in his chest or modal voice. Women should be careful not to speak at too low a pitch level or they can unintentionally segue into vocal fry. Female singers should strive for a mixture of chest and head voice as they find a happy medium in the middle voice for their optimal speaking pitch range.
2. Match the pitch and timbre of your singing voice. This doesn't mean that tenors should answer the telephone on an Italianate high C, but if the vocal resonance of your singing voice is balanced and consistent, it can be a good model for your speech as well. Pick a familiar, easy song with a conjunct, stepwise vocal line, such as "My Country 'Tis of Thee," and avoid rangy showpieces like "The Star-Spangled Banner." Sing through the song, then speak-sing it, giving yourself the freedom to segue into speech but trying to maintain the general pitch level and quality from your singing.
3. Support your speaking voice in a manner more similar to your singing voice (see Secret 2). Again, this doesn't mean that friendly conversation has to become an oration from *Julius Caesar*, but employ healthy breath management instead of mumbling and dropping the ends of sentences, as so many Americans do.

Benefit

Developing a healthy speaking voice will also help the health of your singing voice. So unless you're playing a quirky character like Lilly Onakurama, the soft-voiced whisperer in *Pitch Perfect*, or you're Ben Stein with his comedic monotone ("Bueller? Bueller?"), try to speak in your optimal pitch range with good breath flow and resonance as another key component of your vocal-hygiene regime.

VOCAL HEALTH 49

SECRET 23: USE STRAW PHONATION (AND OTHER SOVT EXERCISES)

Over the past several decades, there has been increased dialogue between teachers of singing and vocal-health professionals: speech-language pathologists, surgeons, and otolaryngologists, also known as ear, nose, and throat doctors (ENTs). Voice scientists have also shown an increased interest in voice pedagogy and scientific applications to teaching. Professional organizations such as the National Center for Voice and Speech (NCVS) in Salt Lake City and the Voice Foundation in Philadelphia have done much to cultivate these interdisciplinary relationships and encourage advanced research on the singing voice.

One of the most important and widely used exercises that has found its way into the voice studio is the use of semi-occluded vocal tract (SOVT) exercises. Roughly meaning "partially closed vocal tract," this term describes any vocal exercise that restricts airflow at the front of the oral cavity, such as humming, lip or tongue trills, or straw phonation (literally, singing through a straw). It should be noted that some vowels—like [e] and [i]—can also be semi-occlusive. While all of these exercises are helpful, straw phonation is perhaps the most beneficial type of SOVT exercise (see figure 3.1).

Technique

Note: This section will present straw phonation exercises. Any of them, however, may also be done on a hum or lip or tongue trill, which are also considered to be SOVT exercises.

Figure 3.1. Opera Singer Renée Fleming and Vocologist Ingo Titze Practicing Straw Phonation. *Martin Kane, UNC Greensboro*

Not all straws are equal. Straws that are too wide in diameter (such as those one finds at McDonald's) are less ideal than narrower straws (one of our colleagues emphatically states her preference for Panera straws). Experienced "straw phonators" may also experiment with extremely narrow tubes, such as coffee stirrers.

Any vocal warm-up can be sung through a straw, but it is best to start with glides. Start midrange and glide over the interval of a perfect fifth (P5). Start at the bottom pitch, slide up to the fifth, and slide down again. Breathe and repeat a half step higher, then begin descending before getting into an extremely high or uncomfortable range. After these simple introductory exercises, extend to scales and arpeggios. Repeat for five to ten minutes. Fifteen minutes is ideal if you can set aside the time.

Singers new to straw phonation should be careful that they are not singing with nasal resonance during this exercise. All airflow should be directed entirely through the mouth. Singing a [u] vowel through the straw can be helpful, as can pinching the nose shut with your fingers to ensure that no air is escaping through the nasal cavity.

Benefit

The benefits of SOVT exercises are both therapeutic and technical. Although they were originally used by speech-language pathologists and other vocal-health professionals when dealing with troubled or injured voices, voice teachers later appropriated them for their studios, citing habilitative and rehabilitative benefits.

According to voice scientist Ingo Titze, SOVT exercises serve four primary physiological functions:[1]

1. SOVT exercises get respiratory muscles into full action rapidly.
2. SOVT exercises minimize upward force on vocal folds because of positive oral pressure.
3. SOVT exercises spread the vocal folds to vibrate only their edges.
4. SOVT exercises lower phonation threshold pressure by providing an inertive acoustic load.

In addition to these efficiency and health benefits, many singing teachers find that SOVT exercises are ideal vocal warm-ups. Ten minutes of straw phonation while warming up for a morning audition can do wonders (see Secret 9) to help the singer "feel ready" to sing, even at an early hour. In addition, some singers notice a positive impact on their breath management and resonance after practicing SOVT exercises, citing ease of production and a more focused tone quality. SOVT exercises seem to be especially effective with young, breathy voices striving to achieve a clearer, more fully adducted sound.

SECRET 24: FOOD AS FUEL NOT FAD—DIET MATTERS

Atkins, South Beach, vegetarian, vegan, pescatarian, Paleo, gluten free. It seems there's always a new diet in the news. There is no trademarked "Singer Diet," although some vocalists have food allergies or health issues that will impact what they can or should eat. Many singers avoid dairy products because they fear an increase in mucus production, while some deal with GERD (gastroesophageal reflux disease) or LPRD (laryngopharyngeal reflux disease) and need to take measures to prevent acid reflux (see Secret 29).

Technique

Get to know *your* body. Try a variety of different foods and meal plans to see what might work best for you—don't simply try something new the day before or the day of a big performance. Develop a ritual. Having a regular routine (food-wise) will help maintain your energy, health, and vocal stamina. You don't want to sing on a full stomach that is still busy digesting, but you need to have something in your system, just like a runner does before a big race. Singing on an empty stomach could lead to fainting, especially under hot stage lights. If you have an 8:00 p.m. performance, maybe try a 4:00 p.m. meal since it may take up to three hours for food to digest. Backstage, many singers like fruit for a pre- or midperformance snack. Bananas contain natural beta blockers, so they help performance anxiety, and chewing an apple releases jaw tension for some.

Benefit

A healthy diet fuels your body for optimal performance. You are a vocal athlete, so you need energy to perform. As famed tenor (and pasta expert) Luciano Pavarotti said, "You need some sugar when you sing. You need the energy. Zap! You cannot be romantic on stage without some sugar." But try to eat complex carbohydrates rather than simple sugars in order to maintain steady blood sugar throughout the day. Perhaps try some whole wheat pasta . . . with plenty of water, of course!

SECRET 25: EXERCISE—YOUR BODY IS YOUR INSTRUMENT

Your body, not just your larynx, is your instrument. That does not mean your body has to look like muscle-man Dwayne "the Rock" Johnson or supermodel Heidi "the Body" Klum. Not many singers are known for their abs of steel, except midriff-baring Shania Twain and "barihunks" like Nathan Gunn. Actually, abs of steel are not necessarily good for optimal breath management, especially if they are too rigid and "rock hard." Still, singers need to be in good shape these days in order to sing while doing their blocking (opera) or choreography (musical theatre). Furthermore, a professional singer's life often involves a lot of traveling, so being in good physical condition helps you stay healthy as you traverse shifting time zones and demanding tour schedules.

Technique

Figure out what type of exercise you like so you will stick with it. If you're on tour and living out of a suitcase, explore your new home away from home by walking or jogging, or try the hotel gym for a low-impact workout on the elliptical or recumbent bike. If you lift weights, make sure you don't hold your breath. Inhale before you lift and exhale as you lift to prevent putting pressure on your vocal folds. Try out new fitness classes on a preliminary trial pass or Groupon deal; that way you can find out if you're a fan of Zumba, Pilates, barre work, boot camp, or spinning. If you have joint issues, swimming is a great option. Also consider yoga, which can be part of your backstage warm-up as well as your exercise regime (see Secret 31).

Benefit

Cardiovascular exercise will improve your lung function, therefore it will help your breathing. Exercise is a wonderful stress reliever since it releases endorphins, our own natural mood elevators. A singer's life can be a stressful one, and physical exercise can keep both your body and mind in good condition. When asked about exercise, baritone Thomas Hampson said: "It's number one! Movement, air, exercise."

SECRET 26: AVOID VOCALLY ABUSIVE (LOUD) ENVIRONMENTS—CAN YOU HEAR ME NOW?

Although they are both dynamic personalities and engaging public speakers, it can be difficult to listen to Rachael Ray and Bill Clinton speak because both seem to have vocal damage, perhaps from vocal abuse. It is actually easy to abuse your voice with overuse (too much talking or singing) or straining (pushing or trying to project outside without amplification or when you are sick). Certain social activities require or encourage screaming (cheering at sporting events, talking over music at a club, or riding roller coasters). Whether you are a singer who is also a cheerleader or an elementary school music teacher, you need to do what you can to avoid abusive environments that might endanger your voice.

Technique

1. Avoid the Lombard effect. The Lombard effect occurs when we raise the intensity and pitch level of our voice to project over background noise. So stay away from loud restaurants or you will probably be tempted to strain to be heard over the conversation and music surrounding you.
2. Avoid smoky environments. Most indoor public places are nonsmoking these days (with the exception of Las Vegas casinos). But this means that bar/restaurant patios or building entrances have become havens for smokers, making them perilous for singers. Even the now-trendy hookah lounges can be a dangerous environment for singers because they can make smoking seem exotic, even though hookah is no safer than smoking cigarettes. Similarly, vaping and e-cigarettes minimize the perception of tobacco's dangers.
3. Protect your instrument: your voice *and* your ears. If you do attend a football game, lip-sync your cheering instead of screaming along with the crowd. If you go to a rock concert or night club, again avoid the Lombard effect so you protect your voice but also wear ear plugs so that you don't abuse your hearing either.
4. Take a vocal break. Try to avoid meeting with friends, family, or fans who want to talk with you before a big performance. Hopefully they will understand the need for you to conserve your vocal energy and wait until after the show for in-depth discussions. Sometimes vocal rest is a good idea for any of us, and it can be a necessity for singers recovering from laryngitis or vocal cord surgery.

Benefit

As singers, sometimes we face circumstances that we can't always control, such as when we catch a cold or a delayed flight disrupts our plans for sleep.

But it is easy to shun loud, smoky environments and avoid sounding like Harvey Fierstein. Besides the Lombard effect, noisy public places can be overstimulating, drawing focus away from your performance. Instead, find a quiet, peaceful environment that nurtures serenity and places no extraneous demands on your voice.

SECRET 27: AHEM! AVOID CLEARING YOUR THROAT—TRY *UJJAYI* BREATHING INSTEAD

Throat clearing: we've all done it. Some people do it habitually or unknowingly, but singers usually do it to relieve a feeling of irritation in the throat or to remove phlegm before singing. However, many singers clear their throats unnecessarily or mistakenly include the habitual action as part of their vocal routine. The problem is that repeated throat-clearing can actually be damaging to your vocal cords. Just like scratching an itch only makes it itch more, one "ahem" begets more and only exacerbates any pharyngeal inflammation. So resist the urge to (ahem) clear your throat, which doesn't really clear it anyway. Address any issues that might be causing irritation (see Secrets 21 and 28), and then consider this alternative technique.

Technique

Instead of clearing your throat, try a yoga breathing technique called *"Ujjayi* breathing." Also known as "Victorious Breath," this yogic breath-control practice calls for you to inhale through the nose, then exhale, keeping your mouth closed while you partially close the glottis as if you were whispering [ha] but with your lips gently closed. If you have trouble doing this, first practice exhaling on [ha] with an open mouth, as if you're trying to fog up a mirror, and then close the lips. The sound of the *Ujjayi* breath resembles ocean waves or the infamous *Star Wars* villain Darth Vader.

Benefit

Ujjayi breathing helps shake phlegm off the vocal cords without the irritation of throat clearing. In addition, *Ujjayi* has other benefits for singers. It helps lengthen your exhalation, thereby increasing breath control, and lowers your blood pressure. Its soothing quality can also help with performance anxiety (see Secret 80), making *Ujjayi* a much better pre-performance ritual than "Ahem!"

SECRET 28: PHLEGM IS NOT YOUR FRIEND (COPING STRATEGIES)

Our colleague Daniel Ihasz, professor of voice at SUNY Fredonia, used to say sarcastically, "Phlegm is your friend." Phlegm is necessary in the body—we actually go through a liter and a half a day—but is a problem when there is too much or it thickens due to illness or allergies. Then, phlegm becomes an irritant to the vocal folds. It drains from our mucous membranes, often causing coughing, swelling, and pharyngitis. Whether caused by illness or allergies, phlegm can lead to temporary or long-term inflammation. Even habitual throat-clearing of phlegm can sometimes lead to vocal damage (see Secret 27). Thus singers need to be in control of their sinuses as much as possible.

Technique

1. Hydration. Keep phlegm at bay by staying hydrated (see Secret 21). Water helps thin mucus. Besides drinking water, you can also keep your mucous membranes moist by using a humidifier and/or a personal steamer.
2. Diet. If you are allergic to dairy, gluten, or another food group, avoid those foods since they might create phlegm. An elimination diet can help you determine potential allergens by eliminating certain foods for a few weeks and then reintroducing them to see your body's reaction.
3. Treatment. If you are faced with phlegm that won't respond to your hydration and diet efforts, then you should consider treatment and check with your ENT. You'll want to make sure your medicine contains the important phlegm-thinning expectorant guaifenesin. Perhaps the best-known over-the-counter medication is Mucinex, made famous by its commercial with a persistent green-colored character named Mr. Mucus. If you are looking for an alternative treatment without medication, and you don't mind having water in your nose, then consider trying a Neti pot. In this Ayurvedic/yoga practice, you use what looks like a miniature tea pot to irrigate your nasal cavity with a saltwater solution to rinse and relieve mucus. Although you can buy them at most pharmacies, Neti pots aren't for everyone, so again check with your physician and definitely read the instructions carefully so you don't end up swallowing the water, burning your nasal cavity, or getting bacteria from contaminated tap water.

Benefit

Excessive phlegm is definitely not your friend, so fight it off by staying hydrated, minimizing allergens, and using guaifenesin or a Neti pot if necessary. A phlegm-free singer is a happy and healthy one.

SECRET 29: COMBAT ACID REFLUX DISEASE (GERD AND LPRD)

Ideal dietary habits and professional singing do not always complement each other. It is not at all uncommon for a singer to indulge in a high-calorie meal after a show lets out at 11:00 p.m. Oftentimes this late-night indulgence takes place in a loud environment and is accompanied by several glasses of wine as well. The morning after such excursions, many singers notice that their voices seem compromised. There may be a bitter taste in the mouth, a sore throat, or a general feeling of fatigue. A common cause of these symptoms is acid reflux disease.

There are two basic kinds of acid reflex disease: gastroesophageal reflux disease (GERD) and laryngopharyngeal reflux disease (LPRD). GERD is caused by gastric acid migrating into the esophagus. LPRD is a bit more severe and occurs when acid proceeds to spill into the larynx and vocal folds. The vocal fold irritation caused by LPRD is of serious concern to the singer.

Does Everyone Have It?

Since digestive acids exist in everyone's body, everyone, in theory, is prone to acid reflux. However, singers tend to be more sensitive to it than other people due to the fact that they are professional voice users. Everyone gets colds, for instance, but a cold will impact and slow down a singer far more than someone who is an accountant or an insurance agent. By extension, acid reflux disease tends to bother singers much more than someone else because singers are much more sensitive to the throat irritations caused by GERD/LPRD. While some singers seem to be able to get away with reckless lifestyle choices and still sing beautifully, many need to carefully consider dietary matters in order to consistently sing at their best.

Technique

Acid reflux disease can be managed and often avoided altogether through awareness of the causes of GERD and LPRD and taking appropriate preventative measures. The following are the most important things to remember:

1. Eat meals at least two to three hours before lying down so that food can properly digest.
2. Consider *what* you eat: spicy foods, alcohol, chocolate, and citrus fruits are some foods that can trigger acid reflux.
3. Don't overeat. If you are a fast eater, consider slowing down so that your body has a chance to tell your brain that you are full.

4. Acid reflux tends to occur more frequently if you are overweight. If this describes you, diet and exercise can help to minimize the symptoms of acid reflux.
5. Elevate the head of your bed four to eight inches. This can help significantly.
6. Don't smoke! As a singer, hopefully you aren't doing this anyway.

Fortunately, the causes of acid reflux are not a mystery and can be easily managed with a moderate amount of discipline.

Benefit

Awareness of the perils of late-night eating, alcohol, and dietary choices can make a significant difference in how you feel and how well you sing the following day. Even singers who don't suffer from regular acid reflux per se can still notice a negative impact the morning after a midnight meal or too much to drink. Taking preventative measures to avoid acid reflux is a precaution that will benefit most singers.

SECRET 30: MANAGE YOUR MEDICATIONS: BALANCING RX AND OTC WITH TLC

Note: The authors are doctors of musical not *medical arts! Always check with your physician if you have questions or concerns about your health, and check with your pharmacist to review the proper usage and potential side effects of your prescription medications.*

Singers have a reputation for being hypochondriacs. The slightest hint of a sniffle can send us into a panic and begin a frenzy of tea drinking and scarf wearing. Sometimes we aren't afflicted with a cold, but we have a different medical condition that requires a regular prescription for the management of our health. It is important to know how prescription, over-the-counter (OTC), and herbal medications may affect your voice, whether they help your recovery from a brief illness or manage an ongoing condition.

Short-Term Medications

1. Antibiotics. It can be tempting to pop a Z-Pak, especially when you're feeling sick before a big performance. But antibiotics can only help with a bacterial infection (e.g., strep throat) not a viral infection (cold, flu). You don't want to take them if they won't do anything except build resistance for when you really need to take them.
2. Steroids. It's also tempting to take a steroid, particularly when hoarseness threatens an impending gig. Yes, steroids can quickly reduce swelling and inflammation of the vocal folds, but their side effects are substantial, so you want to make sure you don't overuse steroids. It's not worth endangering your long-term health for a short-term performance.
3. Nonsteroidal NSAIDs. When your throat hurts, you may take aspirin or ibuprofen for pain, but these OTC pain relievers can increase your risk of vocal hemorrhage. That's why some laryngologists would recommend taking Tylenol instead.
4. Throat sprays. Most OTC throat sprays temporarily numb the throat, thanks to the ingredient phenol. The anesthetic action will relieve throat pain but also make it difficult to feel when you're straining and possibly causing more inflammation.

Long-Term Medications

Many of us have chronic issues for which we need to take medication, be it asthma or acid reflux (see Secret 29). If you are dealing with allergies, you may need to explore allergy shots, experiment with which antihistamine works best for you (Benadryl, Allegra, Claritin, Zyrtec), or seek other phlegm-fighting methods (see Secret 28). Hormonal medications can also affect the voice. If you have hypothyroidism, you'll need to take thyroid medicine regularly or the lack of thyroid hormones could cause hoarseness. Some women feel effects on their voice from birth control pills, especially progesterone-dominant pills. Antidepressants (Prozac, Zoloft), drugs for attention deficit syndrome (Adderall), and acne medication (Accutane) can cause dry mouth and, thus, negatively impact singers. Some singers suffering from performance anxiety take medicines that can cause memory issues (Xanax) or dizziness (beta blockers). When it comes to relieving anxiety, long-term medication seems less safe and desirable than learning to use meditation to calm your nerves (see Secret 80).

Note

Again, check with your doctor and be sure to ask about the benefits and possible side effects of any medication you take. The National Center for Voice and Speech has an excellent database where you can easily research your prescription(s) as well as any herbal treatments you might be taking. Appendix L of *A Dictionary for the Modern Singer* is another helpful resource for quick and easy reference. Don't just pop a pill or throat lozenge; take the time to know what you are taking so that you can verify the effects of your medications and ensure your valuable vocal health.

SECRET 31: EMBRACING BODYWORK—YES, EVERYONE IS DOING YOGA

So-called alternative body therapies are no longer considered alternative and have entered the wellness/fitness mainstream. Many musicians use the Alexander Technique or the Feldenkrais Method to aid alignment and prevent fatigue. Developed by Alexander teachers, Body Mapping is another kinesthetic practice that can help singers with body awareness. Soprano Renée Fleming reportedly is a practitioner of Pilates, a system popular among dancers to help with "contrology" or muscle control. These are all valuable forms of bodywork, but the most common modality is yoga. From the Sanskrit word meaning "union," yoga joins body, mind, and spirit in a practice that has gained increasing popularity in the United States, with over thirty-six million practitioners according to a 2016 *Yoga Journal* study. While over 11 percent of Americans practice yoga (and 34 percent say they are likely to practice yoga in the next year), it seems numerous singers practice yoga (from opera singers Thomas Hampson and Joyce DiDonato to pop stars Madonna and Adam Levine) because of its ability to help improve breathing, posture, and frame of mind.

Technique

Incorporate some yoga into your vocal-practice routine:

1. *Pranayama.* Yoga breath-control exercises can improve breath control by helping to increase lung capacity and lower your heart rate. Besides the popular *Ujjayi* breathing technique (see Secret 27) or the *kala* breath (see Secret 2), try the cooling *Shitali* breath. You can roll your tongue into a tube (some people are born with this genetic trait), reach your tongue toward your chin as in lion pose, or simply shape the lips into a [u] vowel. Inhale and exhale through the mouth while you maintain this tongue/lip position. The *Shitali* breath is thought to help relieve anxiety and cool the body. If you're feeling low energy, then try a technique on the opposite side of the spectrum, the Breath of Fire. Inhale through an open mouth and exhale repeatedly on [ha], bringing in the abdominal wall for each exhalation and building the coordination for staccato singing.
2. *Asanas.* Yoga poses can be helpful spine lengtheners (warrior 1, warrior 3, mountain pose) or empowering rib spreaders (warrior 2, reverse warrior, side plank, gate pose; see figure 3.2). Forward bends (rag doll, down dog, head-to-knee pose) help stretch and strengthen the backs of the legs for a stronger stance, while backbends (up dog, locust, bow, camel, fish) are heart openers that help singers to keep the sternum high and their expressive hearts open and communicative onstage (see Secret 81). And lion pose is the

ultimate yoga pose for singers, releasing tongue tension while also opening the throat for *gola aperta*.

Figure 3.2. Warrior 2 Pose

Benefit

"*Pranayama*" means "breath control" in Sanskrit, and the ancient breathing practice can definitely improve a singer's breath-management skills, while *asana* practice helps fine tune the body for healthy posture. Yoga and other types of bodywork have revealed tremendous benefits to singers of many genres. So embrace your yoga mat, your Pilates Reformer machine, or your tai chi practice as a wonderful means of keeping your entire instrument in its best possible condition.

SECRET 32: HOW TO WORK WITH METAL IN YOUR MOUTH—THE JOY OF BRACES

Oh, the miserable metal mouth of adolescence! The indignity of headgear! Now it's not just tweens suffering through braces, it's also college students and middle-aged soccer moms. Celebrity singers like Faith Hill and Fantasia Barrino have also endured "train tracks" on their teeth while performing (see figure 3.3), while others like Justin Bieber opted for Invisalign. Despite advances in orthodontia and its more modern options like clear aligners, braces can make singing a challenge. They can cause lisps, jaw tension, and lip discomfort, not to mention self-consciousness and a lack of confidence. But there are ways to work with and around orthodontic devices, and usually singers adapt quickly after the initial shock and apprehension of having this new apparatus in their mouths.

Technique

1. Embrace your braces. They are there to improve your jaw alignment, which will only help make you a better singer. They are there to align your teeth, which will only help make you a more confident performer. So don't hide your smile. Besides, Gwen Stefani chose braces as a "fashion choice," leading to a trend in some Asian countries to "wear" braces as a fashion accessory when they are not even necessary.

Figure 3.3. Katy Perry Shows Off Her Braces. *Music video still, YouTube 2011*

2. Take care with consonants and vowels involving the lips. Avoid fricatives, especially the labiodentals [v] and [f], which can be uncomfortable at first. Your lips will have to get used to moving over your braces, so labial vowels will also take some acclimation.
3. Keep your articulators agile. Practice articulatory exercises (see Secret 37) and tongue twisters ("the tip of the tongue, the lips, the teeth," "red leather, yellow leather"). Although you may not be able to open your mouth as wide, having braces may improve your kinesthetic awareness, especially of your tongue, which can help improve your singing in the long run.
4. Talk with your orthodontist in detail. Discuss the schedule of tightening and adjustments so that you can possibly avoid important auditions or performances on those dates. If you have an underbite, braces will actually help improve the lift of the soft palate, and a palatal expander will help create a larger resonant space in the oral cavity. Most important, optimal jaw alignment from braces should help keep these important joints healthy and free from TMJ (temporomandibular joint syndrome).

Benefit

Braces may seem like torture at the time, but luckily the torture is temporary, and the end result is a healthier and more beautiful smile. While awaiting the arrival of your straight teeth and aligned jaw, keep your articulators in shape and know that you're investing in the long-term health of part of your performance package.

NOTE

1. Ingo Titze, "The Five Best Vocal Warm-Up Exercises," *Journal of Singing* 57, no. 3 (2001): 51–52.

CHAPTER 4

Practice Strategies

SECRET 33: REGARDING VOWELS—THE ROOMS IN WHICH SINGERS LIVE

The great voice pedagogue Oren Brown used to say the following: "Vowels are the rooms in which singers live. Consonants are the doorways that propel you from room to room." Describing vowels as "the rooms in which singers live" is appropriate, as perhaps nothing is more basic and essential to vocal technique than good vowel formation. When we speak, we rarely think of our vowels, but singing requires that we actively think about our vowels in a more precise and mindful way.

Vowels are very closely related to resonance in singing (see Secret 4). This is particularly true of classical singing, but it is also true in certain contemporary commercial music (CCM) styles, including musical theatre—the "Broadway belt," for example, is in effect a specific kind of resonance strategy. It is important for singers to know some basic acoustic facts about vowels since vowels are unique to singing; no other instrument—wind, string, or percussion—experiences the vowel phenomenon.

About Vowels

Unlike the clarinet, the human voice is not a "fixed-bore" instrument. Singers can manipulate their vocal tract, thus changing their formants (resonances in the vocal tract) to create various timbres. The manipulation of the first two formants creates distinct vowels (see figure 4.1).

Although singers strive to make their vowels precise and appropriate for the style and range in which they are singing, it is important to note that vowels exist on a continuous spectrum with an infinite number of shadings and possibilities. International Phonetic Alphabet (IPA) symbols can only approximate specific

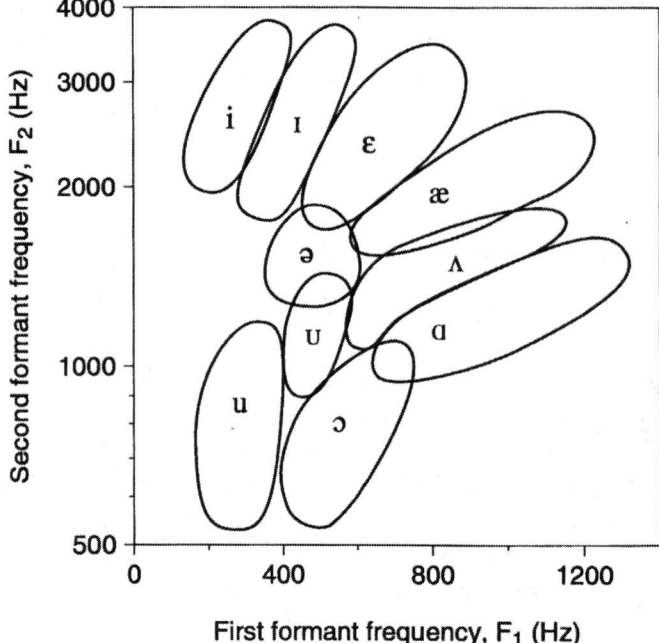

Figure 4.1. Vowel-Formant Chart (adapted from Peterson and Barney, 1952). *Ingo Titze, Principles of Voice Production (NCVS, 2000)*

vowels (see Secret 50). Ultimately, the singer is in control of specific vowel parameters, such as how bright/dark or open/closed the vowel should be.

Technique

1. Sing your song or aria on vowels only. If you are a classical singer, strive for a seamless legato and even vibrato. Classical singers tend to favor a longer vocal tract and a lower, more relaxed laryngeal position. Be careful not to become too spread or bright, particularly in the higher range. CCM singers tend to favor brighter, more speech-like vowels. For example, the [æ] vowel is strongly associated with the Broadway belt and by and large does not exist to the same degree in classical singing.
2. For optimal resonance, experiment with modifying vowels in certain parts of your range. For example, male classical singers tend to modify toward closed vowels—[i] and [u]—in their *secondo passaggio*, whereas sopranos and mezzos tend to modify toward [a] in the top of their range. Of course, do not get carried away with this. Some classical teachers have become so dismayed with the trend toward overmodification that they are now telling

students to forget about this and "just sing the vowel." Ultimately, vowels have to sound natural, or at least "natural" within the style that is being sung.

Benefit

Singers spend far more time singing vowels than consonants. Due to their omnipresence while singing, approaching vowels with precision is paramount to good vocal technique as well as singing in style. Knowledge about the fundamental acoustic properties of vowels can also offer specific strategies for refining one's resonance and tone quality in singing.

SECRET 34: REGARDING CONSONANTS—THE DOORS THAT PROPEL SINGERS FROM ROOM TO ROOM

If vowels are the rooms in which singers live, then describing consonants as "the doorways that propel [singers] from room to room" is a perfect analogy. Singers spend most of their time singing vowels, and consonants, in most instances, need to be as unobtrusive as possible as singers move from vowel to vowel. Legato is one of the great hallmarks of classical singing, and excellent legato is an attribute toward which all classical singers strive (see Secret 7). Thus, consonants are of special concern to classical singers, who need to make sure that consonants interfere with legato as little as possible.

CCM singing is very different than classical singing, and this is especially true with how CCM singers regard consonants. In contrast to classical singing, legato is not a quintessential feature of most CCM styles, and prioritization of textual clarity usually takes precedence over the tone quality or resonance of the singing. CCM singers often sing and speak their consonants in a similar way.

Technique

There are many different types of consonants, all of which are described by phoneticians and lyric diction specialists according to how they are produced. Thus, consonants can be described as bilabial, labiodental, dental, alveolar, post-alveolar, retroflex, palatal, velar, or uvular, as well as nasal, plosive, or fricative. In addition, consonants can also be voiced or unvoiced, which refers to whether or not the consonant has pitch (i.e., whether the vocal folds are active during the pronunciation of the consonant). The same consonant can have several of these attributes. For example, the consonant [b] is a plosive bilabial voiced consonant.

With regard to a technical approach to consonants, the voiced/unvoiced attribute is worthy of analysis and study as it relates to vocal technique. A common mistake for young singers is to neglect to voice consonants, particularly at the beginnings of words. For example, if you sing the word "darling," make sure that the first consonant is indeed a [d] and not its unvoiced "consonant pair," the [t]. Another common mistake is to add an additional (and unnecessary) nasal sound before voiced consonants. Make sure that you are actually singing "[d]arling" and not "[nd]arling."

Another important thing to remember is that, relative to vowels, consonants need to be *as short as possible* and occur, rhythmically, *before the beat*. This means that the vowel sounds on the written rhythmic notation, not afterward. It is important to remember that voiced consonants also need to be sung on the same pitch as the vowel they are preceding.

Choral directors tend to have different attitudes about consonants than solo singers, often prioritizing legato to a lesser degree and wanting more of virtually every consonant except [s]. Singers need to recognize this as simply being one of the stylistic distinctions between solo classical singing and choral singing.

Benefit

Having a technical approach to the complex and varied world of consonants maximizes your potential for a seamless legato and clear enunciation of the text.

SECRET 35: BE AN ACTIVE PARTICIPANT—GO TO YOUR LESSON WITH A PLAN

Being a successful singer requires you to be "all in." Singing is not an art form in which you can engage only passively, and nothing will annoy your voice teacher more than making him or her feel like they are the one doing all of the work or giving off all of the energy. In order to optimize your relationship with your voice teacher (see Secret 14), both participants need to be bringing something to the table. Specialists in teaching and learning refer to "flow," a process in which the student and teacher are feeding off each other in a synergistic relationship.

As teachers, nothing energizes us more than students who arrive at lessons fully prepared and ready to learn. Not surprisingly, these are the same students in whom we see regular improvement from week to week. The following is a list of ways in which you can maximize your learning—and your relationship with your voice teacher or coach.

Technique

1. Go to your lesson with a plan! Our very best students usually come in with a notebook on which they have written a short list of goals for the day's lesson: a list of two to three pieces they would like to sing, specific technical problems they are having within songs, or questions about a specific pronunciation issue. Sometimes this list includes things that are nonmusical: an audition application that they need me to sign or advice on how to handle a professional problem that has arisen with a teacher or fellow student. Sometimes these lesson plans are too ambitious, with more on the agenda than can possibly be accomplished during the next hour. That is okay and far preferred to the alternative: coming to your lesson with little plan or no plan at all.
2. Come to your lesson with the attitude and realization that you have done everything you can possibly do on your own. It is a waste of your teacher's time if you are still learning notes and rhythms, have not rehearsed with your accompanist, or have not transcribed your song into IPA. It is also a waste of your money to do things during the lesson that you should have done on your own. This behavior stifles learning, makes your teacher grouchy, and impedes your improvement. If it's something that you can and should do on your own, do it before your lesson.
3. Record your lesson and refer to it throughout the week (see Secret 46). It is also valuable to keep a notebook to keep track of assignments or ensure that you keep a record of a technical breakthrough or remember an important comment that your teacher gives you.

4. Arrive ready to sing. This means arriving warmed up, fed (if you don't sing well on an empty stomach), hydrated (see Secret 21), and well rested. Adequate rest is difficult for any of us, especially during busy times of the year, but your teacher will not be pleased if you show up sleep deprived because you stayed up all night writing a paper. The ideal voice student could have avoided the situation by not procrastinating in the first place. Your body is your instrument (see Secret 25), and you can't be a good singer without adequate sleep.

Benefit

One of our undergraduate professors had a quotation on his door that consisted of one sentence: "You are here to educate yourself." That doesn't mean that the teacher is unimportant, but it does mean that the student has enormous control over his or her own destiny. Being an active participant by going to your lesson with a plan and ready to sing will ensure an excellent relationship with your voice teacher and maximize your improvement as a singer.

SECRET 36: MIRROR, MIRROR ON THE WALL—USING THE MIRROR AS A PRACTICE TOOL

George Herbert wrote, "The best mirror is an old friend." Actually, the mirror is your best friend, but it seems as if some people avoid the mirror. Most of us are not narcissists; instead, we get distracted critiquing our hair or our outfit. However, using a mirror in both your voice lessons and practice sessions provides you with an important tool that can assist in creating good technical habits (see figure 4.2). Of course, you can't take the mirror onstage with you so you don't want to become dependent on it, but you can use it like a dancer uses the ballet barre (and mirror!) during each warm-up to prepare for a mirror-free performance.

Technique

Use a full-length mirror to monitor a number of issues by making visual observations of key elements that could affect your sound.

1. Tongue position: Is the tongue pulling backward when you sustain a note? Is it shaking?
2. Lip position: Are your lips rounding for your labial vowels? Are they shaking?

Figure 4.2. UNLV Students with Backstage Mirrors

3. Jaw alignment: Is the lower jaw jutting forward? Is it going to one side or the other? Is it shaking?
4. Body alignment: Is your sternum lifted or collapsed? Are your shoulders rounding forward or stretching backward? Is your head on your spine or pulling forward?
5. Clavicular breathing: When you inhale, do your shoulders and/or chest lift? Do you see a "high" vertical breath or a "low" inhalation that involves rib and abdominal expansion?
6. Facial expression: Is there tension in your face when you sing? Are your eyebrows furrowed? Are you making odd or off-putting facial expressions (see Secret 83)?

If you observe any tension, try to release it. If you observe a misalignment, try to realign it. Focus on one thing at a time instead of trying to address three to four vocal faults at one time. If your teacher asks you to use a mirror during the lessons, do so and resist stealing a glance at the teacher for approval.

Note

Not all practice rooms have mirrors, so have a small portable one you can carry in your bag. Then at least you can monitor mouth position and vowel formation. You can also use your mirror (or iPhone camera) to make sure there's no spinach in your teeth before your big audition!

Another Thought

For additional feedback, try videoing yourself for later viewing (see Secret 46). This used to be cumbersome when video cameras were the only option, but it is now easier than ever in the age of iPhones. Video feedback is particularly useful in situations like rehearsals and performances, when use of a mirror is not practical.

SECRET 37: TRAIN YOUR TONGUE—
FREEING CODEPENDENT ARTICULATORS

What are your articulators? To refresh your memory of some, revisit the tongue twister from Secret 32: "the tip of the tongue, the lips, the teeth." Some of your articulators are passive articulators (teeth, alveolar or gum ridge, hard palate, soft palate), while your active articulators are considered the lips and the tongue—not the jaw! The tongue and jaw should be independent, so that the jaw does not necessarily have to move unless it is essential in order to make a specific sound. You want to avoid singing like a puppet, with the jaw automatically "wagging" for every note or syllable.

Technique

Practice singing "la la la" (a common occurrence, be it in a Christmas carol, Glinda's "Popular" from *Wicked*, or Carmen's "Chanson *bohème*") without moving the jaw. Use the mirror to monitor (see Secret 36) or rest the index finger on the chin to encourage stillness of the jaw.

Then try to sing alveolar [da da da] and velar [ka ka ka] plosives by moving the tongue and not the jaw. Finally, if you are able to roll your *r* in a trill, try to sing [ri ri ri] or [ri re ra re ri] without jaw movement. Try these exercises first on a single note, then down a five-note scale from dominant to tonic, and then up and down a five-note scale from tonic to dominant and back. Since it may take time to break the codependent movement, it can be frustrating at first, like trying to learn rib cage isolations in a jazz dance class. Be patient but persistent.

Benefit

With free and independent articulators, you can sing with the dexterous diction needed for *The Barber of Seville*'s "Largo al factotum" or the wordy patter of a Sondheim song. With clear, intelligible diction, you will be able to reach the audience more directly and sing foreign languages more idiomatically. And codependent articulators won't stand in the way of your vocal freedom and textual communication.

SECRET 38: JOHNNY ONE NOTE—FROM MONOTONE TO LEGATO

You may or may not know "Johnny One Note," the Rodgers and Hart song from *Babes in Arms* about a man who could only sing one note. Despite Johnny's limited range, he had a useful pedagogical methodology. Carol Webber at the Eastman School of Music has her students use this exercise on their songs and arias before singing the actual melodic line.

Technique

Sing the text of your piece in rhythm on one note. Pick a pitch that is comfortably midrange or upper middle, avoiding extremes of tessitura. To avoid boredom, you can change the note up or down a step or to another note in the chord after several repetitions. (See figure 4.3.)

Che fie-ro co-stu-me d'a-li-ge-ro nu-me che a forza di pe-ne si fac-cia ado-rar!

Figure 4.3. Exercise on "Che fiero costume"

Benefit

It may seem pedantic, but this technique nurtures legato, aligns the sound, and makes sure that you have the text ready before you start adding intervals (see Secret 7). By temporarily minimizing some of the multitasking involved in singing by keeping the pitch the same, this exercise lets the singer focus on sustaining his or her vowels and stringing them together into a seamless cantabile line. While it can certainly improve legato when you are singing in your native tongue, it is particularly helpful in aligning and solidifying text in a foreign language (see Secrets 50–57).

Note

Richard Rodgers wasn't the first composer to employ this one-note method. There is a piece by Gioachino Rossini with a melody consisting of a single pitch, appropriately titled "*Élégie* sur une seule note." There's also a catchy jazz tune by Antonio Carlos Jobim called "One Note Samba."

SECRET 39: DON'T LISTEN TO YOURSELF! (OR SHOULD YOU?)

"No one is buying a ticket to sit inside your head; they are sitting out in the house," one of my voice teachers said to me when I (Matthew) was a very young singer. This comment was in response to my insistence that something sounded pretty good to me, so therefore it was okay. (He rightfully disagreed.) One of the most commonly heard maxims in the traditional singing lesson is "don't listen to yourself." On one level, this is very good advice. Because we live inside of our bodies, we don't really hear ourselves the same way that others do.

On the other hand, how can we not listen to ourselves? Unless you are deaf or otherwise hearing impaired, there is no way to sing without some sort of personal aural experience. How can one sing in tune without listening and centering the pitch? Also, older singers whose hearing is in decline often experience a decline in tone quality and resonance. The ear and the voice are so interconnected that they cannot truly be separated.

Therefore "don't listen to yourself" is in a sense a hyperbole—you can't help but do it on some level. It is helpful, then, to point out strategies for what kind of listening is beneficial versus detrimental to good singing.

Technique

1. Record yourself. It is true that the voice you hear when you sing is different than the voice others will hear. One way to overcome this is to record and listen to your singing (see Secret 46). This objectifies things considerably, allowing you to more accurately hear what others hear. When you first hear your singing voice on a recording, you may be surprised and say, "Do I really sound like that?" However, over time, you will come to understand your voice and hear it in a more accurate, less subjective way. We are still astonished when we hear recordings of our speaking voices, but we have now listened to so many recordings of our singing that what we hear no longer surprises us.
2. Have another set of ears that you trust. This can be a teacher (see Secret 14), coach, colleague, or friend that you can trust to give you objective feedback about your singing. Don't ask your mother (unless she's a singer, of course). Some people will not have the heart to tell you if something does not sound good. You will need for someone to be both knowledgeable and—on occasion—brutally honest.
3. Feel more, listen less. Obviously, some things you have to listen for, such as ensemble with your pianist, accurate intonation, and the degree to which a vowel is open or closed. However, at some point too much listening can be

detrimental, and you run the risk of overanalyzing your singing (see Secret 43). Singing is a kinesthetic activity: If you are connected to your body and it feels good, chances are it is good; if you are disconnected and it feels terrible, it will always be terrible.

Benefit

Balancing listening with kinesthetic feeling is extremely important for optimal singing. Singers who find this ideal balance set themselves up for the perfect blend of healthy technique, expression, intonation, and musicianship.

SECRET 40: USE A METRONOME—THEY AREN'T JUST FOR INSTRUMENTALISTS

If you wander the practice room hallways of a conservatory or university school of music, you will routinely hear pianists, violinists, saxophonists, and other instrumentalists practicing their scales, arpeggios, and repertoire accompanied by the steady click of a metronome. The regular use of metronomes among musicians has been in place for over two centuries; Johann Maelzel patented the metronome in 1815.[1] To this day, we still refer to metronome markings via the abbreviation MM, which stands for Maelzel's Metronome.

Although the metronome's function is simple—keeping a steady beat—its usefulness for training musicianship and preparing scores is profound. It is an essential tool for securing rhythmic accuracy in music, both on macro and micro levels (see Secret 16). Most musicians, even the most talented and experienced, tend to rush or drag in the heat of the moment while performing a piece of music, and a metronome helps to "keep you honest." It is also useful for singers to learn their scores at various tempi, often practicing difficult passages under tempo and proceeding steadily toward actual performance tempo after mastery occurs at the slower one.

Technique

The following are some suggestions for implementing metronome use into your practice and score-preparation routine.

1. Purchase a metronome and have it with you at all practice sessions and lessons. In the age of smartphones, there are also a variety of free apps you can download. Practice speaking the text along with the metronome before singing the piece on pitch.
2. If the tempo is fast, try practicing with a metronome under tempo before speeding it up incrementally. If the tempo is slow, set the metronome to double (or even quadruple) speed in simple meter or triple speed in compound meter so that you can explicitly feel the subdivision as you practice.
3. Mark your scores with all metronome markings. For example, MM = 104. This not only keeps a record of the tempo (so that you are "checking in" at the same tempo at all practice sessions), but it will also please your pianist, who is used to practicing while regularly consulting a metronome. Metronome markings are also helpful in audition situations when you do not have the luxury of rehearsing with your pianist beforehand. When collaborating with other instrumentalists in chamber music, they will likely expect to

have metronome markings communicated to them in advance of the first rehearsal.

Benefit

As the proverb says, "slow and steady wins the race." Regular use of a metronome in one's practice will benefit the singer in several ways, including improved musicianship, technical accuracy, and better communication with pianists and other collaborative instrumentalists. Some conductors—like Robert Shaw and Helmuth Rilling—were known to have metronome markings so engraved in their psyche that they could accurately recall precise pulses simply by someone stating the MM number (e.g., 72!). Musicianship to this degree represents the apotheosis of what one may be able to achieve after a lifetime of metronome work.

SECRET 41: YOUR FOCUS NEEDS MORE FOCUS— PRACTICE MINDFULNESS

The title of this secret is a line Jackie Chan says to Jaden Smith in the 2010 remake of *The Karate Kid*, but it could apply to most of us. Attention deficit disorder, smartphones, tablets, iPods, iPhones, Netflix streaming, mobile everything, Wi-Fi everywhere, even on planes and cruise ships. Modern technology has made us all scattered, so it can be a huge challenge to focus in a multitasking, digitally driven world.

Technique

First, turn off all electronic devices! Millennials (and some of us older folks) are so addicted to cell phones that this may be a task that requires significant willpower and discipline. Instead of multitasking, practice mindfulness, especially with practicing. No practice room selfies! Actually focus on practicing rather than tweeting, Snapchatting, or updating your Facebook status.

In addition, there are several yoga techniques that can help improve your focus:

1. Alternate nostril breathing. Find a comfortable seated position. Make sure your hands are freshly washed or sanitized with antibacterial gel. Place your right thumb on your right nostril so that it is occluded. Inhale through your left nostril. Then release your thumb from the right nostril and place your right index and middle fingers on your left nostril to occlude it. Exhale through your right nostril. Inhale through your right nostril, then occlude the right nostril with your right thumb and exhale through your left nostril. Continue with this pattern of alternating nostrils. This *pranayama* technique helps focus the mind and is even thought to help integrate the right and left hemispheres of the brain. You might skip this technique if you are congested, unless you have some Kleenex handy and are ready to clear your nasal passages!
2. Tree pose. For this balancing pose, place your weight on your left leg and move the sole of your right foot directly next to the arch of the left foot (called a "kickstand" tree), to the left calf muscle, or to the left inner thigh. Avoid placing the foot on your knee joint and be sure to keep both hips level, as the hip of the lifted leg will want to lift with it. Find a soft visual focal point (*drishti*) in front of you and bring your hands together in front of your chest. Feel free to vary your arm position, perhaps lifting the arms from prayer *mudra* (hand yoga position) directly overhead into a diamond or opening them out horizontally. After balancing for a few minutes, release

and switch sides to balance on your right leg. Don't worry if your balance falters a bit—trees do blow in the wind. But try to regain your balance by regaining your focus and concentrating on centering your energy in the central meridian of the body. (See figure 4.4.)

Benefit

Your focus will find more focus!

Figure 4.4. Tree Pose

SECRET 42: WHOSE LINE IS IT ANYWAY? TIPS FOR MEMORIZATION

Few things are more frightening for a singer than standing onstage and drawing a complete mental blank. A memory slip can cause a forgotten word, skipped stanza, missed cadenza, or an awkward (and seemingly endless) silent pause. Singers' brains are already busy multitasking, so it can be a challenge to remember the many strophes of Schubert's *Winterreise*, Susanna's voluminous recitative in *Le nozze di Figaro*, or the loquacious patter of a Gilbert and Sullivan song.

Techniques

1. Recitation. Whether it's a wordy German *Lied* or a witty Cole Porter standard, learn the text alone first. Practice reciting the words as if they were a poem or monologue. Then memorize the text alone first so that your memorization of the words is not dependent on the music.
2. Repetition (oral). Practice does not make perfect, but it does help build muscle memory and can help your musical and textual recall. Reiteration is a reliable memorization method for many. Speaking the text repeatedly and singing your part over and over can ingrain it in your brain. Some singers find comfort and confidence in rehearsing or "over-rehearsing." Others use speed run-throughs or sing-throughs to help learn by rote, singing or speaking as fast as possible to prevent pauses. Not surprisingly, oral repetition seems to work best with auditory learners.
3. Repetition (handwritten). Some singers prefer an effective old-school approach of writing out song texts or lyrics longhand. Putting pen to paper, rather than typing on a computer keyboard, has been proven to boost retention. The process of thinking of the words and then writing them down repeatedly helps activate the left side of the brain, which controls language and logic, thereby helping boost word recall. So left-brained learners might do well with filling empty journals with handwritten repetitions of the lyrics or libretto they are trying to memorize.
4. Liaison. Sometimes singers can remember song verses perfectly fine within themselves but then draw a blank, for instance, during an interlude between verses. To combat this intermediary memory block, make a practice of linking the last word of a verse with the first word of the subsequent verse. This linking will help bridge the gap in recall that can occur so that you already know how the next verse will begin instead of having to pause and "search the database."
5. Visualization. For right-brained or visual learners, a story or a series of images might be a better memorization tool. Imagine (or if you're an artist, draw) a storyboard for your song, as if you were directing it as a music video. Linking the words and music to images or the through-line of a larger

narrative arc might be your ideal mnemonic device, one that can also enrich your dramatic interpretation.

6. Improvisation. When memory fails, sometimes you just have to make something up. Instead of stopping, make yourself keep going through a lapse. Keep singing, be it "la la la" or a hum. Sometimes improvising can lead you back to the right notes and/or words. Dory in *Finding Nemo* may not have had a reliable memory, but her mantra "just keep swimming" is an apt one, so just keep singing.

7. Yoga. Yes, everyone is doing yoga (see Secret 31), and some yoga breathing practices (alternate nostril breathing) and positions—inversions such as shoulder stand (see figure 4.5) and balance poses like tree pose—are thought to help focus and memory.

Note

Put down the gingko biloba; there are times when we all wish we could improve our memory by taking an herbal supplement or adding more RAM to our brains. But memorizing vocal music requires honing a method befitting your unique learning style. Most of us do not have photographic memories (like Mozart and Bob Dylan, reportedly), so experiment with the techniques above. And take heart in the knowledge that studies have proven that musicians have better long-term memory than nonmusicians thanks to the enhancing effect of all of your musical training.

Figure 4.5. Shoulder Stand and Plow Pose

SECRET 43: GET OUT OF YOUR HEAD AND INTO YOUR BODY—LET'S GET PHYSICAL

There's a lyric from a Stone Temple Pilots song that says "I think I think too much." Overthinking, overanalyzing, and second-guessing can sometimes make a performer "choke" or freeze. Despite careful preparation and planning, the performance does not rise to its potential. The fabulous, five-time World Figure Skating champion Michelle Kwan overthought her appearances at the 1998 and 2002 Olympics, and she never managed to win an Olympic gold medal. She got stuck in her head, admitting "it seemed like I was in my own little world. I didn't open up; I didn't really let go." Learning vocal technique takes a lot of concentration and coordination. While serious vocal study usually involves years of lessons, you want to make sure you don't get stuck in the pedagogy of it all without being able to practice and perform with kinesthetic connection. Instead of thinking of a VoceVista reading (see Secret 47), explore the approach of Kristin Chenoweth. ("Sing from your hoo-hoo.")

Technique

Focus on physicality—the visceral part of singing. Instead of thinking and analyzing every detail of your technique, try to figure out how it feels. When your teacher says what you're doing is right, try to remember the sensation and then try to re-create that in your practice. Act like an athlete. Singing is an athletic event. Focus on encouraging natural, intuitive coordination and developing body awareness instead of on theories about vocal technique. Here are some tips to try.

1. Be hands-on. Instead of using the mirror when you practice, step away from it so you won't have visual cues to analyze. If you're working on breathing, put your hands on your rib cage or on the abdominal wall below your navel so you can feel the physical movement of your intercostal muscles or lower abdominals. If you're working on alleviating and eliminating tension, put a hand on the shoulder, neck, or chin that might be shaking. (Just don't do so with your tongue, although you can check in with tongue tension externally via the soft underbelly of the chin.) You can even employ some gentle massage on a tight jaw joint or trapezius muscle.
2. Get mobile. Instead of standing still, staring at your own reflection, move around the room while singing. As you vocalize, move through space, imagining forward motion in your breath flow. Roll your shoulders backward to loosen the upper body, or do other torso stretches upward and sideways to open up the rib cage. Trust the tangible and interact with the somatic rather than ruminate on your analysis of a physical process.

Benefit

By getting out of your head and into your body, your technique will become more instinctual and your kinesthetic awareness will improve. Of course, it is important to have an intellectual understanding of your instrument and how it works. But in the end, as the Nike slogan tells us, you have to put down the pedagogy book and "just do it."

SECRET 44: LISTEN INTELLIGENTLY TO GREAT RECORDINGS

Whenever students are assigned a new piece of music, their natural first reaction is to find a recording to listen to. This is true of both vocalists and instrumentalists. We are writing this book halfway through the second decade of the twenty-first century, and we are blessed to have such a legacy of recorded music. Thomas Edison invented the phonograph in 1878, which means that we are quickly approaching the sesquicentennial (150th) anniversary of recorded sound. The recording industry, against all predictions, also shows no sign of waning. Every year thousands of new recordings are released, including hundreds of new recordings of previously recorded repertoire.

One of our undergraduate professors, a choral conductor, was adamant that students should avoid listening to recordings as a first reaction and get to know a piece of music via the score first. He did not want students to become influenced by another conductor's or performer's interpretation before forming their own interpretive opinions first. This point is well taken, and this strategy has much to offer in terms of connecting to the score (see Secret 15) and developing creative artistry. There are, however, many benefits to listening to recordings, especially great ones by legendary performers (or excellent lesser-known ones), as long as one does so carefully and intelligently. The singer should keep the following points in mind while listening to recordings.

Technique

1. Seek out the best recordings possible by familiarizing yourself with the classic recordings. Virtually all of the best performers of the past several generations have been chronicled via extensive discographies. What a gift it is to have access to their recorded legacies: Dietrich Fischer-Dieskau and Elizabeth Schwarzkopf for German *Lieder* (see Secret 61), Gérard Souzay and Elly Ameling for French *mélodies* (see Secret 62), Luciano Pavarotti and Mirella Freni for Puccini (see Secret 65), Barbra Streisand and Ethel Merman for musical theatre (see Secret 72), and Ella Fitzgerald and Sarah Vaughan for jazz (see Secret 75). Don't restrict yourself to YouTube, Spotify, or other free sources, as many of the most important recordings are not yet available via these resources. You may have to purchase some of the very best recordings or seek them out via your library.
2. When you listen, it is best to listen with score and pencil in hand. Make sure that the recording is in the same key as the score you are looking at. (Art songs are especially notorious for being published in multiple keys.) Listen

intently to the singer (and accompaniment) and make notes in your score as appropriate.
3. Remember that while some things are okay to imitate, others are not. For example, some of the best things to take away from recordings are stylistic features: understanding that the appropriate tone quality for Italian opera is very different than contemporary musical theatre. Noting where singers breathe is also something very important and worth considering for your own performance. Perhaps most important, you should be careful to never imitate another singer's voice. Every voice is unique, and parodying another singer always sounds derivative and never works. A young light lyric baritone who tries to imitate Bryn Terfel's sound is setting himself up for not only technical problems but perhaps ridicule as well. Always be true to yourself and your voice.
4. Immerse yourself in discographical knowledge. Although they are beginning to become a bit dated, J. B. Steane's books are still a wonderful introduction to the legacy of classical singing on record. These volumes include *The Grand Tradition: Seventy Years of Singing on Record*, *Voices: Singers and Critics*, and the three-volume *Singers of the Century*. Alan Blyth's two multivolume works—*Song on Record* and *Opera on Record*—are also a helpful resource.

Benefit

Great recordings, when approached with intelligence and maturity, have much to offer students of singing, from the raw beginner to the advanced professional. Singers should consult discographies regularly for inspiration when preparing recitals and other performances. Singers cannot be successful if they live in a bubble, and some knowledge of great singers and stylistic traits of genres is paramount for success in the art form.

SECRET 45: VIEWER BE WARY—THE PLEASURES AND PERILS OF YOUTUBE

How much easier life would have been for those of us who grew up in the era of vinyl or cassettes if we would have had YouTube! Back in the twentieth century, aspiring singers had to rely on a university music library (or a large allowance to spend at Tower Records) to access a substantial collection of recordings. Some of us remember the joy and agony of dropping the needle and fast-forwarding through tapes to find a song. Now instead of loading a CD or DVD, YouTube lets you instantly listen to or watch countless performances. These fall into three general categories: (1) the Good (professional releases, historic and classic recordings); (2) the Bad (modern or amateur performances without polish and accuracy); and (3) the Ugly (bootlegs of singers having "off" nights, drunk karaoke, etc.). All three categories are well represented on YouTube, where you can glean insights from the great performers and learn what not to do from the bad, all for free and without getting up from your seat, as long as a laptop or smartphone is within arm's reach.

Technique

On YouTube, you need to be careful with what you emulate and what you emanate.

1. Pick good vocal models on YouTube. If your teacher assigns you an aria, don't listen repeatedly to an imprecise version from someone's junior recital, or you may unintentionally mimic the same errors. Even when it comes to professional versions, don't presume they are perfect, and resist the urge to imitate great singers. But you can certainly learn a lot from viewing and comparing. How did Arleen Auger, Kathleen Battle, and Natalie Dessay ornament Cleopatra's arias differently? Is there a recording posted of the obscure piece you have to learn for a callback tomorrow? These are excellent uses of the site. If you're doing research, try not to get distracted by watching the multitude of tempting videos (of cute baby goats, flash mobs, marriage proposals, etc.) unless that's part of your relaxation ritual.
2. Monitor your own performances on YouTube. Make sure the videos show your singing at its best. There are a billion users of YouTube worldwide, so you don't want to leave your performance open for attack. If you leave the comments section enabled, be ready for the fiercest critics. If you have your own YouTube channel, make sure it's up to date and appealing. Link your channel to your professional website. Periodically do what is called "ego surfing," or searching for yourself on the site. This way you can see others'

videos of you of which you might not be aware. If you don't like it, you can ask the user to take down the video or remove your name from the listing.

Benefit

YouTube is an amazing resource and a wonderful tool when used wisely. On your computer, tablet, or smartphone, you can instantaneously access over twenty thousand renditions of "Caro mio ben" and over a million versions of *Frozen*'s "Let It Go." You can watch operas in their entirety, or you can post an unlisted audition video for quick and easy submission. Keep your YouTube presence as a performer pristine. And you can still watch cat videos for fun.

SECRET 46: RECORD YOURSELF—I LOOK AND SOUND LIKE THAT?

Again, the twenty-first century and the digital revolution have made recording easy and ubiquitous. Gone are the days of having to lug a tape recorder to your lesson. Most smartphones or tablets have voice memo and/or video capability, and the sound quality only continues to improve. Along with mirror work (see Secret 36), recording yourself is one of the very best practice tools.

Technique

Record your lesson regularly, using audio and/or video as you are able. Some teachers are able to record lessons for you on their own studio system or computer. Then actually listen to or watch the recording. This may sound obvious, but conscious listening/watching (not while washing dishes or scrolling through Facebook—see Secret 41) will help you hear subtle nuances of resonance or see small alignment issues that can have a major impact on the quality of your sound. Also, record rehearsals, just never post rehearsals on YouTube or SoundCloud out of respect to your colleagues. Use them for personal reference only as a means of hearing what you can't hear when you're busy being the instrument. Listen and notice what you see and hear in an empirical, nonjudgmental manner. You don't want to become your own worst critic; you want to use recordings to gather information and make adjustments that will lead to improvement. Here are some sample questions to ask yourself as you listen/watch.

1. Auditory observations: Is my sound clear or breathy? Does my vibrato sound steady, slow, or fast? Does my resonance sound balanced, bright, or dark (see Secret 4)?
2. Visual observations: Does my posture look aligned (see Secret 1)? Do my facial expressions look appropriate for the pieces (see Secret 83)? Do my arms look free to gesture (see Secret 82)? Does my stance look grounded?

In addition to recording lessons and rehearsals for personal listening and study, always have some up-to-date recordings ready for audition/competition submission. For these recordings, you should use a high-quality recording system either in a recording studio or a recital hall. Audio or video screenings are common as preliminary application materials for many young artist programs, so for this you want to bypass the smartphone for a more professional-sounding product. Make sure the recordings are recent and showcase your best performance, not last year's technical challenges. Make sure you have the files in MP3 (audio) or MP4 (video) format. If you are an aspiring CCM singer, it's always good to have some demo tracks ready to go in case you meet a potential producer or collaborator who might be interested in your work.

Benefit

By recording yourself, you leave yourself free to focus on your singing. Instead of overanalyzing in the middle of phonation and perhaps impeding yourself (see Secret 41), you can sing first and critique later, making more of a mindful and immediate performance.

SECRET 47: DO YOU HEAR WHAT I SEE? USING SPECTROGRAPHIC ANALYSIS (VOCEVISTA)

Singing, like music, has always been (and always will be) an aural art form. We judge other singers, and our own singing as well, by listening and analyzing what we hear. Because singers cannot always hear themselves the way that others hear them (see Secret 39), we depend on the critical ears of others, such as our voice teachers (see Secrets 14 and 37) as well as recordings of ourselves, for a more objective perspective (see Secret 46).

Wouldn't it be wonderful if we also had a visual perspective of how we sound? Until recently this was not possible; however, over the past several decades, spectrographic analysis software has increased its presence in voice studios and practice rooms.

One of the most popular spectrographic programs is called VoceVista. This program was invented by singer, pedagogue, and voice scientist Donald Miller, who designed it with the intention of giving voice pedagogues and their students visual feedback via a computer monitor while singing. VoceVista is a translation of "seen voice" and uses two types of electronic signals: a microphone for a real-time spectrum analysis (or spectrograph) and an electroglottograph (EGG).

Technique

A laptop computer with installed software and a quality microphone (even a built-in one) are all that is needed to use VoceVista during a voice lesson or practice session. This equipment will allow the singer to see his or her overtones and first several formants. Formants are resonances of the vocal tract: the first two formants determine the singer's vowel, and formants 3–5, known as the "singer's formant," are an essential element of resonance, particularly in lower voice types. A singer can also examine his or her vibrato rate and extent through this basic setup. (See figure 4.6.)

More advanced users are also likely to use an electroglottograph, or EGG. This is a noninvasive device that is strapped to the singer's neck while singing (see figure 4.7). It uses electrical signals that measure relative contact between the vocal folds, assessing both the frequency of the glottal cycle as well as the closed quotient—the percentage of time that the glottis is closed during each cycle of vocal fold oscillation.

The beginner can rely on the basic software default settings, while more customized advanced settings are also available for the advanced user or for research. Donald Miller's book *Resonance in Singing* also functions as a treatise-long instruction booklet for advanced uses of VoceVista.[2]

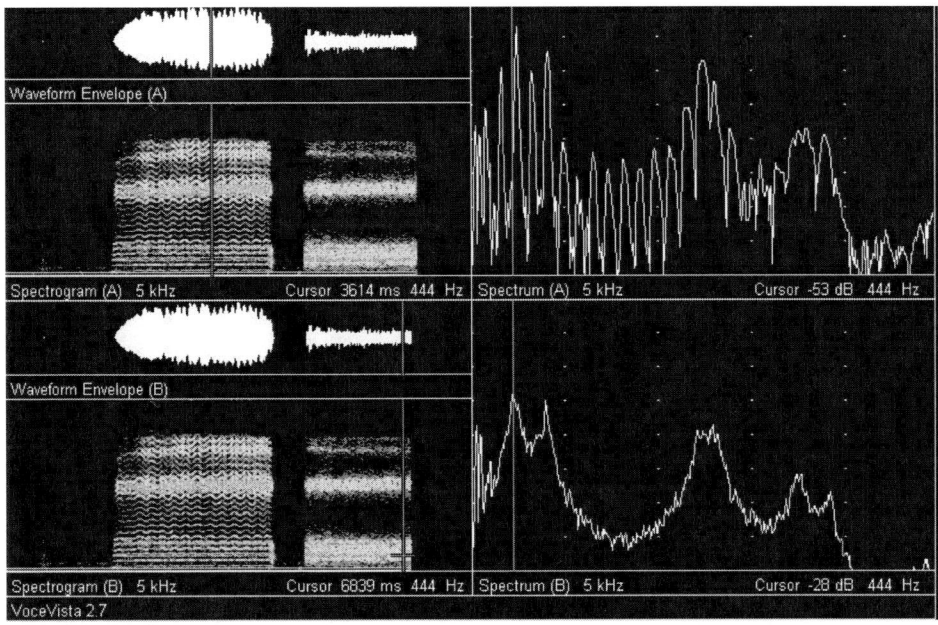

Figure 4.6. Screen Shot of VoceVista Software

Figure 4.7. "Wired" Student with Electroglottograph (EGG)

Benefit

VoceVista is not for everyone, but some students respond well to additional visual feedback while singing because it allows them to see what is happening acoustically. We have witnessed student breakthroughs with spectrographic software on issues such as vibrato—they couldn't hear that they were singing straight tone on certain notes, but the fact that they could see it on the spectrogram heightened their awareness and convinced them that the nonvibrato sound was actually occurring. Students who are math/science "left brainers" or voice pedagogy "geeks" are particularly attracted to software programs like VoceVista.

Note

Unfortunately for the world of Mac users, VoceVista only runs on PC platforms. Possible solutions to this program include Parallels Desktop, Boot Camp, or other Mac programs designed to run Windows software, but this is probably not a cost-effective solution. There are, however, several very good spectrogram programs that run on Apple products, including Gold Wave and Spectrum View. Spectrographic software has also begun to make an appearance in app form for use on mobile devices such as iPads and iPhones.

SECRET 48: BE GLEEFUL! REMEMBER THAT YOU LOVE TO SING! (JUST LIKE THE KIDS ON *GLEE*!)

Sometimes even the most enthusiastic singer can lose the joy in his or her singing. Maybe you too remember a vocalise from days of old: an arpeggio with the words "I love to sing." Even a young singer at the high school or college level can lack joie de vivre after some negative feedback at a solo and ensemble festival or a Simon Cowell–esque comment from a friend or teacher. But we all need to remember that we love to sing. Sure it takes hard work and lots of practice, but as the hymn "His Eye Is on the Sparrow" says, "I sing because I'm happy, I sing because I'm free."

Technique

1. Go back to your beginnings. Think back to when you first began singing. Do you have an old recording? Listen to it. Pull out your first big solo or competition piece. Sing it through and rediscover it, be it Mozart's "Un moto di gioja," Schubert's "Seligkeit," or the spiritual "Oh, Happy Day."
2. Go back to your favorites; then, sing along with one of your favorite soundtracks. Maybe like the kids on *Glee* (who were actually almost thirty, but that's okay), jam to "Don't Stop Believin'" or *Wicked*'s "Defying Gravity." Relive that zeal, the endorphin rush, and try to bring that to your practice and your performance. What song was your favorite as a hairbrush anthem or lip-sync dance? (Cue the effusive "Happy" by Pharrell Williams.)

Benefit

When you rediscover gleeful singing, your performance will be freer and more connected to your body and spirit. Audiences react ecstatically when they sense a performer's joy and freedom onstage. They want to witness your glee! Yes, studying voice takes a lot of hard work, but remember, singing should still be fun.

NOTES

1. It should be noted, however, that early prototypes of the metronome were actually invented by Abbas ibn Firnas (810–887) during the ninth century CE.
2. Donald G. Miller, *Resonance in Singing: Voice Building through Acoustic Feedback* (Princeton, NJ: Inside View Press, 2008).

CHAPTER 5

Language and Diction

SECRET 49: SINGING IN ENGLISH—AMERICAN VERSUS BRITISH DICTION

If you are reading this book, there is a good chance that you speak English as your primary language. The English-language speaker describes the typical voice student in American, British, and Australian voice studios. On the surface, it would seem as if singing in one's native language would be an easy thing to do, but it is actually quite difficult. Dialects, accents, and regionalisms abound, and ten different English speakers from ten different regions are likely to speak in very different ways. As the English opera critic Rupert Christiansen says, "Singing in English presents all sorts of insoluble problems."

Therefore, Americans who are assigned an English-language song should consider starting from scratch, approaching English as if it were a foreign language. In addition, one should also consider the nationality, style, region, and era of the song or composer. Most listeners would agree that a different pronunciation style should be used when singing a Gilbert and Sullivan aria, one of Copland's *Old American Songs*, an African American spiritual, or a contemporary musical theatre selection. Indeed, singing a spiritual with a British accent and rolled [r]s would sound ridiculous, but many singers neglect consideration of these elements when programming English-language repertoire.

Historically, some style manuals and diction books have advocated for a standard, unified approach to English diction regardless of composer, style, region, and era. This culture extended beyond singing; the Mid-Atlantic accent, for instance—a hybrid of British and American diction—was popular in Hollywood before World War II. For the reasons stated above, the authors find this approach to singing in English dated and out of step with contemporary singing practices. We argue that the composer, style, region, and era of the song should be of prime consideration when singing in English.

Technique

1. Consider the nationality of the composer and poet. They are often the same, but not always.
2. When was the song composed? Are the text and music a product of the same era?
3. What is the style of the piece? Is it formal, intended for the concert hall, or is it written in more of a folk or popular vein?
4. Approach English as if it were a foreign language. Speak through the text slowly, carefully analyzing each vowel and consonant that you are speaking. Be aware of your own personal regional accent and dialect. Is it creeping in somewhere it is not welcome?
5. Consider marking vowels, particularly ones set on sustained notes, with International Phonetic Alphabet (IPA) symbols (see Secret 50). Vowel purity is an essential aspect of good singing in any language (see Secret 33), and going on "autopilot"—not paying attention to which vowels you are actually singing—is almost never beneficial, particularly when initially learning repertoire.
6. Listen to your repertoire performed by a top-flight performer who exemplifies the style (see Secret 44): John Mark Ainsley singing Roger Quilter, Thomas Hampson singing Samuel Barber, Bernadette Peters singing Stephen Sondheim, or Mahalia Jackson singing a gospel song. Make notes of how each performer (all of whom are native speakers) approaches the English language differently.

Benefit

When singing in English, a one-size-fits-all approach is no longer adequate in today's vast world of musical styles and repertoire. The approaches listed above will give the singer the tools necessary to sing English in a fresh and stylistically correct way.

SECRET 50: EMBRACE IPA—SINGING IN FOREIGN LANGUAGES

In classical singing, the traditional repertoire is centered around what is known as the "big four" languages: Italian, German, French, and English. Choral musicians and oratorio/concert singers also regularly encounter Latin. In recent decades, the art song repertoire has also expanded dramatically, and it is now not uncommon to hear Spanish, Russian, and Scandinavian songs in recitals. Very few English-speaking singers speak all of these languages fluently, yet all advanced singers need to be comfortable enough with pronunciation to sing in these foreign languages.

Virtually all programs that train classical singers now offer diction curricula, and the International Phonetic Alphabet (IPA) has emerged as the standard tool for teaching lyric diction. The beauty of IPA is that it remains standard across all languages. Many sounds will occur in multiple languages; therefore, once learned, they can be applied elsewhere. A singer who possesses a good command of IPA will be able to sing any foreign language song or aria for which he or she can find an IPA transcription.

It should be noted that IPA can be applied to all languages—including English—and many schools do offer English diction coursework that uses IPA. English-speaking musical theatre and contemporary commercial music (CCM) singers, however, are less likely to know and use IPA, and it is therefore most often used as a tool by classical singers who are interested in it as a gateway to acquiring proficiency in foreign languages in which they will regularly sing.[1]

About the International Phonetic Alphabet

The International Phonetic Alphabet was devised by the International Phonetic Association (also abbreviated IPA), which publishes the *Handbook of the International Phonetic Association: A Guide to the Use of the International Phonetic Alphabet*. Also useful is the current edition of the *Phonetic Symbol Guide*, by Geoffrey K. Pullum and William A. Ladusaw. We will refer to the vowel and consonant charts below (figures 5.1 and 5.2) over the course of this chapter.

Benefit

Diction curricula in English-speaking countries have universally embraced the International Phonetic Alphabet as a standard way of transcribing song texts in foreign languages. Modern classical singers can no longer get away with not having a fluid and thorough knowledge of this system. The singer who possesses thorough IPA grounding will almost invariably sing his or her vowels and consonants with more precision than those who do not. Today's classical singing world is far too competitive to not have indigenous-sounding foreign languages. Fluency in IPA is a must for the serious student of classical singing.

the international phonetic alphabet (2005)

consonants (pulmonic)	LABIAL		CORONAL				DORSAL				RADICAL		LARYNGEAL
	Bilabial	Labio-dental	Dental	Alveolar	Palato-alveolar	Retroflex	Alveolo-palatal	Palatal	Velar	Uvular	Pharyngeal	Epi-glottal	Glottal
Nasal	m	ɱ		n		ɳ		ɲ	ŋ	N			
Plosive	p b			t d		ʈ ɖ		c ɟ	k ɡ	q ɢ		ʡ	ʔ
Fricative	ɸ β	f v	θ ð	s z	ʃ ʒ	ʂ ʐ	ɕ ʑ	ç ʝ	x ɣ	χ ʁ	ħ ʕ	H ʢ	h ɦ
Approximant		ʋ		ɹ		ɻ		j	ɰ				
Tap, flap		ⱱ		ɾ		ɽ							
Trill	ʙ			r						ʀ		ʜ	
Lateral fricative				ɬ ɮ		ɭ̊		ʎ̥	ʟ̝				
Lateral approximant				l		ɭ		ʎ	L				
Lateral flap				ɺ		ɺ̢							

Where symbols appear in pairs, the one to the right represents a modally voiced consonant, except for murmured ɦ.
Shaded areas denote articulations judged to be impossible. Light grey letters are unofficial extensions of the IPA.

Figure 5.1. Consonants of the International Phonetic Alphabet (IPA). *Creative Commons (CC BY-SA 3.0)*

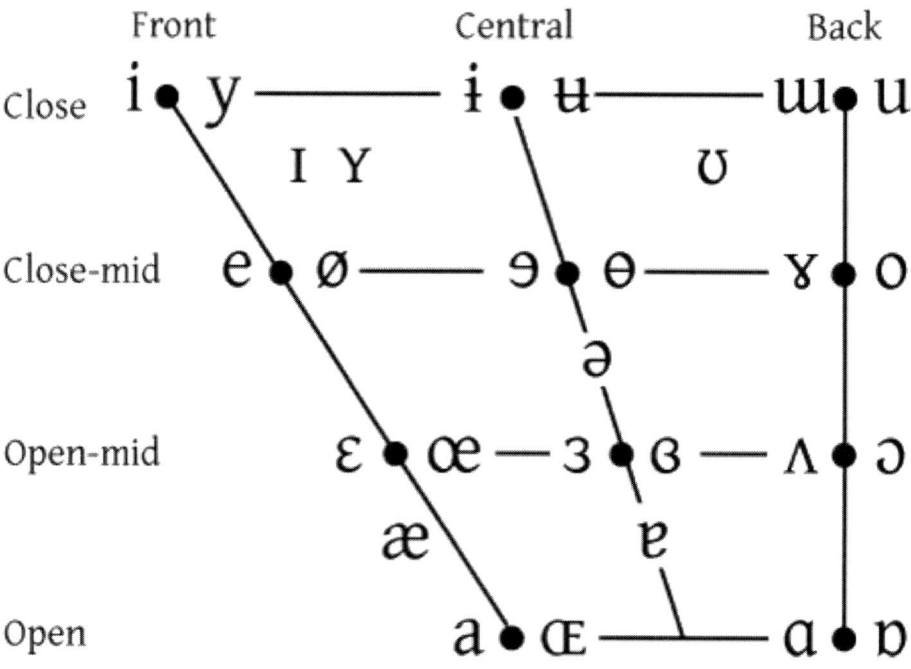

Figure 5.2. Vowels of the International Phonetic Alphabet (IPA). *Creative Commons (CC BY-SA 3.0)*

SECRET 51: *SI CANTA COME SI PARLA*—SINGING IN ITALIAN

Italian is widely regarded as the quintessential language for classical singing, and for good reason. It should come as no surprise that the Italian operatic repertoire remains some of the most popular and frequently programmed classical works. Even non-Italian operas are often composed and sung in an Italianate style—Bizet's *Carmen* is a notable example. (In graduate school, one of our professors remarked that *Carmen* is an Italian opera that is set in Spain and sung in French! These observations are absolutely correct.)

Voice teachers frequently assign Italian songs to their students at their initial lessons, also for good reason: the Italian language has much to teach students—particularly American students—about good vocal technique (see Secret 59). The Vaccai method is also useful, as these systematically arranged vocalises are also settings of poetic Italian texts, thus helping the singer to gain proficiency with the language while honing specific aspects of technique.

While an in-depth lyric diction course is needed to truly master Italian, here are some of the most fundamental concepts that singers should keep in mind when approaching Italian repertoire for the first time.

Technique

1. The Italian language is *bright*. A common pitfall for English-speaking students learning their first Italian song is that they forget to brighten their [a] vowels, instead replacing them with a dark American [ɑ]. *Sempre* [a]!
2. The Italian language is perhaps the most *legato* of all languages, which is why many regard it as the perfect language for opera and the ideal language for learning to sing (see Secret 7). The prevalence of words that end in vowels will help the singer in his or her quest for perfect, seamless legato. In Italian, one also should never start words that begin with a vowel with a glottal stop. Instead, elide with the previous word or begin with a gentle, balanced onset when these words begin a phrase (see Secret 3). There are also no aspirated consonants in Italian. *Sempre legato!*
3. The Italian language is the most phonetic of the "big four." Often words look the way they sound, which is not something that can be said of English or French. Also helpful is the fact that there are only seven vowel sounds: [a], [e], [ɛ], [i], [o], [ɔ], and [u]. The two respective flavors of *e* and *o*—which can be either open or closed—can be vexing to student singers, however. These two letters are often referred to as "dictionary vowels" due to the fact that rules will not work 100 percent of the time. Fortunately, IPA transcriptions are now widely available. Also, the open versions of [ɛ] and [ɔ] only occur on stressed syllables, which makes things a bit less anxiety-provoking for the student.

Benefit

The title of this chapter—*Si canta come si parla*—suggests that one should sing the way he or she speaks. If Italian is your native language, this is good advice, as perhaps no language has more in common with good classical vocal technique. Italian is rightly the fundamental building block for singing in the classical style in any language. Voice pedagogues often refer to the International Italian School when speaking of various aspects of technique, including breath connection, legato, and resonance. And think of the world of repertoire—particularly opera—that opens itself to the singer proficient in Italian!

SECRET 52: *SINGET NICHT IN TRAUERTÖNEN* — SINGING IN GERMAN

After Italian, German is perhaps the most important language for the classical singer. The expansive repertoire of German *Lieder* perhaps comes to mind first, with its glorious gifts by Ludwig van Beethoven, Franz Schubert, Carl Loewe, Robert Schumann, Johannes Brahms, Hugo Wolf, and Hans Pfitzner (see Secret 61). Operas by Carl Maria von Weber, Richard Wagner, Richard Strauss, and Alban Berg likewise form an important cornerstone of the repertory (see Secret 65). And one must not forget about sacred music, which contains German masterworks by Heinrich Schütz, Dietrich Buxtehude, and—most important of all—Johann Sebastian Bach.[2] As one of the "big four" languages, proficiency singing in German is a must for classical performers.

Technique

Perfecting German, with all of the subtle nuances involved, is a major project that lasts well into one's graduate student and young artist years. Even seasoned professionals routinely check in with vocal coaches who help them refine the subtleties of the language. The intricacies of German cannot adequately be distilled into a single "secret," but here are a few thoughts about the language that the student new to German should keep in mind.

1. Mixed vowels. Unlike English and Italian, German makes use of four mixed vowels: [y:], [ʏ], [ø:], and [œ]. They are called "mixed" vowels because each—via the tongue and lips—combines the quality of two other vowels; for example, [y:] = [i:] + [u:]. To accurately pronounce these vowels, the singer should ask him- or herself, "What is my tongue doing, and what are my lips doing?" Only when both of these questions are answered with precision will he or she be able to correctly execute mixed vowels.
2. Long, closed vowels. In German, the length of the vowel (long or short) is just as important as the quality of the vowel (open or closed). In almost all circumstances, a closed vowel—such as [e:], [i:], [o:], [u:], [y:], and [ø:]—also means a long vowel. Closed vowels in German should be extremely closed; it is almost impossible to be too closed. By extension, open vowels—[ɛ], [ɪ], [ɔ], [ʊ], [ʏ], and [œ]—are always short.
3. Like Italian, the German [a] is very bright. A common mistake for English-speaking students is to pronounce this vowel as a dark American [ɑ]. Instead, always err on the bright side; it is almost impossible to make a German vowel too bright.
4. Know that there are *numerous* exception words. Rules are a good thing, but remember that German has an extreme number of exceptions compared to

other languages. These exception words simply have to be memorized, but this takes years of study and practice. While it is always good to have a dictionary on hand whenever singing in a foreign language, singers of German are likely to end up consulting their dictionary even more often than singers of French and Italian.

5. The *ich-laut* [ç] and *ach-laut* [χ] are two consonants that are idiosyncratically associated with German. These sounds are associated with the *ch* consonant combination. The *ach-laut* [χ] occurs when *ch* is preceded by *a, o, u,* and *au*; and the *ich-laut* [ç] occurs when *ch* is preceded by any other consonant, vowel, or vowel combination.
6. Unique diphthongs: [ae], [ao], and [ɔø]. These three diphthongs—the only diphthongs in German—are unusual and completely idiomatic to the language.
7. The "chameleon schwa." Although schwas exist in English and French, the German schwa is unique because it is not a consistent sound within the language. German schwas are always influenced by the vowel occurring in the syllable immediately before the schwa.

Benefit

While it may seem easy to master the basics of German, excellent pronunciation of the language takes many years of study and coaching. Much attention must be paid to the very specific length and vowel colors of German vowels, and many, many exception words must be memorized. The reward is access to some of classical music's most magnificent repertoire.

SECRET 53: *SAVOIR FAIRE*—SINGING IN FRENCH

Classical singers are expected to be able to sing in excellent French. The operatic repertoire consists of major works by Jean-Baptiste Lully, Jean-Philippe Rameau, Hector Berlioz, Georges Bizet, Jules Massenet, Charles Gounod, Léo Delibes, and Gustave Charpentier (see Secret 65). Since Paris was a major international center for opera during the nineteenth century, Italian composers, including Gioachino Rossini, Gaetano Donizetti, and Giuseppe Verdi, set French librettos as well. And French art songs—called *mélodies*—are an especially rich repertoire as well. Gabriel Fauré, Claude Debussy, Maurice Ravel, Francis Poulenc, and Jacques Leguerney are all regarded as masters of the genre (see Secret 62).[3] The singer cannot explore this vast and magnificent repertoire unless he or she is comfortable singing in French.

Technique

Like any foreign language, the ability to perform exquisite French is only accomplished after many years of focused study. The following topics, however, represent some of the biggest hurdles for singers approaching the French language for the first time.

1. Identify and learn the four nasal vowels: [ɛ̃], [œ̃], [ɑ̃], and [õ]. These four vowels do not occur in German, Italian, or English, and they represent the most distinct aspect of the French language. Further, these nasal vowels are an idiosyncratic hallmark of the "French sound." The phrase "un bon vin blanc" (meaning "a good white wine") is a helpful one for the singer to learn, as all four nasal vowels are present within this short phrase; each word in this four-word phrase includes a different nasal vowel: [œ̃ bõ vɛ̃ blɑ̃].
2. Transcribe every vowel into your score. Due to the inclusion of three of the four German mixed vowels—[y], [ø], [œ]—in addition to the four nasal vowels, there are more vowel sounds in French than in any of the other "big four" languages. Strive for vowel precision at all times.
3. Learn basic rules for the omission of consonants. The fact that many consonants in French are unpronounced is one of the most difficult aspects of French for the young singer to learn. A helpful mnemonic device for students of French diction is the word "careful." The four consonants in the word careful—*c*, *r*, *f*, and *l*—are often—but not always—ones that are pronounced when they occur at the ends of French words. Examples include *parc* [park], *chef* [ʃɛf], *ciel* [sjɛl], and *mer* [mɛr]. However, there are exceptions to this rule, including *blanc* [blɑ̃], *baiser* [beze], *clef* [kle], and *gentil* [ʒɑ̃ti].

4. Study and mark *liaison* and *elision*. Like silent consonants, this is another extremely difficult concept for young singers of French to absorb. "*Liaison*" refers to a final unpronounced consonant that becomes pronounced when followed by a word that begins with an initial vowel, and "*elision*" refers to a final mute *e* that is dropped when followed by a word that begins with an initial vowel. Sometimes composers confuse things further by having their own ideas regarding *liaison* and *elision*. When in doubt, listen to a recording of a reputable French art song singer who is also a native speaker and make note of what they do. (Sometimes even these great performers contradict each other!)
5. Perhaps more so than any of the other "big four" languages, there is a big difference between spoken French and sung French. Some of the biggest differences involve the *r* consonant (these are always flipped in sung French as opposed to guttural), *liaison* (more common in singing than in speech), and the pronunciation of mute *e* (composers often set the mute *e* as its own syllable on a specific pitch and rhythm). When singing classical music in French, the best rule of thumb is to imitate the pronunciation found on recordings of French singers as opposed to asking nonsinging native speakers for advice.

Benefit

Ranking in importance alongside German and Italian, the advanced classical singer must have complete mastery of French. In spite of—or perhaps because of—the nuances and subtleties inherent in the pronunciation of good French, it is a favorite language for many performers to sing.

SECRET 54: *CANTO ERGO SUM*—SINGING IN LATIN

The historical language of Latin is essential for any singer engaging in the performance of sacred repertory. For over a millennium, Latin was the official language of the Catholic Church, and the earliest recorded Western music—the Gregorian chant repertory—standardized a body of texts that were set over the next twelve hundred years by countless composers. Performing the sacred Latin works of Johann Sebastian Bach, Wolfgang Amadeus Mozart, Franz Joseph Haydn, Ludwig van Beethoven, Franz Schubert, Anton Bruckner, Gabriel Fauré, or Maurice Duruflé—to list only a few of history's most prominent composers—means that one must feel comfortable singing in Latin.

Technique

Fortunately, Latin is far more straightforward than German or French. German can drive the singer crazy with its seemingly endless lists of exception words, and French has a mind-boggling array of rules that takes years for even seasoned singers to fully memorize and integrate. Fortunately, neither of these situations applies to Latin: rule lists are much shorter, and there are very few exceptions to rules.

The standard Roman pronunciation of Latin—or Church Latin—is particularly simple and straightforward, easily digested by high school singers and volunteer community choirs. One of the things that makes Church Latin simple is the presence of only five vowel sounds: [ɑ], [ɛ], [i], [ɔ], and [u]. The consonant rules are also straightforward, with few surprises. Most works written by Italian, French, English, and American composers are performed in Church Latin.

Germanic Latin, the other standard pronunciation, is a bit more complex but still easier to master than German, French, or even Italian due to a finite set of rules and a lack of exception words. Germanic Latin is a "hybrid" language that exists somewhere in between Church Latin and German. The full array of German vowels is explored in Germanic Latin (usually following the same rules as German), and many of the consonants are also pronounced in a Germanic way. Most works written by German, Austrian, Hungarian, and Czech composers are performed in Germanic Latin.

For a one-volume resource that compares Church Latin with Germanic Latin using IPA transcription, please refer to the *Latin Lyric Diction Workbook*, by Cheri Montgomery and Matthew Hoch. A complete set of rules and transcriptions of sacred Latin texts is also published in that volume.

Benefit

As the traditional language of the Roman Catholic Church, Latin is perhaps the most frequently sung language of historic sacred music. No choral director, choral singer, or concert soloist can avoid singing in Latin, and singing in Latin frequently. Mastery of both standard forms of Latin—Church Latin and Germanic Latin—is also a must in today's performance culture, where both versions are sung with increasing regularity.

SECRET 55: *SI PUEDES HABLAR, PUEDES CANTAR*—SINGING IN SPANISH

Out of all the languages discussed in this chapter, Spanish is the most ubiquitous globally. More people in the world speak Spanish than English, and Spanish is surpassed only by Mandarin as the most widely spoken language internationally. Spanish is the majority language in twenty-one countries and spoken by an estimated 442 million people from Spain to Mexico to Argentina. Because of the widespread nature of the language, many dialects and regional pronunciations exist, and these subtle distinctions from country to country can make singing in Spanish a challenge for the singer approaching the repertoire for the first time. Since most of the core repertoire of Spanish art song—as well as *zarzuela*—is sung in Castilian Spanish (CS), this secret will be devoted to the specific challenges of singing in this particular Continental dialect.

Technique

Since Spanish is frequently studied as a second language in American public schools, many students are already familiar with Spanish on some level. This makes Spanish a logical "fifth language" to add to your singing repertoire. One of the most attractive attributes of singing in Spanish is the simplistic nature of the vowels. Like Church Latin, there are only five vowels in Spanish: [a], [ɛ], [i], [ɔ], and [u]. Any singer who has been tormented by the complexities of vowels in French, German, and even Italian will find this fact about Spanish to be a huge relief.

Consonants, however, are a different matter and must be learned through study of the language. Since most American students are more likely to learn a Latin American pronunciation of Spanish in their studies, it therefore may be most useful to point out some of the primary differences between certain Castilian Spanish (CS) consonants and Standard American Spanish (SAS) consonants within the short confines of this unit. Here are some of the common mistakes encountered by singers who are new to singing in Spanish:

c preceding *e* or *i* = [θ], never [s]
cc = [kθ] in all situations
g = [x] preceding *e* or *i*; [ɣ] within a word or phrase and before *a*, *o*, *u*, and consonants
j = [x], never [h]
ll = [ʎ], never [j]
v = [b] or [β], never [v]
z (initial, intervocalic, or final) = [θ], never [z]

In addition, singers approaching Spanish for the first time will encounter the ñ (*n* with a tilde), a character unique to Spanish; ñ exists in both CS and SAS and is always pronounced [ɲ].

Benefit

The Spanish art song (*canciones*) and *zarzuela* have much to offer the classical singer. This repertoire—which is not performed with enough frequency—makes for a wonderful addition to any recital program.

SECRET 56: *ВЕК ЖИВИ́—ВЕК УЧИ́СЬ—SINGING IN RUSSIAN*

A few years back, I (Matthew) brought Onegin's aria to a coaching with an accomplished Russian baritone. One of the first things he said to me was: "Why do you want to learn this? You do realize that no one will ever hire you for the role because you are not Russian." I explained that I was a teacher of singing and interested in learning some Russian repertoire for my own edification, but his point was well taken. Singing in Russian is something of a niche market at the present time. Very few opera companies mount full-scale Russian opera productions in the original language, and when they do, they are most likely to favor singers who are native speakers for the roles. Nevertheless, the Russian aria and art song repertoire is becoming more accessible than ever thanks to a number of published resources that have made IPA transcriptions of Russian songs and arias available to non-Russian-speaking singers.

It is preposterous to adequately introduce the Russian language within the short confines of Secret 56, so the purpose of this unit is to point out some of the idiomatic challenges of the language and point the singer toward appropriate resources.

Technique

The greatest challenge that singers face when approaching this repertoire is the use of the Cyrillic alphabet (see figure 5.3), which is published in virtually all of the reputable Russian vocal scores.

Figure 5.3. Russian Cyrillic Alphabet. *Creative Commons (CC BY-SA 3.0)*

Reading Cyrillic is an endeavor that is easily accomplished with a little practice, so a far more important issue for classical singers is finding IPA transcriptions of respective songs and arias. Fortunately, there has been an explosion of IPA transcriptions of Russian vocal literature published in recent years, many of which are published by Leyerle. The aria volumes published by Leyerle even print the IPA transcription in the score, directly underneath the Cyrillic text, thus making things easier for the singer. Another important volume is Anton Belov's *Russian Romantic Art Song*, an anthology published by Classical Vocal Reprints. All of these publications are geared toward the non-Russian-speaking singer.

While many of the IPA symbols encountered in a Russian-language transcription will be familiar to the singer from other languages, special attention needs to be paid to several phenomena. The first is the important distinction between soft (palatalized) or hard (nonpalatalized) consonant sounds. In Russian, most consonants will exist in these two varieties. The letter П, for instance, can be either [p] or [pʲ] depending on the vowel or consonant that follows it. Often the meaning of the Russian word depends on whether a single consonant is palatalized or non-palatalized.

Secondly, a new IPA symbol that represents an important vowel must be mentioned: [ɨ]. This central vowel—an important hallmark of the Russian language—is not encountered in any of the other standard singing languages. Russian lyric diction expert Anton Belov provides this instruction for the singer wishing to produce this idiomatic sound:

> To form this vowel first intone [i]; then modify it to an English [I] as in king. In order to modify the vowel from [i] to [I] the back-central part of the tongue moves forward. If you move the back of the tongue a bit more forward the resulting vowel will be an [ɨ]. Notice that [ɨ] is not a diphthong. It is strictly a tongue vowel, and in its production the lips must remain unrounded.[4]

Additional resources for learning Russian diction can be found in the bibliography of this book.

Benefit

The title of this unit, Век живи—век учись, means "no pain, no gain." Russian can present many challenges, but the rewards are great. You will have access to an astonishing goldmine of art songs and arias. Thanks to the published resources that are now available, it has never been easier for singers to add Russian to their repertoire.

SECRET 57: EXPLORE LANGUAGES THAT ARE OFF THE BEATEN PATH

In 2010, a colleague of mine and I prepared and performed a program that we titled "From Many Foreign Lands: Songs and Arias That Are Not in German, French, Italian, or English." Our goal was to present an entire hour-long recital during which nothing was sung in any of the "big four" languages. Western singers are slaves to tradition, and this self-imposed rule presented a significant challenge for us; to date, I have not yet experienced another recital in which the standard repertoire was avoided in this way. Nevertheless, the twelve-language recital that we devised—one that included Swedish, Danish, Norwegian, Icelandic, Finnish, Greek, Russian, Czech, Spanish, Chinese, Japanese, and Hawaiian—remains one of the most fun and fulfilling ventures I have had during the past decade.

With the canon of classical vocal repertoire expanding so rapidly and so many resources available, why not pursue languages that are off the beaten path? This short section will briefly list some other languages worthy of exploration by the twenty-first-century classical singer.

Recommendations

Finnish: Finnish is actually one of the simplest foreign languages in which to sing. More phonetic than even Italian—it looks the way it sounds—its finite number of vowels and consonants makes it an attractive option for classical singers. The art song repertoire is also surprisingly vast, with dozens of quality songs by important composers. Finnish diction guides are available through the Academy of Finnish Art Song.

Hawaiian: Although the repertoire is somewhat finite, *The Queen's Songbook* offers a generous sampling of traditional Hawaiian songs. Like Finnish, the palette of vowels and consonants is simple and straightforward. I once attended a vocal literature presentation that convincingly made the pedagogical case for Hawaiian songs as first songs for young singers, preceding even the twenty-four hits (see Secret 59).

Scandinavian languages: The art song repertoire of Sweden, Denmark, and Norway is rich, worthy of standing alongside German *Lieder* and French *mélodies*. Unfortunately, the language barrier—the necessity of gaining proficiency in Swedish, Danish, and Norwegian—has frequently scared away all but the most die-hard of English-speaking singers. A new book, *Scandinavian Song: A Guide to Swedish, Norwegian, and Danish Repertoire and Diction*, by Anna Hersey, goes a long way toward making this repertoire more accessible in the Western Hemisphere.

Portuguese: Brazilian song is an undiscovered treasure trove of repertoire! Marcía Porter of Florida State University is currently a leading scholar on this repertoire, presenting workshops all over the world with several forthcoming publications.

Greek: Interested in singing Ravel's *Cinq mélodies populaires grecques* in the original Greek instead of French? Check out Lydía Zervanos's book, *Singing in Greek: A Guide to Greek Lyric Diction*, which also lists other repertoire that you might not have been aware existed.

Polish: We finally have access to Chopin's songs thanks to Benjamin Schultz's *Singing in Polish: A Guide to Polish Lyric Diction*. Important arias by Stanisław Moniuszko and Karol Szymanowski are also in Polish.

Czech: From the operas of Bedřich Smetana and Leoš Janáček to the art songs of Antonín Dvořák and Bohuslav Martinů, singing in Czech is now occurring with ever-increasing frequency in the classical world. Timothy Cheek's *Singing in Czech: A Guide to Czech Lyric Diction* is the standard resource.

Benefit

A new world of fresh and exciting repertoire awaits those who are eager and willing to explore, learn, and program it. With so many resources available for teachers and singers, now is the perfect time.

SECRET 58: KNOW YOUR TRANSLATION INSIDE AND OUT

If you are a classical singer, then you are most likely a multilingual performer. Language study is an important part of a singer's education, and word memorization is an important aspect of being a singer. Instrumentalists often spend four or more hours a day practicing their instrument. Singers often spend this much time as well but divide their time between physically practicing (singing) and academically studying their scores and translations. A good portion of the singer's practice routine is devoted to the memorization of words, which can be extremely time consuming, especially if the texts are in a foreign language.

Because it is challenging and time consuming, sometimes the intense word-by-word study of a foreign-language song or aria is neglected. Yes, the piece is memorized, but it is very clear that the singer has no idea what he or she is singing about! Some students even become adept at "faking it" by knowing the general mood of a song that he or she is singing, but this surface-level knowledge of the text will only take the singer so far. In order to really express a song in a genuine way, a singer has to know his or her translation inside and out.

Technique

1. The very best way to perform foreign languages convincingly is to go beyond studying the translations of your songs and arias and study the foreign languages themselves. Most bachelor of music (BM) voice performance curricula will require a certain number of semesters of foreign language, but go beyond these requirements by taking additional semesters. Consider a semester or summer of studying abroad—there is no better way to learn a foreign language than by immersing yourself in the culture. Software programs like Rosetta Stone and smartphone apps can also be useful.
2. Seek out good translations, and don't be afraid to translate things yourself. Over the course of the last thirty years, translations and IPA transcriptions of most of the standard vocal repertoire have now been published. What a gift this is to the current generation of performers! The Leyerle series of opera librettos and art song lyrics is owned by most university libraries and is particularly useful to singers. Singers should also own good Italian, French, and German dictionaries and use them regularly while studying and memorizing their repertoire.
3. Be prepared to invest lots of and lots of time studying your texts and translations. This is self-explanatory: there are no shortcuts.

Benefit

There is no shortcut to thoroughly learning the translations of your foreign-language repertoire, but the payoff is exponential. You will become a more convincing and sincere performer and far more competitive with your peers who are not as linguistically adept. Knowing your exact translation also unlocks many of the composer's intentions—why he or she set something to music a certain way. Also consider the alternative. Imagine your embarrassment when a master-class clinician (or your voice teacher) asks you what a particular word or phrase means and you don't know!

NOTES

1. It should be noted that some theatre curricula also use IPA for accents and dialect courses as opposed to foreign-language-only application.

2. The composers listed are identified only once according to the principle genre with which they are associated. Most of them, however, were active in multiple genres. Johannes Brahms, for instance, also wrote sacred music, Franz Schubert wrote operas, and Richard Strauss wrote many *Lieder*.

3. It should be noted that many of the opera composers listed here also wrote art songs, and vice versa: the art song composers listed also wrote operas. This paragraph intentionally oversimplified matters by categorizing each composer within the genre for which he is principally identified.

4. Anton Belov, ed., *Russian Romantic Art Song* (Fayetteville, AR: Classical Vocal Reprints, 2015), 5.

CHAPTER 6

Singing Classical Genres (and Singing Them Well)

Note: Chapter 5 focused on the language skills necessary for the classical singer to explore the standard vocal repertoire, while this chapter focuses on the repertoire itself. Many of the language-based genres presented here are intended as companion units to those presented previously. While the previous chapter focused on language and diction, this one is devoted to introducing and exploring the representative composers and repertoire of various genres.

SECRET 59: GO BEYOND THE TWENTY-FOUR HITS—USING ITALIAN *ARIE ANTICHE* AS YOUR FOUNDATION

"Caro mio ben" . . . "Sebben crudele" . . . "Amarilli mia bella" . . . "Se tu m'ami, se tu sospiri" . . . These Italian songs (and twenty others) are part of the DNA of every classical singer. In 1894, the publisher G. Schirmer published *24 Italian Songs and Arias*, and this collection has since become part of virtually every classical singer's training for over one hundred years. OK, so the songs are famous and overdone, but are they really that wonderful?

Well, yes, they are. These songs are part of a specific art song genre called *arie antiche* (translated as *ancient arias*) and—when taught and sung properly—can form a solid basis for bel canto classical technique.

Origins and Overview

The melodies of most *arie antiche* were originally written for baroque and early classical Italian operas. The accompaniments, however—all piano reductions—were largely reconceived and romanticized for piano. The most famous *arie antiche* with which we are familiar are part of an important collection edited and published by Alessandro Parisotti in 1890, titled *Arie antiche: Ad una voce per canto e pianoforte*. In New York, the publisher G. Schirmer collected twenty-four of Parisotti's songs and republished them as *24 Italian Songs and Arias* (1894), which became the most frequently owned vocal anthology in American studios. Composers represented in the anthology include Giulio Caccini, Alessandro Scarlatti, and Giovanni Battista Pergolesi. *Arie antiche* are a specific kind of romantic Italian art song and should not be confused with Neapolitan songs or the bel canto art songs of Gioachino Rossini, Gaetano Donizetti, Vincenzo Bellini, Giacomo Puccini, Paulo Tosi, Ottorino Respighi, or Stefano Donaudy.

Advice

Since most classical teachers ascribe to the International Italian School of vocal technique, all students of singing should purchase *24 Italian Songs and Arias* for their libraries as one of his or her first acquisitions. G. Schirmer publishes this classic collection in two keys: medium high and medium low.

Serious and advanced students, however—as well as every teacher—should also purchase the full Parisotti collection of one hundred *arie antiche* published by Ricordi in three volumes. Largely neglected in the United States, this larger collection provides a wealth of additional *arie antiche* to build technique and enliven recital programs. The medium keys published in this anthology also prove in many instances to be better fits for young baritone voices. Go beyond the twenty-four hits by purchasing and exploring this important collection.

Benefit

Arie antiche merge the best of all worlds for student singers. First, they are settings of Italian lyrics, and Italian is an ideal first language for classical singers looking to build a solid classical technique (see Secret 51). Second, they are appropriate for all ages; while it would be reckless to give a teenage student a Verdi or Puccini aria, he or she can build a solid technical foundation through this repertoire. Third, even though the melodies have their origins in the baroque and early classical eras, the accompaniments and editorial markings of Parisotti's arrangements are unapologetically romantic in style. Nineteenth-century bel canto ideals permeate the entire volume, making them an ideal stepping-stone to the core of the operatic repertoire.

SECRET 60: BRITS AND YANKS—ENGLISH AND AMERICAN SONG

Native English speakers should relish the opportunity to sing in their own language. Sometimes, however, young singers can lose sight of their own language during their effort to perfect language skills in Italian, French, and German. Fortunately, the vast repertoire of British and American art songs awaits the English-speaking singer seeking to program repertoire in his or her native tongue. This secret gives an overview to this important body of literature.

Origins and Overview

British art song originated during the sixty-four-year reign of Queen Victoria (1837–1901). The early experiments that occurred during the nineteenth century are now classified as "Victorian art song" and include composers such as John Liptrot Hatton, Henry Hugo Pearson, William Sterndale Bennett, and Arthur Sullivan (of Gilbert and Sullivan fame). Victorian art song is often neglected due to the long-held bias that it is of inferior quality to the great flowering of English art songs that occurred toward the turn of the century. The composers of this "mature" period of British art song include Ralph Vaughan Williams, Roger Quilter, John Ireland, George Butterworth, and Ivor Gurney. In the twentieth century, Gerald Finzi and Benjamin Britten contributed important works to the genre.

American art songs likewise have their origins in the nineteenth century. After early, European-styled experiments by Boston composers such as Amy Beach and Edward MacDowell, Charles Ives is considered to be the founder of a more distinctive and truly "American" art song. Many of Ives's compositional innovations were so radical that they were rejected by the conservative musical circles of the time, and he was forced to self-publish his *114 Songs* in 1922. Posterity would later judge this volume to be perhaps the most historically significant song collection ever published. Other important twentieth-century American art song composers include Charles Griffes, Virgil Thomson, Ernst Bacon, Aaron Copland, Theodore Chanler, Samuel Barber, Paul Bowles, Ned Rorem, Dominick Argento, and Richard Hundley. In recent years, younger composers such as Stephen Paulus, Libby Larsen, John Musto, and Lori Laitman have made an indelible mark on the American art song repertory.

Advice

While there is stylistic variety within the respective genres of English and American song, there are also broad stylistic differences between the two repertoires as well. Issues of diction are one of the most important distinctions (see Secret 49). In addition, both repertoires tend to incorporate folk elements, reference nationalistic figures and events, and employ idiomatic vocabulary. The English pianist Gerald Moore humorously said that "often [singers] bring me American songs, and I nearly always get a friend to come in and translate these songs into English." One of the best ways to immerse yourself in the stylistic distinctions between these two genres is to seek out great recordings of English singers singing English songs and American singers singing American songs.

Benefit

If English is your first language—or even if it isn't—waste no opportunity to include English and American song in your recitals. It is a magnificent and diverse repertoire.

Note

It should also be noted that there are many additional English-language songs that are not British or American per se. The Canadian and Australian repertoires, to name two, are also rich treasure troves waiting to be explored.

SECRET 61: *LIEDER* OF THE PACK: GERMAN ART SONG

The vast repertory of German art song is bountiful with riches from some of music history's greatest composers. *Lieder*—which is German for "songs" but typically denotes art songs specifically, as opposed to folk or pop songs—originated during the romantic era as settings of German romantic poetry. Any formal study of the voice will most likely involve thorough study of the *Lied* repertoire.

Origins and Overview

Of all the art song languages, the *Lied* genre is probably the vastest; there are literally thousands of *Lieder* that make up the standard repertory. The *Lied* genre is closely linked with the advent of German romanticism and the great flowering of German romantic poetry. This proliferation of romantic literature occurred at the same time as the rise in popularity of the newly invented piano, which made the early nineteenth century ripe for *Lieder* composition. Composers were attracted to the small-scale nature of the genre and the expressive possibilities offered by the combination of the human voice and piano. Important pioneers of the German *Lied* genre include Johann Friedrich Reichardt, Johann Rudolf Zumsteeg, and Carl Friedrich Zelter. These early experiments were basically strophic in style with a simple accompaniment (intended for amateur performance) and few real text-to-music relationships.

The *Lieder* of Franz Schubert marked a major step forward in compositional style, with the use of varied forms (strophic, modified strophic, scenic, and through-composed) and a true synthesis between poetry and music. In Schubert's *Lieder*, the piano accompaniment played a significant role in text painting, and many of the piano parts were virtuosic in difficulty. Schubert wrote more than six hundred songs and is considered by many to be the "father of the German *Lied*." Ludwig van Beethoven and Carl Loewe also composed some important *Lieder*, and Robert Schumann, Johannes Brahms, Hugo Wolf, and Richard Strauss also made significant contributions to the genre throughout the remainder of the nineteenth century. The orchestrated *Lieder* of Gustav Mahler also make up an important corner of the repertory. Although *Lied* composition became less popular in the twentieth century, important *Lieder* were written by Hans Pfitzner, Arnold Schoenberg, Alban Berg, and others.

Advice

The German *Lied* is a quintessentially romantic genre (in both the musical and literary sense), and one cannot adequately sing *Lieder* without some understanding of German romantic poetry.

Deborah Stein and Robert Spillman outline four themes of German romanticism that can be very helpful to singers:[1]

1. Heightened Individuality (dramatized by the figure of the Wanderer)
2. The Evocative World of Nature (typified by the Lonely Forest)
3. The Seductiveness of Mystery (represented by the Night)
4. Spiritual Salvation (projected by Yearning for Peaceful Death)

The symbols of the wanderer, forest, night, death, and yearning are ubiquitous in the poetry of *Lieder*. Understanding these symbols is a starting point that can greatly help the singer in his or her interpretation.

There is also a significant recorded legacy of German *Lieder*, which can be helpful for performers both experienced and new to the repertoire. Regularly listening to the great *Lied* interpreters can be deeply inspiring. By far the most famous interpreter of the style is the late German baritone Dietrich Fischer-Dieskau, who recorded virtually every *Lied* suitable to the male voice over the course of a career that spanned five decades. Two of the most significant female interpreters from Fischer-Dieskau's generation include soprano Elisabeth Schwarzkopf and mezzo-soprano Christa Ludwig.

Benefit

From Schubert's *Die schöne Müllerin* and *Winterreise* to Schumann's *Dichterliebe* and *Frauenliebe und -leben* to Wolf's *Italienisches Liederbuch*, the German *Lied* repertoire contains some of the most important and profound pieces in the canon of Western music.

SECRET 62: A PRETTY GIRL IS LIKE A *MÉLODIE*—FRENCH ART SONG

The term "*mélodie*" refers to French art song. This word contrasts with the French word "*chanson*," which usually is used to describe a folk or pop song (or, among musicologists, a secular song of the medieval or Renaissance era). Like German *Lieder*, French *mélodies* are a staple among art song enthusiasts.

Origins and Overview

The French equivalent of the German *Lied* genre, the *mélodie* was directly inspired by the early nineteenth-century compositions of Franz Schubert and Robert Schumann, as well as by the French *romance*, a kind of strophic, piano-accompanied parlor song that dates from the late eighteenth century. Hector Berlioz, Charles Gounod, George Bizet, and Jules Massenet contributed the earliest works in the *mélodie* genre. Just as German *Lieder* achieved maturity through keener text-to-music relationships and a more expressive and innovative use of the piano accompaniment, the French *mélodie* likewise reached maturity in the 1880s, most notably through the songs of Gabriel Fauré, Henri Duparc, and Claude Debussy. Other notable composers of the mature *mélodie* include Ernest Chausson, Emmanuel Chabrier, and Maurice Ravel. Francis Poulenc and Jacques Leguerney represent a twentieth-century climax of the French *mélodie*, contributing some of the greatest works in the entire art song genre.

Advice

Just as the performance of German *Lieder* requires some study and understanding of German romantic poetry, French *mélodies* are settings of French poetry—a distinctly idiomatic literature that can be quite complex to non-French speakers. Fortunately, two magnificent resources have been written that can help English speakers better understand French poetry. The first is Jacques Barzun's *An Essay on French Verse: For Readers of English Poetry*. This book, assuming no prior knowledge from the reader, provides an overview of the history of French poetry from the neoclassicists to the post-symbolists. The second, David Hunter's *Understanding French Verse: A Guide for Singers*, is a must-read for every student of singing. Hunter clarifies the specific meters, forms, and rhyme schemes embraced by French poets, most of which are distinctly French inventions that can be confusing to nonnative speakers. These two volumes significantly help to demystify the enigma of French poetry.

The French *mélodie* repertoire is well recorded, but every singer new to exploring this repertoire should begin with the recordings of pianist Dalton Baldwin on

EMI. Baldwin, accompanying singers such as baritone Gérard Souzay, soprano Elly Ameling, and a host of other luminaires, including tenor Nicolai Gedda and baritone William Parker, laid out comprehensive collections of the *mélodies* of Fauré, Debussy, Ravel, Poulenc, Duparc, and Chausson. These recordings are classics of the genre and are a great starting point for any singer wishing to explore the *mélodie*.

Benefit

Students are often daunted by the French vocal repertoire due to the complexity of the language (see Secret 53) and the unique style of the poetry and music. The above resources can be a helpful entry point to some of the art song genre's most beautiful and important works.

SECRET 63: GO BEYOND THE BIG FOUR—ART SONGS IN OTHER LANGUAGES

Historically, recital singers have confined themselves to the "big four" languages: Italian, German, French, and English. This was in part due to tradition but also in part due to the language barrier: resources and pedagogies had not yet emerged to make these repertoires user-friendly to students and teachers of singing. In recent decades, however, it has become standard to program art songs in other languages. The following art song repertoires are the most expansive and the ones most commonly programmed and heard.

Origins and Overview

Russian art song: Russian art song reached its full flowering in the mid-nineteenth century as a result of the nationalistic movement that swept many of the non-European countries. The romances of Mikhail Glinka—the "Father of Russian Opera"—and Alexander Dargomyzhsky were pioneering works that inspired future generations of Russian art song composers. The "Mighty Handful" or "Russian Five"—Aleksandr Borodin, César Cui, Mily Balakirev, Modest Mussorgsky, and Nikolay Rimsky-Korsakov—all composed songs, with Mussorgsky emerging as the group's most important composer of vocal music. A second, more European type of Russian art song flourished in the late nineteenth century with the songs of Pytor Il'yich Tchaikovsky and Sergey Rachmaninov. These songs were more melodic in nature and owed less to the folk idioms and rustic harmonies favored by the Mighty Handful. While not as vast as the German *Lied* repertoire, the Russian art song genre contains hundreds of works from some of Russia's greatest composers, not to mention settings of some of the greatest Russian poets. The recent proliferation of publications related to Russian art song IPA transcriptions and Russian diction books has finally made this genre more accessible to Western singers and audiences.

Spanish art song: While Spain's singing tradition is rich, most Spanish vocal music written before the twentieth century was either popular in nature or written for the theatre. Spanish art song did not reach its zenith until the early twentieth century, making it a much younger cousin of the German *Lied* and French *mélodie*. The most important composers of Spanish song include Enrique Granados, Manuel de Falla, Joaquín Nin, Jesús Guridi, Federico Mompou, Fernando Obradors, Joaquín Rodrigo, and Xavier Montsalvatge. Songs written by these composers should always be performed using Standard European Spanish (SES), or Castilian Spanish (CS). In recent years, some resources have emerged for Latin American art song repertoire in addition to continental Spanish art song. These art songs should be performed in Standard American Spanish (SAS).

Nordic art song: A vast repertoire of recital music not often heard in the West due to the number of languages represented in the repertoire. A singer of Nordic art song must be comfortable singing in Danish, Norwegian, Swedish, and Finnish. While there is some repertoire from Iceland and the Faroe Islands, this literature is minimal compared to the songs that exist in the four principal Nordic languages. Nordic art song is frequently called Scandinavian song, but Scandinavia proper only includes the countries of Denmark, Sweden, and Norway. Since Finnish art song is of such high quality—and since the ease of Finnish diction makes it a reasonable conquest for young singers—it is practical to include Finnish repertoire in discussions of Nordic art song. The most important composers of Nordic art song include Edvard Grieg, Jean Sibelius, Yrjö Kilipinen, Wilhelm Stenhammar, Hugo Alfvén, Ture Rangström, and Carl Nielsen.

Benefit

With so many resources available to the twenty-first-century singer, why not explore this diverse and interesting body of repertoire in your recital programs?

SECRET 64: HANDELING RECITATIVE—SINGING ORATORIO

In the world of classical singing, oratorio is its own niche. Although historically and stylistically there is not much that separates opera from oratorio—the latter is an unstaged, usually sacred version of the former—modern oratorio and opera singers usually focus on their respective genres with very little crossover: opera singers are known as opera singers, and oratorio singers tend to have the identity of concert singers. This secret will focus on the oratorio repertoire and the unique skills needed to perform it well.

Origins and Overview

Oratorio is a genre of music for chorus, orchestra, and soloists. Oratorios generally have a biblical or religious narrative but are written for the concert hall as opposed to a liturgical worship service. Unlike opera, oratorios are generally not staged and do not feature sets and costumes. Historically, the oratorio proper is always set in the vernacular as well; for example, Handel's operas were performed to London audiences in Italian—the "proper language of opera"—whereas his oratorios were settings of English libretti.

Musicologists and singers tend to draw different boundaries regarding the oratorio repertory. The oratorio has several closely related "cousins," including sacred Latin works, cantatas, odes, and secular concert works. While these genres do not fit neatly into the narrow definition above, professional oratorio soloists universally claim them as part of their repertory as well, singing Bach's Mass in B Minor and Finzi's *Imitations of Immortality* in addition to Mendelssohn's *Elijah*. No oratorio singer will restrict him- or herself only to the sacred narrative works that are described by the narrow musicological definition.

The earliest oratorio experiments were Italian baroque works, but the first oratorios that are still in the repertory were composed in Lutheran Germany by Heinrich Schütz and Johann Sebastian Bach. Bach's *St. John Passion* and *St. Matthew Passion* represent two of the greatest works in the genre. Perhaps the most important composer of oratorio in any era was George Frideric Handel, who devoted himself almost exclusively to the genre during the later part of his long career in London. Franz Joseph Haydn composed the classical era's most important oratorios with *Die Schöpfung* (*The Creation*) and *Die Jahreszeiten* (*The Seasons*), and Felix Mendelssohn became the romantic era's most important oratorio composer with *Paulus* (*St. Paul*) and *Elias* (*Elijah*). In the twentieth century, it was England that remained most devoted to the genre, with four essential oratorios: *The Dream of Gerontius*, by Edward Elgar; *Belshazzar's Feast*, by William Walton; *A Child of Our Time*, by Michael Tippett; and *War Requiem*, by Benjamin Britten.

Technique

There are several important things to consider when performing oratorio: the fact that there are no sets or costumes presents a challenge, and the tradition that the genre is performed "on book"—with performers holding folders—also limits the use of blocking and gesticulation (see Secret 82). The singer must tell the story with his or her eyes, face, and—most important—voice! In spite of these restrictions, oratorio should not be less expressive, and great oratorio singing can only occur if the singer is just as prepared as if he or she were singing a staged opera. Although oratorios are usually not memorized, the great oratorio singers commit their roles to memory anyway so as to internalize the music and maximize facial and vocal expression. Mastery of recitative, particularly in the extensive body of Handel's baroque oratorios, also depends on exquisite declamation, portraying every nuance of every word through the color of your voice.

Benefit

Classical singers will at some point in their career have the opportunity to sing Handel's *Messiah* or Bach's *Christmas Oratorio*. Knowing this repertoire and understanding the stylistic conventions of the oratorio genre broadens opportunities for the classical singer, and some particularly adept concert singers make careers out of singing these works.

SECRET 65: *VISSI D'ARTE*—SINGING OPERA

Among classical singers and teachers, opera is widely considered to be the summit of the singer's art. The literature—ranging from *Giulio Cesare* to *Der Ring des Nibelungen* to *Porgy and Bess*—is vast, and there are dozens of subgenres within the operatic repertory. Many singers and teachers devote their lives to studying opera, and the few brief paragraphs presented here can only scratch the surface of what it means to be an opera singer. This secret will briefly outline the repertory and articulate some ways in which opera performance differs from other classical genres, such as art song and oratorio.

Origins and Overview

Opera is often defined simply as "a drama that is entirely sung." A thorough definition is far more complex, however, as the genre of opera has assumed radically different forms over the course of its four-hundred-plus-year history. Most people would think of Beethoven's *Fidelio*, for instance, as an opera even though it contains dialogue. On the other hand, most people would also regard *Les Misérables* and *The Phantom of the Opera* as musicals, even though they are entirely sung. Perhaps a more accurate contemporary definition would also incorporate the intentions of the composer (whether he or she conceives of the work as an opera) and the singing style required to realize the intentions of the composer (e.g., some sort of classical technique).

The birth of opera occurred during the last decade of the sixteenth century as a result of musical experiments developed by members of the Florentine Camerata, a group of scholars, poets, and composers, who met at the court of Giovanni de' Bardi. These operas, written in a monodic style, retold Greek myths that were the subject of dramas performed during the Renaissance era. Claudio Monteverdi composed opera's first universally acclaimed masterwork in 1607 with *Orfeo*. Thirty-six years later, Monteverdi proceeded to push boundaries with the new genre in *L'incoronazione di Poppea*, the first opera that was based on a historical rather than mythological subject. Opera continued to grow in popularity throughout the baroque era. In addition to the major cities of Italy—Venice, Florence, Milan, and Naples—Paris and London also became important centers for opera. French operas, in their own distinctive style, were written by Jean-Baptiste Lully and Jean-Philippe Rameau. Henry Purcell experimented with English opera in London with *Dido and Aeneas*, but it was George Frideric Handel who emerged as the late baroque's most successful and distinguished composer of opera with his Italian operas for London audiences.

The most important opera composer of the Viennese classical era was undoubtedly Wolfgang Amadeus Mozart, whose mature operas are still among the most frequently performed works in the world's opera houses. In Italy, bel canto operas emerged as the aesthetic convention of the day, with Gioachino Rossini, Gaetano Donizetti, and Vincenzo Bellini emerging as the three greatest exponents of the style. As the nineteenth century progressed, more-distinct traditions flowered in Italy, France, and Germany. Giuseppe Verdi built upon the bel canto traditions of his predecessors, becoming the romantic era's most important composer of Italian opera. After early experiments in Germany by Carl Maria von Weber, Richard Wagner became the towering figure in German opera, reinventing the form—and perhaps music itself—with his mature music dramas. In France, the most important opera composers were Hector Berlioz, Georges Bizet, Charles Gounod, and Jules Massenet. Nationalism in opera also emerged toward the end of the nineteenth century, with a proliferation of Russian, Czech, and even Polish operas, all of which explored their vernacular language, idiomatic histories, and musical traditions.

The genre of opera continued to become more diverse by the beginning of the twentieth century. Giacomo Puccini continued the Italian tradition with his *verismo* operas, and Richard Strauss and Alban Berg wrote the most important German operas of the first half of the century. Claude Debussy created opera's only experiment in impressionism with *Pelléas et Mélisande*. American opera also flourished, offering its own brand of nationalism. And the avant-garde operas of Karlheinz Stockhausen and the minimalistic experiments of Philip Glass stretched the very definition of the genre. Ultimately, however, these modernist works have made very little impact on the international repertory, which still favors repertoire from Handel through Puccini. Romantic opera predominantly forms the core of the performance repertory.

Technique

1. Vocal quality and resonance. Even more so than art song and oratorio, performing the core works of the operatic repertoire requires a sterling technique and a well-produced, resonant voice that can carry to the back row of the house. A solid technique will also give you the stamina you will need to sing entire roles multiple times in one week without tiring or relying too much on your capital (see Secret 13).
2. Acting. Plain and simple, opera is about more than just singing; it is also about exploring the nuances of a character and getting inside the mind of the composer and librettist who created the role. Opera singers are likely to have

acting as part of their training, and good theatrical skills and stage presence are essential for a successful operatic performance (see Secrets 80–85).
3. Movement. Closely related to acting, opera singers must be agile and mobile, ready to be blocked and engage in an almost infinite variety of onstage interactions and situations. Some operatic roles even require dance (and opera choruses dance regularly). Maintaining good physical health and formal training in movement and dance are also an essential part of the opera singer's comprehensive education (see Secrets 25 and 31).

Benefit

Although there are other types of classical singing, opera permeates the entire classical singing world, and few singers can avoid encountering it on a regular basis. Since the operatic repertoire is so vast and encompasses multiple eras, any classical singer can find a portion of the repertoire that suits his or her voice. Becoming an operatic character through the singing of a role is one of the most gratifying experiences a singer can have.

SECRET 66: UTOPIA UNLIMITED—THE JOYS OF LIGHT OPERA

Operetta . . . *opéra bouffe* . . . *zarzuela* . . . *Singspiel* . . . The genre of light opera exists in many languages and forms. But all of these labels celebrate a genre that is unified behind a single purpose: to present a lighthearted form of entertainment free from the ambitions of grand opera. Occupying a unique place somewhere between musical theatre and grand opera, light opera stakes a claim as its own genre, complete with delightful idiosyncrasies.

Origins and Overview

One of the first forms of light opera to emerge in Europe was the German-language *Singspiel*. In this genre, spoken dialogue alternates with songs and ensemble numbers. Settings are usually in rural or exotic places. Some of the most famous examples of the genre include two *Singspiels* by Wolfgang Amadeus Mozart: *Bastien und Bastienne* and *Der Schauspieldirektor* (*The Impresario*).[2]

In the mid-nineteenth century, *opéra bouffe* emerged as a form of French light opera. An *opéra bouffe* is usually satirical, comical, and (often) quite bawdy in nature. The genre derived its name from the Bouffes Parisiens, where many of the first *opéra bouffe* productions were premiered. The *opéra bouffe* was invented by the French composer Louis Auguste Florimond Ronger—better known to history as Hervé—but the genre achieved popularity with the works of Jacques Offenbach. Offenbach's *Orphée aux enfers* (*Orpheus in the Underworld*), which satirizes the Greek myth of Orpheus, is considered to be the quintessential *opéra bouffe*. It is no accident that Offenbach chose this myth—the same one chosen by Claudio Monteverdi and Christoph Willibald Gluck—for his subject; the possibilities for satire could not have been richer!

Viennese operetta—sometimes simply referred to as "operetta"—came to Vienna during the 1870s. Viennese operetta is a waltz-based, "cleaner" version of its predecessor, the bawdy French cousin *opéra bouffe*. Viennese operetta features dialogue, dancing, and memorable tunes, and the genre's libretti usually feature members of the aristocracy who embark on comical romps of mayhem and infidelity, only to have it all work out in the end. *Die Fledermaus* (*The Bat*) by Johann Strauss represents the apotheosis of the genre and the golden age of Viennese operetta. The genre was at its peak in the 1870s and 1880s but began to wane in popularity by the beginning of the twentieth century, when it was almost single-handedly revived by *Die lustige Witwe* (*The Merry Widow*), by Franz Lehár. This work ushered in a new silver age of Viennese operetta. In addition to Strauss and Lehár, other significant composers of Viennese operettas include Oscar Straus, Robert Stolz, Franz von Suppé, Karl Millöcker, Emmerich Kálmán, Leo Fall, Eduard Künneke, and Walter Goetze.

English comic opera is a specific genre of light opera that emerged around the same time as Viennese operetta. This British spin on the genre is best exemplified by the thirteen surviving comic operas of librettist William Schwenck Gilbert and composer Arthur Sullivan (see figure 6.1). These works are ubiquitously known as Gilbert and Sullivan or G&S works. Usually in a two-act structure with dialogue, the librettos satirized various aspects of Victorian British society, and excessive confusion and mayhem are almost always resolved neatly (though not always logically) in the final moments of the evening. Essential to the Gilbert and Sullivan formula was their own set of stock characters: the attractive ingénue (the soprano), the pining tenor (her love interest), the bad bass, the uglier and older mezzo-soprano, and—most idiomatically to Gilbert and Sullivan—the patter baritone, who is usually the central comic figure of the work. Gilbert and Sullivan's comic operas are unapologetically dated but still enjoy frequent revivals. The most famous and often-performed include *The Pirates of Penzance*, *HMS Pinafore*, *The Mikado*, and *The Gondoliers*.

In New York City, American operetta emerged as a form of light opera in the early decades of the twentieth century. American operetta is a repertory distinct from Viennese operetta and English comic opera. While New York certainly enjoyed numerous imports from Gilbert and Sullivan and Franz Lehár, the principal

Figure 6.1. Caricature of Gilbert and Sullivan

composers of American operetta were Victor Herbert, Rudolf Friml, and Sigmund Romberg, all of whom lived and worked in New York. Ironically, none of these composers were born in the United States: Herbert was born in Ireland, Romberg in Hungary, and Friml in Czechoslovakia. Herbert's operettas appeared first, during the first decade of the twentieth century; his most famous works were *Babes in Toyland*, *The Red Mill*, and *Naughty Marietta*. Friml's star rose after Herbert's, during the 1920s; his most famous works—*Rose Marie*, *The Vagabond King*, and *The Three Musketeers*—all date from this period. Romberg was the most European of the three, and his most popular works—*The Student Prince*, *The Desert Song*, and *The New Moon*—are very much in the style of Viennese operetta.

Lastly, *zarzuela* is a form of light opera that developed in Spain. Although the earliest examples of this genre were written for the court of King Philip IV in the seventeenth century, *zarzuela* finally achieved popularity in the nineteenth century and international recognition in the twentieth century. "*Zarzuela*" literally translates as "bramble bush," but its name derives from the name of the palace of Philip IV—"La Zarzuela." The genre eventually found its way into the cosmopolitan theatres of Madrid and Barcelona. Important composers of *zarzuela* have included Juan Hidalgo, Francisco Asenjo Barbieri, Emilio Arieta, Tomás Bretón, Amadeo Vives, Francisco Alonso, and Federico Moreno Tórroba.

Technique

1. Put on your dance shoes! Several operettas will require choreography as part of the plot, be it waltzing (*The Merry Widow* and *Die Fledermaus*) or a cancan (*Orpheus in the Underworld*).
2. Develop your ability to speak dialogue. Most operas don't ask singers to speak, but operetta will typically feature spoken dialogue in between the musical numbers. It is a very different skill and takes practice and coaching to do it well!
3. Practice your accents. Operettas often require the performers to sing and/or speak with a foreign accent. Perhaps you are doing a truly British rendering of Gilbert and Sullivan's *HMS Pinafore* or an English translation of Offenbach's *La vie parisienne* with French accents for comedic effect and flair. In *Die Fledermaus*, the character Rosalinda masquerades as a faux Hungarian countess—she's "very much from Hungary!" Who knows what accent, real or imagined, you might be asked to do as someone from fictional places such as Pontevedro (*The Merry Widow*) or Barataria (*The Gondoliers*).
4. Embrace the absurdity! Opera plots are notoriously contrived, but operetta plots can be downright ridiculous. This may be because they are satirizing something or just because it adds to the comedy. For example, much of the

plot of *The Pirates of Penzance* stems from confusion over a profession—did he say "pilot" or "pirate"?—and *Orpheus in the Underworld* contains a "fly" duet in which the characters spend most of their time singing "*zzz*." And Offenbach's *Mesdames de la Halle* contains, in addition to a traditional pants role, three skirt roles as well! How absurd is that!

Benefit

The musical theatre of previous generations, light operas continue to be beloved repertoire pieces enjoyed by both amateurs and professionals, from local Gilbert and Sullivan societies to university productions to the Metropolitan Opera in New York, which still stages *Die Fledermaus* annually in celebration of the New Year. As a classically trained singer, you will likely find many opportunities over the course of your career to experience the joys of light opera.

SECRET 67: COLLABORATE WITH OTHER MUSICIANS THROUGH CHAMBER MUSIC

When one thinks of chamber music as a genre, images of string quartets, piano trios, and brass quintets instantly come to mind. Singers tend to forget that there is also a rich body of chamber music written for voices and assorted instruments as well.[3] This secret will explore some strategies for exploring this repertoire.

Exploring the Repertoire

Chamber music is defined as a piece of music written for a small ensemble. In vocal music, chamber music usually refers to a song or song cycle with instrumental accompaniment other than orchestra, usually with one instrument on a part. The repertoire of vocal chamber music is vast, but some of the most famous examples of vocal chamber works are *Der Hirt auf dem Felsen*, by Franz Schubert (for soprano, clarinet, and piano); the *Chansons madécasses*, by Maurice Ravel (for voice, flute, cello, and piano); and *Dover Beach*, op. 3 (1931), by Samuel Barber (for baritone and string quartet).

There are several good resources available for singers and teachers interested in integrating vocal chamber music into their repertoire. Two books that are particularly helpful are *Vocal Chamber Music: A Performer's Guide*, by Barbara Winchester and Kay Dunlap, and *Chamber Music for Solo Voice and Instruments, 1960–1989: An Annotated Guide*, by Kenneth S. Klaus.

Technique

Although art song and chamber music can be technically and stylistically similar, the rehearsal technique involved in singing chamber music can be very different. A singer who is used to listening only to the piano can become disoriented when other instruments are added to the mix. Just adding one violin to the piano-vocal duo can change everything; all of a sudden you must listen for two other parts instead of one, and tuning and balance can become a greater challenge. These complexities increase the more instruments are added to the ensemble. Many chamber works are not scored for piano at all, which can also seem disorienting at first to the inexperienced chamber music singer. Careful listening, educating yourself about the capabilities and idiosyncrasies of each instrument, and—most significant—repeated *experience* singing with chamber ensembles are the most important keys to conquering this repertoire.

Benefit

Incorporating chamber music in recital programs offers the opportunity for performers and audiences to be exposed to a unique body of extraordinary works. Chamber music can add immense variety to the traditional song-recital program. Perhaps most important, this repertoire allows singers to explore collaborations and build relationships with talented instrumental colleagues.

SECRET 68: BE HIP—EXPLORING EARLY MUSIC

Historically informed performance—abbreviated as HIP—is a relatively recent movement that seeks to re-create compositions as they may have originally been heard during the era in which they were composed. Also known as "period performance" or "authentic performance," HIP practice considers the size of the forces (often very small choirs, sometimes one on a part), period instruments, baroque tuning (such as A = 415), performance space (small churches as opposed to large concert halls), and diction/pronunciation considerations.

Early music performers tend to be specialists, as many of the techniques required represent a significant departure from mainstream vocal repertoires and styles. The natural inclinations of a singer's individual instrument also play a significant role. Voices that are valued in the early music community will not necessarily be valued by the mainstream operatic community and vice versa. For example, a vocalist who excels when singing Puccini might not be heard to best advantage in the music of Josquin des Prez or Hildegard von Bingen. Many early music specialists are often academics as well, researching new repertories, reading from original notation, and having a thorough understanding of ornamentation. (The great early music singer Julianne Baird, for example, is also a scholar with a PhD in musicology from Stanford University.) Understanding period language and diction and having knowledge of social and historical contexts is paramount. In contemporary performance culture, early music singers often double as professional choral singers (see Secrets 70 and 98).

Technique

1. Baroque tuning. The most important thing that early music singers should be aware of is that the modern standard tuning of A = 440 usually doesn't apply to early music performances. While early music tunings can vary, A = 415 is quite common. This means that the music you are singing is approximately one half-step lower than what you are seeing on the page and are used to hearing. This can be jarring to the singer who is used to preparing scores with the help of a modern piano and can drive the singer with perfect pitch batty! Ask the conductor what tuning will be used in advance of the first rehearsal so that you can practice and prepare.
2. Period instruments and smaller forces. Early music ensembles will sound different than modern orchestras due to the use of historical instruments and the fact that there are usually fewer musicians playing each part; one on a part is not uncommon. Experiencing this new aural world can require some adjustment.

3. Resonance and vibrato. Since orchestras and performance spaces are smaller, traditional resonance in the nineteenth-century bel canto operatic sense is less important in the early music community (and, frankly, out of style). The small resonant churches in which early music is performed are often enough for the singer's voice to carry. Vibrato is usually considered to be an ornament in early music and may not be consistently present in the sound, or at least not on a perceptual level.
4. Ornamentation. A huge and important topic for the early music singer, ornamentation is an expansive and complex skill that must be studied and practiced. Frederick Neumann's book *Ornamentation in Baroque and Post-Baroque Music* is a helpful starting point.

Benefit

The early music community has exploded over the course of the past several decades. Many specialists in HIP practice have emerged, and many recordings of authentic performances are now available. Several universities, such as Indiana University, the University of North Texas, and the Peabody Conservatory, also offer training programs in early music. Early music can be an important performance outlet for the right mind and voice.

SECRET 69: EXTEND YOUR TECHNIQUE—THE WORLD OF AVANT-GARDE MUSIC

In the twentieth century, the world of classical music took a turn toward a host of revolutionary new styles, and new schools of composition emerged. The rules and traditions of Western harmony and form—from Johann Sebastian Bach through Johannes Brahms—no longer seemed to apply to a new generation of avant-garde composers. For vocalists, one of the most pioneering and groundbreaking works was Arnold Schoenberg's infamous 1912 composition, *Pierrot lunaire*, a dark piece of chamber music (see Secret 67) that set the expressionist poetry of Albert Giraud. This work introduced *Sprechstimme*—a style of "singing" that fell somewhere in between traditional singing and human speech—to a wide audience for the first time.[4] *Sprechstimme* challenged everything that classical audiences thought they knew about singing. Over the next several decades, other composers would continue to explore these new vocal possibilities, most famously Alban Berg (Schoenberg's pupil) in his 1925 opera, *Wozzeck*.

Other prominent composers who explored new possibilities for the voice—usually called "extended techniques"—included John Cage, György Ligeti, Luciano Berio, Hans Werner Henze, Karlheinz Stockhausen, George Crumb, and Peter Maxwell Davies. Most of these composers worked directly with a new generation of singers who were eager to stretch their voices. Notable singers who specialized in these extended techniques for voice included Cathy Berberian, Bethany Beardslee, Jan DeGaetani, Phyllis Bryn-Julson, Patrice Pastore, Joan La Barbara, and Joan Heller. Meredith Monk (b. 1942) deserves special mention as a creative artist who both composes and then performs works that explore the limits of the capabilities of the human voice. The following list explores some of these techniques specifically.

Techniques

Buccal speech: An alternative way of speaking that does not use the lungs or larynx. In buccal speech, air is stored in the oral cavity (usually the cheek), which acts as an alternate lung. The air is then sent into the mouth, where speech is created without the engagement of the vocal folds. Buccal speech is also widely known as "Donald Duck talk," as the famous Disney character is the quintessential example of buccal speech in the mass media.

Glottal fry: Phonation at the lowest pitches of the voice, either male or female. Glottal fry produces an imprecise phonation reminiscent of clicking. Minimal airflow is needed to produce glottal fry.

Growling: A low, guttural vocalization. In addition to new music, growling is also applied in some types of heavy metal music.

Inhaled singing: A technique that involves singing while inhaling as opposed to exhaling. The result is a sound rooted in glottal fry. While some pitch variation is possible, the technique is limited in scope compared to traditional singing.

Multiphonics: More than one pitch produced at the same time. While usually an instrumental technique, vocalists can also produce multiphonics, typically in one of two ways: either through throat singing or whistling while phonating.

Screaming: Self-explanatory, although there is a technique to screaming in a nondamaging way. Consultation with a knowledgeable acting voice teacher is highly recommended.

***Sprechstimme*:** A vocal quality or style that lies somewhere in between speech and singing. Although exact pitches are notated—with an *x* over each note stem—and are expected to be performed with accuracy, it is also incumbent on the performer to give the vocal line a speech-like quality.

Tuvan throat singing: An eccentric singing technique that involves specific manipulation of the singer's jaw, lips, mouth, and sinuses to produce several overtones simultaneously. The fundamental note that produces these overtones is always a specific pitch in the TA (thyroarytenoid)/mode 1 register.

Ululation: A long, wavering, high-pitched vocal sound produced by the deliberate and rapid manipulation of the tongue. Ululation is a distinct and idiomatic sound heard in certain types of world music.

Yodeling: A style of singing often associated with the folk music of the Swiss Alps. Yodeling features the singing of leaps and a rapid alternation between the two principal vocal registers (thyroarytenoid and cricothyroid). A "yodel" can also be a short section of yodeling, sung on a single breath. Derived from the (middle-high) German verb "*jôlen*," meaning "to call," yodeling is thought to have originated as a call between mountain peoples. Whether there was a practical use for yodeling is unclear, but its popularity as a folk music endures. Due to the use of both registers, yodelers often have an extensive range of three octaves or more. A singer who practices yodeling is called a yodeler.

Benefit

Although only a small segment of the singing population engages in the regular performance of new music, the singer with the right skill set and vocal flexibility might find a comfortable niche in this genre. Universities and conservatories with thriving composition departments are likely to feature new music festivals and series, and certain cities—such as New York, Boston, and Minneapolis—are a haven for avant-garde composers who can offer interesting opportunities for singers.

SECRET 70: APPROACH CHORAL MUSIC IN A HEALTHY WAY

Of all of the options available to the classical singer, choral music opportunities are perhaps the most ubiquitous. From children's choirs to public school ensembles, churches to community choruses, professional chamber choirs to symphony chorus work, there are far more opportunities to sing as a chorister than there are for any of the other opportunities mentioned in this chapter—and probably more than any of these other opportunities combined.

Students who study classical singing in college usually sing in choirs in addition to their solo voice training with their private teacher. Much confusion—and sometimes conflict—can result due to shifting between the two styles. Many choral styles are very different than mainstream solo classical styles, and choral conductors and voice teachers are likely to want very different things from their singers. This secret will attempt to address some of the most common issues.

Technique

The most important thing to remember is that choral conductors are interested in the overall sound of their ensemble as opposed to the unique sound of your individual voice. While voice teachers, opera directors, and coaches will most likely encourage you to sing loudly and resonantly while exploring the individual nuances of your own voice, being unique in a choral situation—and running the risk of "sticking out"—will probably not be viewed positively by your conductor. The vast majority of choral directors will encourage each section of their ensemble to sound like "one voice." This often means that you must blend with your neighbors within your section.

So how does one "blend"? Rather than thinking that you are constraining your voice (and thus probably engaging in compensatory and unnecessary tension), think instead of the following.

1. Match vowels with the person on either side of you. If vowels within your section are unified, chances are the conductor will be satisfied with what he or she is hearing within your section.
2. Instead of thinking "less free," simply try singing softer. The ability to sing softly is not unique to choral situations. A soloist with solid technique should be able to do this with little difficulty.
3. Realize that it is OK to be less resonant (don't see Secret 4). In classical solo singing—especially opera—the "singer's resonance" is an ideal toward which all singers strive. Striving for maximum "ring" in an ensemble, however, is not likely to endear you to the conductor. Resonance is something that can be controlled through vowel choices and formant tuning.

4. Realize that—in this situation—it is OK to sing non-legato (don't see Secret 7). This is one of the biggest differences between good solo singing and good choral singing. The classical soloist strives for legato at all times, but in most styles of choral music, legato is simply not an important element of the style and may in fact hinder good ensemble. This is especially true in baroque and classical repertoires, as well as many pieces from the contemporary choral repertory. Choral conductors are far more likely to want crisp rhythmic delineation between notes, and leaps should be executed with cool precision, never with portamento (unless you are doing a program of Verdi opera choruses).
5. Be willing to control the extent of your vibrato (see Secret 12). Perhaps the most controversial advice on this list is also the most obvious and should come as no surprise. Many choral conductors will expect this—period. The authors acknowledge that this will be easier for some voices than others.
6. Remember that choral *Fachs*—or *Fächer*—are different than solo *Fachs* (see Secret 11). Just because you are a full lyric or spinto soprano when you sing your solo repertoire doesn't necessarily mean that the S1 part is going to feel comfortable in your college chamber choir, particularly if your director has programmed an all-Renaissance concert. Perhaps S2 or A1 will allow you to sing in a more reasonable tessitura and with a little more warmth. A caring director and advocating voice teacher will usually bend over backward to make sure that you are singing a choral part that is comfortable for you.

Note that none of the above tips recommended that you sing with poor technique or increased strain. It is possible to accomplish all of the above while singing with noble posture (see Secret 1), minimal tension, good breath management (see Secret 2), and freedom. If you are attending long choral rehearsals, be sure that you hydrate (see Secret 21) and pace yourself accordingly.

Finally, remember that choral conductors tend to value a different skill set than opera conductors or art song coaches. Size, color, and resonance of the voice are likely to be less important to the choral director, and acting skills and movement probably are not assessed at the choral audition at all. Alternatively, sight-reading skills, musicianship, and the ability to control one's voice within a section are significantly more important factors at the choral audition. (Note that this list of factors incudes many qualities that are completely out of the singer's control.) Just like everyone is not built for grand opera, not every voice is suited to choral singing. The two genres tend to value completely different kinds of singers.

Benefit

Most singers will sing in a choir at some point in their training or career, so understanding the differences between choral and solo singing can be important. Understanding what choral conductors want is important for approaching the genre in a healthy and stylistically correct way. Not every voice is ideal for singing choral music, but not every voice is meant for opera or jazz either. For many singers, however, the world of choral singing is an exciting option and an ideal fit. Singers who find themselves in larger metropolitan areas can also find many opportunities for employment through choral genres (see Secret 98).

NOTES

1. Deborah Stein and Robert Spillman, *Poetry into Song: Performance and Analysis of Lieder* (New York: Oxford University Press, 1996), 6.

2. Some scholars also consider Mozart's *Die Zauberföte* to be a *Singspiel* as well. While this work fits some of the definitions of "*Singspiel*"—containing dialogue and magical/fantastic elements—its grandiose nature makes it atypical of the genre (to say the least).

3. Some musicologists also consider one-on-a-part choral singing to be chamber music, but this secret will focus on chamber music written for voices and small ensembles of instruments.

4. Technically, *Sprechstimme* was invented by Engelbert Humperdinck in a little-known 1897 work *Königslieder*, but the technique is most famously associated with Arnold Schoenberg.

CHAPTER 7

Singing CCM (Nonclassical) Styles

SECRET 71: UNDERSTAND DIFFERENCES BETWEEN CLASSICAL AND CCM STYLES

Coined by voice pedagogue Jeannette LoVetri in 2000, the term "contemporary commercial Music," or CCM (not to be confused with the acronym for the Cincinnati College–Conservatory of Music), comprises nonclassical music styles, including pop, rock, jazz, musical theatre, R&B, gospel, country, and folk music. Some singers successfully negotiate the so-called crossover between classical and CCM styles with ease. For instance, Juilliard-trained Audra McDonald won a Tony Award for her portrayal of jazz legend Billie Holliday in *Lady Day*, and Broadway favorite Kelli O'Hara debuted at the Metropolitan Opera in their 2014 production of *The Merry Widow*. Fellow Florence Birdwell–trained Kristin Chenoweth displayed the ultimate in stylistic versatility in "The Girl in 14G," switching between comedic character voice, the Queen of the Night, and jazz scatting. The important thing is to recognize the differences in vocal technique and style required to sing idiomatically in different genres.

Technique

Here are some steps to follow as you try to distinguish between different styles of singing. Identify the appropriate

1. tonal aesthetic—is it speech-like? Operatic? Are the vowels vertical? Horizontal?
2. resonance—is it bright? Dark? Chiaroscuro? Nasal?
3. vibrato—is it present? Present throughout? Absent? Used only at the end of long notes?
4. registration—is it predominantly chest voice? Or head voice? Mix? Falsetto? Belt? (For more on this topic, see Secret 6.)

Try to differentiate between these elements by comparing singers in your similar *Fach*. For instance, a tenor might contrast the stylistic and vocal differences between Juan Diego Florez, Matthew Morrison, Usher, Gary LeVox of Rascal Flatts, and Bruno Mars.

Benefit

Recognizing the differences in musical styles is like knowing what attire is appropriate for differing occasions. You wouldn't wear a formal dress to a barbeque or a bathing suit to the Tony Awards, but you can still have both in your closet and look great wearing them in the fitting venue. It will also help you avoid sounding like Michael Bolton on his aria album or Will Farrell and Ana Gasteyer as uncool middle school music teachers in the *Saturday Night Live* skits featuring their operatic pop songs.

SECRET 72: BELTING, BODY TYPE, AND BALLET—MUSICAL THEATRE

Singing in musical theatre has evolved greatly over the last century. The so-called legit singing of the classic Rodgers and Hammerstein/Lerner and Loewe musicals has been joined by shows with more pop and rock influences. The popularity of jukebox musicals (ABBA's *Mamma Mia*, Billy Joel's *Movin' Out*, Frankie Valli's *Jersey Boys*), shows based on familiar films (*Dirty Dancing*, *Flashdance*, *Ghost*), and Disney movies (*The Little Mermaid*, *Aladdin*, *The Lion King*) has widened the stylistic requirements for Broadway singers. Another evolution is the prevalence of body mics. In an era before amplification, Ethel Merman was famous for being able to project her voice to the back row of the theatre. Today hair/wig microphones have become standard, affording singers the ability to sing with a wider palette of dynamics and still be heard. Musical theatre singers still need to have training and experience with belting. What used to be a highly controversial subject in the world of voice pedagogy is finally gaining the study and legitimacy it warrants. Belting means different things to different people, but it most often is described as having a speech-like quality and what Jeannette LoVetri calls "a trumpet-like intensity that makes the sound seem to be very powerful."[1] Think of iconic belters like Barbra Streisand, Betty Buckley, and more recently Sutton Foster. Belting should not be

Figure 7.1.   Bernadette Peters. *Creative Commons (CC BY 2.0)*

pure chest voice extending to extremes of high range but should involve a mix. Modern terminology that has been embraced is "belt mix," "chest-dominant," or "TA (thyroarytenoid) dominant." The larynx will be in a slightly higher position than in classical singing, and there may be more straight tone and much less vibrato. Also, your singing voice, speaking voice, and body type need to be in alignment (see Secret 22) since the theatre world is less forgiving than the opera world when it comes to looks, although opera is evolving to a more stringent standard as well.

Technique

1. Develop vocal technique suitable for musical theatre. Make sure your teacher is familiar with the registral and stylistic issues important for this genre. (Check out International Voice Teachers of Mix or Somatic Voicework™.) Learn to control your vibrato and work on a healthy belt mix.
2. Develop an audition book of sixteen-bar and thirty-two-bar cuts. (Some auditions ask for thirty to forty-five second cuts as opposed to specific numbers of bars.) Compile a three-ring binder with double-sided pages so the pianist can avoid page turns. As tempting as they may be, avoid shiny plastic page covers. Make sure your music is clearly marked so there is no question about where any cuts start or finish. Your audition book should contain both classic and contemporary up-tempo pieces and ballads. Depending on your particular vocal strengths, you might also consider some of these possibilities: character piece, jazz standard, Top 40 pop/rock, country, Disney, or an operetta excerpt.
3. Take acting classes. Musical theatre is theatre, and the standards for believable acting are very high. Approach your songs as you would any scene in a play. Be sure you are always pursuing your character's objectives and taking action to overcome his or her obstacles. Unless you are in a vaudeville or stylized production, avoid "mugging" or "indicating" and try to be sincere and true to the character's reality.
4. Take dance classes. You do not have to become Tommy Tune, but dance training is a must. Ballet is great for posture, balance, and grace, but if it's too intimidating, try jazz dance. You should know some basic steps that are common choreography (jazz square, grapevine, step-ball-change, fan kick, etc.). You might also consider tap, especially if you're great at singing standards from the Great American Songbook (Porter, Gershwin, Ellington, etc.), which feature heavily in shows like *Anything Goes*, *My One and Only*, *42nd Street*, and *Sophisticated Ladies*.

Benefit

With well-rounded training in musical theatre singing, acting, and dancing, you can become a triple threat, or at least a singer who moves or acts well and who is thereby more likely to be cast.

SECRET 73: KNOW YOUR MIC AND YOUR NICHE—ROCK AND POP MUSIC

Who wouldn't want to be a rock star! The appeal of rock music is undeniable, as is its popularity. Unfortunately, until recently some voice teachers avoided addressing issues relating specifically to pop/rock music. Luckily, voice pedagogy is evolving and becoming more relevant to the times. Like musical theatre singers, pop/rock vocalists don't typically use a lot of vibrato. They also favor a chest voice-dominant (or TA-dominant) approach to registration or employ a belt mix. With a few exceptions or special effects (Mariah Carey's common use of whistle tones and Sarah McLachlan's or Jewel's yodeling into head voice), the preferred timbre is a heightened speech-like quality so that text is clearly understood.

Technique

1. Develop a solid vocal technique. Work to develop consistent breath management and tone production. Strengthen your middle and upper-middle registers, but also explore both the low and high ends of your range for special expressive effects. Tenors should build the strength of their falsetto, be it for occasional or frequent use.
2. Work on microphone technique. Sing directly into the mic, not over it, but try not to block your own face. To keep the sound system in check, be careful not to sing plosives with too much force, and pull the mic back a bit on higher notes as needed.
3. Find your niche. Rock/pop music encompasses a wide variety of styles and subgenres. Katy Perry and Jessica Simpson started off in contemporary Christian music before making their names in the Top 40, while Hootie and the Blowfish frontman Darius Rucker went from pop to country. It may take time to find your niche, but just as it is important to know your voice type (see Secret 11), you need to find where your forte is stylistically: bubblegum pop, R&B, hip hop, heavy metal, folk, reggae, punk, funk, techno, and so on.
4. Be in good physical shape. Unless you're a singer/songwriter sitting on a stool with a guitar, your performances will probably involve stage movement. If not, you'll still need to be in good condition for the travel demands of touring (see Secret 25). Plus, for better or for worse, your appearance is also considered an important part of your image or brand as a rock/pop performer. Keep yourself in shape so you can look your best but also so you can maintain your energy level for performing.

Note

Despite the temptation of the possibility, don't enter *The Voice* or other high-profile singing competitions until you are seasoned and in control of your sound.

Karaoke can be good practice (and great fun), but try to develop something unique so that you don't sound like a poor man's Michael Bublé or an Alanis Morissette alternative. Hone your technique. (Pat Benatar trained in opera. Céline Dion still has a vocal coach.) And then be distinctive (Michael Jackson, Adam Lambert).

SECRET 74: BE AN INSTRUMENT OF INSPIRATION—GOSPEL

In the words of four-time Grammy Award winner Yolanda Adams: "There is a sound that comes from gospel music that doesn't come from anything else. It is a sound of peace. It is a sound of, 'I'm going to make it through all of this.'" Drawing on influences from rock, country, R&B, and soul, gospel as a genre grew from Christian hymns and spirituals. While it can be part of a concert or a religious ceremony, gospel music is rooted in the Christian church, specifically the African American tradition. Even sung in a secular context, gospel music is meant to praise God. The Gospel Music Association states their mission is "to expose, promote, and celebrate the gospel through music." The exciting vocals and powerful message of gospel have led to the genre's infusion into other musical avenues, such as the film *Sister Act* and Broadway shows like *The Color Purple*. Many pop performances (especially on award shows) feature a soloist backed by a great gospel choir, as in Josh Groban's "You Raise Me Up" or Mariah Carey's "Joy to the World." But when most of us think of gospel, we think of an inspirational singer with a commanding voice rejoicing in worship.

Figure 7.2.   Mahalia Jackson. *Creative Commons (CC BY-SA 3.0)*

Technique

Most great gospel singers grew up singing in church, so they have a strong background in hymn tunes and spiritual songs. But if you didn't have access to that rich tradition, then immerse yourself in historic recordings by the king of gospel, Reverend James Cleveland, as well as more recent renditions by BeBe, CeCe, and Marvin Winans. Gospel singers need a strong chest voice plus the ability to belt and sustain a high tessitura for a long duration. Make sure your breath management stays well coordinated so that you can build the vocal stamina necessary for this demanding but rewarding genre without straining. You'll also want to work on your ability to sing tight harmonies so that you can sing backup or in a gospel quartet. Of course, since the main purpose of gospel is the spiritual message, you have to deliver the word of God with passion and conviction. Not only does your voice need to be sincere, but your expression needs to reveal your faith. As Mahalia Jackson said, "How can you sing of amazing grace and all God's wonders without using your hands?" With or without a microphone, your hands need to help communicate your intent, and your face needs to show that you revel in and revere the divine impact of the text you are singing.

Benefit

Gospel music provides profound spiritual inspiration and comfort for many people. Recent psychological studies have also shown that gospel music can provide mental health benefits by easing anxiety and promoting a sense of control and satisfaction. So you should sing gospel not just because it sounds great but also because it makes you feel better!

SECRET 75: STANDARDS, STRUCTURE, AND SCATTING—JAZZ

The golden years of jazz brought us many legendary singers: Frank Sinatra, Mel Tormé, Nat King Cole, Louis Armstrong, and of course Ella Fitzgerald, Billie Holiday, and Sarah Vaughan. Thanks to the untiring Tony Bennett, young people are being introduced to the Great American Songbook through his collaboration with pop artists such as Lady Gaga. In the twenty-first century, jazz continues to be championed by a wide variety of modern performers such as Harry Connick Jr., Jamie Cullum, Diana Krall, and Jane Monheit. There is rich repertoire to explore, and many musical rewards for those with the creativity and imagination to illuminate the genre.

Technique

George Gershwin once said, "Life is a lot like jazz: it's best when you improvise." Knowing how to improvise is a key element to singing jazz. Yes, you'll probably have a lead sheet with the melody and chords, but you won't simply sing through the tune as it looks on paper. So you really need to understand the structure of the song: intro, verse, refrain, bridge, outro, possible tag ending. It's especially important to know when the bridge section or chorus is returning so you won't get lost in the middle of a guitar solo or drum break or so you don't get lost if you're experimenting with back phrasing. In addition to song structure, you need to understand the harmonic structure of the song. If you know the chords, then you can more skillfully maneuver your melodic improvisation. Take risks and try different approaches to varying the arc of the melody. Because of the nature of improvisation and the complexity of jazz chords, most jazz singing is done with little or no vibrato. A "straighter" tone without pitch fluctuation helps tight harmonies be heard, not to mention the song lyrics. In addition, you will want to practice scat singing. "Scatting" is improvising on nonsense syllables, singing in an almost instrumental manner emphasizing rhythmic and motivic elements. While you will need to practice scatting to become comfortable doing it, you don't want it to sound too "practiced." Be willing to make different kinds of sounds, exploring your vocal range and timbre. And although you may not be singing real words, you will need clear and nimble articulation to negotiate the quick scat syllables. For a master class in scat singing, listen to Ella Fitzgerald's 1960 live version of "How High the Moon." Her vocal versatility and agility are amazing, and the performance cleverly weaves other standards into the main tune. More recently, Dianne Reeves has shown another ingenuity by turning pop songs into jazz tunes, such as Peter Gabriel's "In Your Eyes," Carole King's "Will You Still Love Me Tomorrow?" and Joni Mitchell's "River." So as a jazz singer, you can turn new songs into new standards, as well as bring new life and insight into old songs so they become standards for a new generation.

Benefit

Whether you're singing with a big band or a piano/upright bass duo, singing jazz is a true collaboration requiring active listening and immediate musical interplay between musicians. So it's not surprising that jazz can only help make you a more astute and accomplished musician.

SECRET 76: SHARE YOUR STRUGGLES AND CELEBRATIONS—COUNTRY MUSIC

The legendary Johnny Cash once said: "Of emotions, of love, of breakup, of love and hate and death and dying, mama, apple pie, and the whole thing. It covers a lot of territory, country music does." Country music has always had a loyal following, mostly in the South and West, but it also has gone more mainstream. Country artists such as Blake Shelton and Keith Urban found widespread fame as judges of television singing competitions (*The Voice* and *American Idol*, respectively), while others made their name by winning such competitions (Carrie Underwood). To sing country, you need to connect to your audience in an authentic and heartfelt way. While part of the appeal of Lady Gaga or Prince may have been their exoticism or chameleon-like flair, country singers need to be more relatable. A cowboy hat and boots may not be absolutely necessary, but as Brad Paisley said, "Country music has become the music that best represents the reality of American life." So a pair of blue jeans might be obligatory. Or if you're Dolly Parton, you're at least honest about your wigs or anything that might not be entirely homegrown. ("It takes a lot of money to look this cheap.")

Technique

If you are classically trained, you will obviously need to adjust your vocal timbre for country music. You don't want to sound like Maria Callas when you're singing Patsy Cline's "Crazy." Don't be afraid of a little nasality since country music's aesthetic usually involves some twang. Like rock/pop music, you should cultivate a natural, speech-like quality. Female country singers usually have a solid belt technique (Reba McEntire, Martina McBride) and sometimes showcase the ability to yodel (LeAnn Rimes singing "Blue"). While male rock singers are almost always tenors, country music also shows appreciation for the baritones, as evidenced by the deep voices of Conway Twitty, Trace Adkins, and more recently Josh Turner. But most important, country music requires storytelling. Country singers like Johnny Cash and Loretta Lynn brought a sincerity and authenticity to their performances, which were informed by their personal experiences. You don't have to have a tragic life to be a country singer, and please don't follow the path of Hank Williams or Mindy McCready. You should not be afraid, however, to share your hardships, because country fans are looking to connect to a multidimensional performer who illuminates the joys and sorrows of his or her own life.

Note

While many opera singers head to Europe and most musical theatre performers move to Manhattan to try to make it on Broadway, country artists usually need to make a name for themselves in Nashville. Tennessee's "Music City" is the epicenter of country music, and being made a member of the Grand Ole Opry is considered the industry's highest honor.

SECRET 77: CONQUER THE WORLD—GLOBAL MUSIC STYLES

World music is about taking things from different places and bringing them together, which is great.

—Youssou N'Dour

"World music" is a term used to denote virtually any form of non-Western music, either in the art music or popular music vein. World music is an extraordinarily vast collection of genres that is rapidly gaining more ubiquity and influence in Western culture. Many forms of world music, in both indigenous and popular styles, feature singing as a prominent element.

The growing field of ethnomusicology has increased the prevalence of world music ensembles in the West, and the fusion between world music and various Western popular styles has made world music styles increasingly relevant to the modern singer and student of singing. World music vocal styles are as varied as the cultures from which they originate, and each must be studied on its own terms within its own social context.

World music styles are far too numerous to mention, and not every kind of world music features singing as a prominent element of the style. Some of the most well-known examples of world vocal music include Beijing/Peking opera (China), *bossa nova* (Brazil), *fado* (Portugal), *Noh* or *Nogaku* (Japan), *qawwali* (Pakistan), *raï* (Algeria), *ranchera* (Mexico), *tahrir* (Iran), tango (Argentina), *xoomei* or Tuvan throat singing (Tuva/Mongolia), and yodeling (Switzerland).

Strategies for Exploring World Music

Listen voraciously! The world music recording industry is mammoth, so fortunately there are currently thousands of recordings of virtually any style of world music in distribution all over the globe. Some of the greatest singers of world music include Sezen Aksu (Turkey), Asha Bhosle (India), Björk (Iceland), Concha Buika (Spain), Fairuz (Lebanon), João Gilberto (Brazil), Camarón de la Isla (Spain), Victor Jara (Chile), Salif Keita (Mali), Nusrat Fateh Ali Khan (Pakistan), Umm Kulthum (Egypt), Kongar-ool Ondar (Tuva), Youssou N'Dour (Senegal), Edith Piaf (France), Alim Qasimov (Azerbaijan), Elis Regina (Brazil), Amalia Rodriguez (Portugal), Oumou Sangaré (Mali), and Mohammed Reza Shajarian (Iran).

Technique

The styles present in world music are so diverse and varied that they cannot possibly be succinctly summarized in one paragraph. Further, no single performer or pedagogue could hope to master the vast pluralism of world music within a single career or lifetime. Specialists are emerging, however, and CCM pedagogues are beginning to recognize the increased prevalence of world music styles in the twenty-first century and thus the need for specific pedagogies to address these burgeoning styles. Current trends indicate that world music voice pedagogy will emerge as a prominent force in the coming decades.

Benefit

As a citizen of the world, it is a social responsibility for singers to acquaint themselves with the singing styles of their international brothers and sisters. It is also a deeply enriching and moving experience, and one gains significant perspective with regard to how Western styles only tell part of a universal story. Western singers have nothing to lose and everything to gain by exploring the vocal music of other cultures. The presence of these styles in Western culture will only increase over the course of the twenty-first century.

SECRET 78: TAG ALONG—BARBERSHOP HARMONY

There is no bad day that can't be overcome by listening to a barbershop quartet. That is just truth, plain and simple.

—Aldous Huxley

Barbershop singing is a four-part, unaccompanied vocal style of American popular music. Barbershop harmony is traditionally performed by four male singers with one person singing each part. The four parts are the lead (who sings the melody), the bass, the baritone (usually called "bari"), and the tenor (a kind of descant to the melody that is sung—usually in falsetto—above the lead part).

Barbershop singing reached its height in popularity during the early decades of the twentieth century, drawing its repertoire primarily from Tin Pan Alley and the Great American Songbook repertory. Unapologetically anachronistic, barbershop harmony recalls a specific era in American popular music, surviving today largely through the sponsorship of the Barbershop Harmony Society, also known as SPEBSQSA (the Society for the Preservation and Encouragement of Barbershop Singing in America). The tendency for each part "to sing its own note" and the avoidance of triadic harmonies are the most significant hallmarks of the barbershop style and give the genre its own idiosyncratic flavor. Stylistically, a four-part a cappella song cannot truly be called a piece of barbershop music unless it is composed of at least 35–60 percent dominant seventh chords (which are called "barbershop chords" by barbershoppers).

Although usually performed by a quartet of solo voices, the same repertory may be performed by a barbershop chorus with multiple singers on a part. Barbershop choruses can be very small (with as few as sixteen voices) to very large (numbering in the hundreds). While historically a male genre, barbershop is now often sung by females as well. Female barbershop quartets and choruses sing the same repertoire up an octave with the same voice part labels: lead, bass, baritone, and tenor. Female barbershoppers are represented by two organizations of their own: Sweet Adelines International and Harmony, Incorporated.

Strategies for Singing Barbershop

1. Visit a local chapter of the Barbershop Harmony Society, where you will find hordes of eager men and women interested in recruiting you to sing barbershop with them. The great news is that barbershop, historically and philosophically, is intended as a hobby for amateur singers, so you will find a welcoming environment to explore the style.

2. Steep yourself in the style! It's really simple. There are literally hundreds of published recordings of championship quartets and choirs, most of which can be purchased online and through the website of the Barbershop Harmony Society.

Technique

Many singers find that the greatest technical challenge to singing barbershop is the "straight tone" nature of the style. While one could argue that no vocal sound is truly straight tone, vibrato in barbershop must be so minimal in its rate and extent that it is imperceptible to the listener. Acute listening and careful control of vibrato are absolute musts if one is to sing the style well.

Intonation can also be a challenge; advanced barbershoppers are keenly aware of which part of the chord they are singing (root, third, fifth, or seventh) and tune it accordingly against the other parts.

Benefit

Barbershop can be a lot of fun, and the people associated with the genre are great folks. Many singers find themselves easily hooked on the style and quickly make it a hobby. It is definitely worth exploring this uniquely American art form.

SECRET 79: BE COGNIZANT OF THE RAW FACTS OF THE INDUSTRY

Most students who study singing at universities and conservatories earn a bachelor of music in vocal performance. This degree is designed to prepare the student to sing opera and art song and is actually growing in popularity among college-aged students. According to a 2013 study, over 9,000 students are currently earning degrees in voice performance at 383 American universities.[2] The same study notes that musical theatre programs enroll twenty-three hundred students at seventy-four institutions and that there are currently only five programs in the United States that offer degrees in CCM styles (excluding jazz programs).

Food for Thought

These numbers are perhaps surprising when one examines the reality of the marketplace. In 2009, pop/rock revenues in the United States totaled $12.3 billion compared to revenues of $289 million for classical singing. These figures suggest that pop/rock employment opportunities outnumber classical singing opportunities by a ratio of forty-two to one! This is especially interesting—and perhaps ironic—when one considers the fact that classical training programs outnumber CCM programs by a ratio of seventy-six to one.

Recommendation

Be realistic and open-minded. The modern classically trained singer needs to be aware of the tough realities of the marketplace. In addition to talent and work ethic, a significant amount of grit, tenacity, patience, business savvy, and good luck is needed for a successful classical career.

Having as broad of a skill set as possible only increases employability. Facility with musical theatre and CCM styles is a plus, assuming that one sings these styles well. This does not mean that one should flippantly engage in other singing styles without some grounding in or prior knowledge of the style, but if the singer is genuinely passionate and equally skilled and talented in a variety of areas, it can only help in terms of employment opportunities. Many performers who do not make their living through singing alone also find fulfilling employment through teaching, church work, and arts management opportunities.

Benefit

One should reach for the stars, but be realistic. The music world has always been a tough one and is not for the faint of heart, and the singing curricula offered by most universities, colleges, and conservatories often fall short of training students for the realities of the marketplace. Having as broad of a skill set as possible increases the possibility for performance and other art-form-related opportunities.

NOTES

1. Jeannette LoVetri, "What Is Healthy Belting," MajoringinMusic.com, accessed 2016.

2. Matthew Edwards, "Why It's Time to Add Pop-Rock to Your Voice Studio," *VOICE Prints* 11, no. 2 (2013): 5.

CHAPTER 8

Stage Presence

SECRET 80: MEDITATION NOT MEDICATION—COMBATING PERFORMANCE ANXIETY

You probably know all too well the familiar symptoms of performance anxiety: elevated heart rate, shallow breathing, dry mouth, sweaty hands, shaky legs, racing thoughts, foggy memory. Stage fright isn't just for beginners or amateurs either. Barbra Streisand avoided performing live for almost thirty years after an onstage memory slip left her paralyzed with fear. Even opera superstar Renée Fleming has battled the beast: "We're not talking about the jitters. We're talking about deep, deep panic, and that every fiber of your being is saying, 'I cannot be onstage.'" The excitement, nervousness, and perceived risk of public performance can all trigger the fight-or-flight response and manifest in familiar physical reactions that are very detrimental for any singer. It can cause even a talented, well-trained singer to "choke" or fold under pressure. Therefore, the successful singer must not only master good breath management but also learn to combat the biology of the stress response in order to achieve good breath management in high-pressure performance situations. Two yoga techniques can help you regain control of your breath and brain.

Technique

1. Breathe. Take a deep breath. This may be easier said than done when you're nervous, because the fight-or-flight response automatically makes breathing more difficult. But try to inhale and exhale to an equal count, employing the *Kala* breathing technique (see Secret 2). This will help lengthen your inhalation. To help lengthen your exhalation, try the *Ujjayi* breath (see Secret 27), lowering your heart rate with the power of Darth Vader. Yoga breathing is called *pranayama*, which means breath control and life control. If you can control your breath, you control your life and your reaction to stress.

2. Meditate. You don't have to meditate in lotus position (see figure 8.1) or corpse pose. Simply close your eyes and begin to cycle a mantra through your mind. The repetition of this positive affirmation becomes a kind of self-hypnosis or positive brainwashing that can silence your negative inner monologue ("I'm going to crack," "I can't hit that note," "What if they hate me?"). Mantras can bring focus and serenity to your mind. Try to keep your mantra positive (so "I won't mess up" isn't what you need) and in the present tense. Many songs provide great inspiration for mantras, from musical theatre pieces such as "This Is the Moment," "I Can Go the Distance," and "I Believe in You" to pop hits like "Roar," "Brave," and "Invincible."

Note

Anxiety is a natural human reaction to stress. This primitive response was a great survival mechanism when *Homo erectus* was combating or fleeing a saber-toothed tiger. An audition or performance is never a life-or-death matter, but it sure can feel that way. You can manage stage fright without medication (beta blockers) by using meditation to empower your confidence and curtail your anxiety before a big gig. Don't let fear of failure prevent you from finding success as a singer. You can use your breath and your mind to let your voice be free so that you can realize your full potential as a performing artist unfettered by stage fright.

Figure 8.1. Lotus Pose

SECRET 81: SING FROM THE HEART—WHY DO YOU SING?

Why do you sing? If you are active as (or actively studying to be) a professional singer, presumably you intend for singing to be your profession. And sure, making a living as a singer is wonderful, and being a famous singer is probably amazing. But most of us are not just singing to pay the bills. So why do you sing? In the musical *The Mystery of Edwin Drood*, music master John Jasper tells his budding student Rosa Bud, "When you sing the words, you must make me feel you mean them!" For your voice to truly speak to an audience, you need to let your heart sing too. While she had many detractors who criticized her voice, Maria Callas was an enthralling singer because her heart was completely open to the audience. In fact, she once said, "I prepare myself for rehearsals like I would for marriage." Her love for singing was evident, and her emotional delivery was heartfelt. We fall in love with singers that can reach us on this level, and we aspire to be them. Whitney Houston once said, "When I heard Aretha [Franklin], I could feel her emotional delivery so clearly. It came from deep down within. That's what I wanted to do." So bring not just strong technique but also true sentiment to your singing for the fullest realization of your power as a performer.

Technique

1. Connect to your intent. Be less generic. Be as specific as you can about what you are trying to communicate emotionally. Make your own mission statement to help define your emotional intent as an artist. A great example is the mission of singer/songwriter Ellis: "My deepest wish is to open people's hearts. It is my life's work and daily practice to allow myself to be undefended and open; to write songs from that place and offer them to others." To hone your own intent or mission, start a manifest journal or try the morning pages exercises of Julia Cameron's *The Artist's Way*.
2. Try heart-openers. If you're feeling closed off emotionally, heart-opening yoga poses can help provide both emotional and physical release. Take care with these backbends, as they can be challenging, but here are some heart-opening *asanas* listed in ascending order of difficulty: cobra, sphinx, up dog, locust (see figure 8.2), bow, camel (see figure 8.3), and wheel. Be careful not to compress the lower back as you arch into these poses, and really try to lift your sternum and lead with your heart.

Benefit

Mezzo-soprano Grace Bumbry said, "It's the star singers who sing from the heart out." Your stage presence represents your soul and spirit. It is what sets you apart as a distinctive artist, a performer with purpose. Knowing why you sing and why you love to sing will draw the audience to you. Sing from the heart and they won't be able to resist falling in love with you and your voice.

Figure 8.2. Locust Pose

Figure 8.3. Camel Pose

SECRET 82: GESTICULATE! OVERCOMING FEAR OF GESTURES

We've all seen it: a singer whose arms are frozen like those of a mannequin. Or you've seen the opposite end of the spectrum: a vocalist whose fingers are moving so much that it looks like sign language. Gestures are a natural part of expression that can greatly enhance the impact of your singing and highlight the meaning of the text you are communicating. Whether you are hypergesticulative (very active) or hypogesticulative (almost still), you may feel self-conscious about using gestures when you perform, fearful of looking either vaudevillian or straightjacketed. Song recitalists used to be confined to the nook of the piano, with one hand resting on the lid or with both hands clasped in front of the solar plexus. More often these days, recitalists are encouraged to gesture freely and naturally, just as if they were onstage in an opera or musical. Gesture is also an important part of gospel music. The hand movements need to be an organic outgrowth of the musical expression, helping to emphasize emotion and heighten the effect of your vocal interpretation.

Figure 8.4. Leonardo da Vinci's Rendition of the Hands

Technique

1. Speak your text as a poem or monologue. Tell a story, painting a picture with how you communicate the text verbally and gesturally. Try to let your hands be an extension of your vocal expression. If you are prone to stillness, imagine you're at a children's story hour and try to enliven your gestures to Disney heights. If your style is more exaggerated (à la Jim Carrey in *The Mask*), then pretend you're a news anchor and focus on communicating through facial and vocal expression rather than continuous hand movements.
2. Avoid stock gestures. Unless you're in a commedia dell'arte or stylized production, you don't want to look too choreographed or "canned." The opera world is known for some common stock gestures, such as "the Claw" (favored by villains and Verdi baritones) and "the Tray" (a favorite of soubrettes). And, of course, there's the open-armed *Titanic* pose (which actually is helpful in keeping the rib cage open). Truly, any of these gestures can be convincing as long as they're done in an authentic manner, but try to avoid imitation and instead follow your intuition.
3. Find the appropriate level of gesture for the repertoire. The starkness of a song like Schubert's "Der Doppelgänger" or a role like the Commendatore in Mozart's *Don Giovanni* should have a slower and more subdued use of gesture than more high-energy pieces such as a Gilbert and Sullivan patter song or a part like the Genie in *Aladdin*.
4. Watch yourself on video. Are you instinctually still like a statue or animated like a master of ceremonies? Do you look like a conductor beating time? Do you fidget with your clothing? Do you have any nervous tics or other unintentional movements of which you are unaware? Use the footage to help make adjustments to your gestural patterns so that they become believable, both unaffected and affecting.

Note

For inspiration, listen to or watch the witty song "Gesticulate" from the musical *Kismet*. Howard Keel does an amusing rendition in the 1955 film version.

SECRET 83: EXPRESS YOURSELF (FACIALLY)—SOMEWHERE BETWEEN BOTOX AND OVERACTING

There's an old saying, "a look is worth a thousand words." For a singer, sometimes no gesture is needed; instead a look can portray infinite emotion, even when you're only singing "ah." But sometimes it can be difficult to align your facial expressions with your singing. Many singers are so concentrated on their vocal technique that their faces reflect only that concentration in their furrowed foreheads. Some fall into exaggerated "eyebrow acting," while others who have had Botox injections can't move their eyebrows a millimeter. As with gestures, facial expression should be sincere and instinctual, helping to depict what your voice is already revealing. So you need to be aware of what your face is reflecting to the audience. In commercial contemporary music (CCM) styles, closing your eyes is a common expressive device, but this effect should not be overused, especially in opera and musical theatre. To quote another old saying, "the eyes are the window to the soul," so you don't want to deny the audience soulful expressive access. Here are some ways to work on authentic and free facial expression.

Technique

1. Watch yourself. Of course the mirror is an incredibly helpful tool for observing your facial expressions (see Secret 36). And watching a video recording of yourself can be very enlightening (and/or painful! see Secret 46). Whether you're watching yourself live in practice or on a recording, try to observe empirically. Is there extraneous facial tension? What is your forehead doing? What are your eyebrows doing? Are your eyes open and expressive? What are your lips doing? Does your face look blank or deadpan? Does your face actually reflect what you think you're trying to portray? Eventually, you need to step away from the mirror and build kinesthetic awareness of what your face is doing when you sing. If you're unaware of routine frowning, you could even put a piece of tape in between your eyes temporarily so you can feel when you wrinkle. Or you can try to imagine keeping this area open, in yoga what they call your "third eye" or a point of wisdom and elevated consciousness. Singers who may be on the autistic spectrum or who are managing Tourette's syndrome will need to heighten their awareness of potential facial mannerisms that might interfere with clear communication and expression.
2. Work with expression cards. Write down different intents or emotions on cards. Then sing a song while flashing different cards, trying to depict what they say. For instance, you might start singing "The Star-Spangled Banner" with a card that says "jubilant," as would naturally fit the song. Then you

might switch cards to try to reflect "mournful," "angry," and "giddy." This exercise works especially well when you have an observer trying to guess the emotion. Instead of adjectives, you could use varying subtexts or acting objectives (e.g., "I want to celebrate America," "I want your hat," or "It's so hot").

Benefit

Just as you want a vocal and dynamic range, you want a wide range of facial expressions so that you can communicate the complexity of human emotion in a natural and relatable way. But some performers fall into generic or stock facial expressions, while others use over-the-top expressions that might only be suitable for an operatic mad scene. Both mezzo-soprano Cecilia Bartoli and blues singer Jonny Lang often employ extreme facial contortions (see figure 8.5), which can distract from rather than enhance their performances. While impressively belting high notes, *Glee* star Lea Michele always seems to have the same look on her face. The goal is to avoid looking predictable or unnatural. An enviable model would be the earnest expression of Judy Garland singing "Over the Rainbow" with simplicity and sensitivity. By nurturing awareness and authenticity, you can develop a wide palette of facial expressions that elucidate your interpretation even when the audience does not understand the language in which you are singing.

Figure 8.5. Jonny Lang. *Creative Commons (CC BY-SA 3.0)*

SECRET 84: OPEN UP AND WRITE IT DOWN—TAKING STAGE DIRECTION

Stories abound about Angela Gheorghiu clashing with stage directors. She famously refused to wear a blonde wig as Micaëla in a 2011 Metropolitan Opera production of *Carmen*. The director was the very famous Franco Zeffirelli; the wig went on without her. Previously, Gheorghiu had been fired from the Lyric Opera of Chicago's 2007 production of *La bohème* when she skipped rehearsals and costume fittings. The director was Renata Scotto, a famous Mimì herself. Obviously, you should not follow the Romanian soprano's example. Being a diva is not a welcome attribute (see Secret 86) while being well prepared certainly is (see Secret 87). Be prompt for rehearsal, and bring a professional and positive attitude into the rehearsal space. That does not mean you will always have an easy time taking direction. Sometimes it's hard to be open to new ideas when you've done a role already or have beliefs that might differ from the director's. But remember the stage director is the captain of the ship. They are dealing with steering many details beyond your characterization. As the iconic acting teacher said in his book *Stanislavski on Opera*, "Think of yourselves always as being an integral part of an overall picture." Trust in his or her vision and the director may be able to guide you to new depths of emotion and new heights of artistry, so embrace the journey and enjoy the ride.

Technique

1. Write down your blocking. This may seem obvious, but many singers don't write down detailed blocking in their scores because they are already crowded with phonetic transcriptions and word-for-word translations or staging from previous productions of the same opera. Are you entering/exiting/crossing right or left? Upstage or downstage? Take notes on where entrances, exits, and movements happen in the music as specifically as you can. Note any formations or spacings that might be important to remember. If there is choreography, try to transcribe it however best makes sense to you—don't just rely on your memory. If you need more room to write, you can make a new book for each production, putting the music on the right-hand page while leaving the left page empty so you can make copious notes about staging and characterization.
2. Make clear choices. Your character's objectives should be clearly portrayed. Go through your score and identify what your character wants, scene by scene. Write down your choices. Hopefully the director will go through this with you as well, and then you can clarify your choices or change them as needed.

3. Ask questions. If some part of the staging or timing is not clear to you, ask for clarification. If you see something differently than the director, you can certainly invite discussion in a polite manner, but it is best to do so in a private moment rather than in a public rehearsal (unless you're working with Bartlett Sher—see item 4 below).
4. Be open. Be willing to experiment. Explore. Imagine. Be ready to be challenged, stretched, and shaped. Of working with Tony Award–winning director Bartlett Sher, Kelli O'Hara said: "Once you get in there with him, it's like being in a wonderfully dysfunctional family. It is sometimes tumultuous and sometimes beautiful. But you can say anything."
5. Have fun. Angela Gheorghiu was taking herself way too seriously to realize how enjoyable her Zeffirelli Micaëla and Scotto Mimì could have been. Support your production team by being serious about your preparation but joyful in your embrace of the vision for the show.

Benefit

Taking direction is part of your job as a singing actor. Resisting direction will only give you a bad reputation, and the music world is very small and interconnected. Instead of adopting Gheorghiu's approach of viewing the director as a dictator, see him or her as a landscape gardener cultivating your characterization and helping you bloom while growing a full garden with other budding blossoms.

SECRET 85: INTERACT WITH YOUR PARTNERS ONSTAGE— SAFETY AND CHEMISTRY

Whether you are singing a duet in a musical, in a rock concert, or a jazz cabaret, you have the pleasure of interacting with other performers. There have been some great onstage collaborations to revere and emulate where the singers seemed completely in sync: Luciano Pavarotti and Joan Sutherland (*Lucia di Lammermoor*), Anna Netrebko and Rolando Villazon (*La traviata*), Liza Minnelli and Chita Rivera (*Chicago*, *The Rink*), Matthew Broderick and Nathan Lane (*The Producers*), Lionel Richie and Diana Ross ("Endless Love"), Barbra Streisand and Neil Diamond ("You Don't Bring Me Flowers"), Beyoncé and Jay Z ("Crazy in Love"). While singing a solo or aria is exciting, there is something extra special and rewarding about creating and sharing a unique onstage moment with another artist. To do so, you'll have to avoid diva or divo behavior (see Secret 86) and embrace the artistic alliance with your singing partners.

Technique

1. Get acquainted. Work closely with your scene partner(s) to find out about his or her character's viewpoint or his or her take on the song. Don't stay in your own world. Rather, try to welcome your collaborator(s) to an even playing field so you can truly "tread the boards" together.
2. Establish a safe zone. See what they are comfortable with, especially if there's any partnering or stage combat involved. If it is a romantic pairing and there is kissing, then no tongue! And don't upstage your partner. That won't make him or her feel comfortable with you and will hinder your onstage partnership.
3. Cultivate chemistry. Whether you're playing sisters (Fiordiligi and Dorabella), lovers (Tony and Maria), rivals (Don José and Escamillo), or Siamese twins (*Side Show*), develop energy and interaction that fits your characters' correlation. But don't cross the line into developing an off-stage romantic relationship with your onstage partner, unless you are prepared to take the risk of a short-lived "showmance." If it is the opposite situation and you don't get along with your partner offstage, that's okay. Do your best to be professional and courteous regardless. You may still be able to mold the energy between you into believable onstage chemistry. Jennifer Grey and Patrick Swayze famously clashed while filming the movie *Dirty Dancing*, but it made for a dynamic onscreen connection and an iconic love story.

Benefit

Versatile vocalist Linda Ronstadt said, "The thing I like about singing duets is that I get things out of my voice I never get singing by myself." Working with other talented singers will instinctually help you raise the level of your own singing. There is hardly a more incandescent moment in opera than the trio from *Der Rosenkavalier*, a piece that celebrates the beauty of vocal lines intertwined for the highest musical effect. So don't just be a soloist-partner with other performers to help bring your own voice to new musical heights.

CHAPTER 9

Business Tips

SECRET 86: DON'T BE A DIVA—YOU'RE NOT THAT IMPORTANT

The designation "diva" originally identified a singer of distinguished talent celebrated as divine. It evokes "Casta diva," the *Norma* aria associated with opera divas such as Joan Sutherland, Maria Callas, and Renée Fleming. But the term "diva" has evolved from a term of adoration to one of denigration. One of the most famous temperamental diva tales involves Kathleen Battle. Her career disintegrated in a dramatic downward spiral during the 1994 Metropolitan Opera production of Donizetti's *La fille du régiment*. She definitely did not take stage direction well (see Secret 84), reportedly demanding the director change her entrances and exits. She also didn't interact well with others onstage (see Secret 85), supposedly asking cast members not to look at her and throwing another soprano's costumes out of the dressing room. The Met fired Battle for her "unprofessional actions." She had clearly lost touch with reality, as evidenced in the legendary limo ride in which she allegedly called her management company so they could call the limo driver and tell him to turn down the air conditioning. We have also heard rumors of pop divas and their ostensibly extravagant backstage demands: Jennifer Lopez's mandate for an all-white dressing room, Mariah Carey's stipulation of chilled Cristal and two-dozen white roses, Katy Perry's insistence on no carnations. Sure, we're all entitled to our preferences, but requests shouldn't become ridiculous requirements.

Technique

1. Follow the golden rule. Treat others the same way you'd like to be treated. Be a courteous and cooperative colleague. Instead of making commands, command respect through collegiality and congeniality.

2. Eschew the standard hierarchy. Even if you are a star, don't act like one. Don't distance yourself from the people who make your production possible. Talk to the stage crew, your dressers, the chorus members. In the Greensboro Opera's 2015 production of *La fille du régiment* (the same opera that doomed Kathleen Battle), tenor René Barbera hugged every single chorus member onstage during his singing of (and the roaring ovation following) "Pour mon âme." He embraced his colleagues during his aria, and they bolstered him like a football team boosting their quarterback. It was a magical moment made out of mutual support and celebration.
3. Keep your ego in check. Be a down-to-earth diva, not a demanding one. You don't want to lose touch with yourself or your audience. With the exception of a few roles (the Prima Donna and Tenor in *Ariadne auf Naxos*, Carlotta in *The Phantom of the Opera*), your character probably isn't a diva/divo. You want the audience to like you. If you're a pop singer, you will want to remain popular, and being inconsiderate to others won't help you keep your adoring fans.

Note

Sing like a god or goddess, but don't expect to be worshipped like a deity. Remember this maxim from basketball coach John Wooden: "Talent is God-given. Be humble. Fame is man-given. Be grateful. Conceit is self-given. Be careful."

SECRET 87: ALWAYS BE PREPARED (AND NEVER BE LATE)

The early bird gets the worm. This old proverb infers that success comes to those who are prompt. Another proverb says people count the faults of those who keep them waiting. Punctuality is an absolutely essential attribute for a professional singer. It is incredibly inconsiderate to your colleagues if your attendance at rehearsals is unreliable. Lateness shows a disrespect for their time. Being late is one of the two cardinal sins in the performance world. Being unprepared is the other. Furthermore, it is discourteous to be ill prepared. It is your job to know your music.

When you come to rehearsal fully prepped and primed, then you can fully contribute to the process instead of being a hindrance to it. As Machiavelli wrote, "Tardiness often robs us opportunity." Being undependable is a sure way to lose gigs and roles. And if you are late to auditions, then you will not get the opportunities to begin with. Pride yourself on being the singer who is the first to arrive at rehearsal and the first to be off book. Be the early songbird.

Technique

1. Be early. If you're early, you're on time. If you're on time, you're late. These adages have been part of the theatre world for years. If rehearsal starts at 7:00 p.m. and you enter the room at 6:56, technically you're early, but you're not really there in time to be ready to go at 7:00. Develop an arrival ritual. Make it part of your process. For instance, if rehearsal is set to begin at 7:00 p.m., plan to arrive by 6:40 or 6:45. This will give you time to unpack your belongings, leave the rest of your day behind, and get your mind ready to rehearse. Take a minute to meditate or focus your thoughts. Then study your score, lead sheet, or lyrics. These moments of review will help facilitate productivity and creativity. Then, at 6:55, anticipate the beginning of practice. Know what is on the schedule and be ready for it, or consult the stage manager before things begin if you are not certain what's on the docket.
2. Be prepared. Know your music inside out. If it's in a foreign language, know the pronunciation and translation (see Secrets 50 and 58). Work with a vocal coach as needed if you can't learn it all on your own. Make sure you know how your vocal part fits with others (see Secrets 18 and 19). When learning a role, most singers focus on their solos when often it's the ensembles that need the most coaching, so don't overlook those parts. If you're in a show, read the entire script or libretto. Familiarize yourself with any source material. For example, read the original Beaumarchais play if you're singing Mozart's *Le nozze di Figaro*, or watch the 1962 film if you're in Guettel's

The Light in the Piazza. Know the relevant musical traditions, comparing bel canto cadenzas or scat solos (depending on what you're preparing). Immerse yourself in the exploration of your art on a multitude of levels so that you are vocally, musically, historically, dramatically, and stylistically equipped.

Note

In the words of mezzo-soprano Joyce DiDonato: "Greatness comes from the months and years leading up to auditions; inspiration doesn't strike on the spot. So rehearse, prepare!" Make sure people never associate your name with lateness or lack of preparation. Make these your mantras: Practice, prepare. Be prompt, be professional.

SECRET 88: CULTIVATE AN IMPORTANT RELATIONSHIP—GETTING ALONG WITH YOUR VOICE TEACHER

Finding the right voice teacher is very important (see Secret 14). Getting along with your voice teacher is even more important. The one-on-one time spent in your lessons should be a precious and integral part of your development as a singer. Some singers establish long-term working relationships with their teachers. For instance, Beverly Peck Johnson taught opera greats Renée Fleming and Anthony Dean Griffey until her death in 2001, when both were well into successful international careers. Broadway stars Kristin Chenoweth and Kelli O'Hara both still give great credit and reverence to their collegiate voice professor Florence Birdwell. Others work with different teachers as they progress through different life and career transitions (college, graduate school, young artist programs, etc.). Whether you have one major teacher or more, your approach and attitude in your voice lessons will have a huge impact on your potential progress and success as a singer.

Technique

1. Be fully present. Make sure you're focused and ready to work. Try to leave any personal drama out of the voice studio so you can be fully attentive to your teacher's instructions. Try not to "zone out" or go on auto pilot, relying on your teacher to bring you back to a place of concentration. Use mindful kinesthetic awareness so you can accomplish the technical or expressive goals your teacher has for you.
2. Be prepared. The importance of preparation has already been discussed (see Secret 87), but it never hurts to repeat and reinforce this vital concept: practice! Make sure you've practiced any assigned vocalises and/or repertoire. If you are fully prepared for your lessons, then your teacher can more easily spearhead your advancement as a technician and artist. The lesson time will then be efficiently used instead of being wasted on reviewing or relearning.
3. Be open to input. See your teacher as an ally or mentor, not a judge or a guru. Sometimes we subconsciously resist change, even when we aren't content with our current standing. Take your teacher's input to heart, but don't let it hurt your heart. Be empirical and understand he or she is not criticizing you personally but simply trying to provide constructive feedback to help you improve vocally. It can be particularly hard on us as singers because our instrument is encased in our body. We can't put it back into a case or blame problems on a broken violin string or bad piano tuning. Remember, your teacher's critique isn't a personal attack. If his or her input does feel too severe and is too much for your temperament to take, then consider whether

you're being overly sensitive or whether you need to find another teacher with a different means of communication.

4. Be self-reliant. Don't expect your teacher to solve all of your problems. Give yourself specific goals for your practice sessions so that you can work toward improvement on a steady basis. Use the tools your teacher gives you, but don't rely on them solely. Your teacher can't learn your music for you or be onstage to help you through a prominent performance, so eventually you need to be able to do it on your own.

Benefit

When you're open to your voice teacher's advice and insights, a wonderful symbiotic, synergistic interaction can develop. With a relationship of mutual respect and readiness to work, the voice student can fully realize the wisdom, support, and guidance of the teacher. Impressively coaching Michael Jordan and the Chicago Bulls to six NBA championships, Phil Jackson had a simple mantra for success: "Always keep an open mind and a compassionate heart." With an open mind on your part as the pupil and a compassionate heart on the part of the pedagogue, you can find fruitful and ongoing evolution as a singer under the aegis of your voice teacher.

SECRET 89: BE A GRACIOUS COLLABORATOR—GETTING ALONG WITH YOUR ACCOMPANIST

First of all, to get along with your accompanist you might want to avoid the word "accompanist." Some pianists are offended by this term, while others are not, but you can be part of moving terminology forward into a positive future by using the term "collaborative pianist." We owe so much to our collaborators at the keyboard because we couldn't rehearse or perform without them. Whether it is a pianist who is sight-reading your audition or one with whom you've shaped a song recital, he or she has the power to help your performance sail or fail. By being clear and considerate in your collaboration, you can help the pianist be your true supporter.

Technique

1. Respect their time. Be prompt to rehearsals (see Secret 87) and make efficient use of your time together. Don't display diva-like behavior such as showing up late, cancelling at the last minute, or making unreasonable demands on their time (see Secret 86). Your pianist probably collaborates with a number of other musicians, so you are not his or her sole focus.
2. Respect their talent. Treat your pianist as an equal partner in music making. While the singer's name usually appears above the pianist's on recital programs, don't view yourself as superior and him or her as inferior. Have open discussions about tempi, dynamics, expressive effects, and so forth. Nurture a creative collaborative environment.
3. Respect their profession. Don't make them do your work for you. Provide legal copies of your music to them in a timely manner. Make sure it's neat and legible, verifying that any cuts or other important details are clearly marked. Unless it's a special skill he or she likes to display or you're doing jazz, don't ask your pianist to transpose on the spot; find and provide your own transpositions if you need a higher or lower key. At an audition, show your appreciation to the pianist for helping you; thank him or her for his or her time and effort. If you're hiring someone to play for you, perhaps the greatest way to show respect for collaborative pianists is to pay them on time. Find out your pianist's payment policies and follow them to the letter. You don't want to show disregard for the time and training your pianists have put into their profession by not treating them professionally.

Note

Collaborative pianists spend a lot of time learning about singers, learning when and how they breathe to shape a phrase, learning what they need to help them succeed. Singers should try to learn more about their collaborators' viewpoints. Check out the online *Collaborative Piano Blog*, or read Gerald Moore's *Am I Too Loud? Memoirs of an Accompanist* or Martin Katz's *The Complete Collaborator: The Pianist as Partner.* Challenge yourself to attend a vocal recital and focus more on the pianist than the singer. Or accompany a pianist by singing in their collaborative piano lesson.

SECRET 90: SERVE THE PRODUCTION NOT YOURSELF—GETTING ALONG WITH YOUR OPERA DIRECTOR

Clearly, if you want to get along with your opera director, don't follow the example of diva Angela Gheorghiu (see Secret 86). Her temperamental behavior is infamous, showing particular defiance to directors. She withdrew from the 2011 Metropolitan Opera's production of *Faust* over its updated concept. In an interview with ABC, she maligned directors who "want to express their own fantasies." It is the director's job to have a vision, be it fantastical or familiar. Whether it's a traditional *La traviata* or a space-age *Semele*, be a team player in the production and you're well on your way to making the director's job easier and more enjoyable.

Technique

1. Join in the vision of the production. Instead of being shortsighted and self-serving by focusing only on yourself, be a true proponent of the production. Share in discussion of the show's concept with the director and, if possible, the designers. Their visions can help inform your interpretation. Appreciate the artistry that goes into mounting the platform for your stage appearance.
2. Bring something special to the table. Know your role. Of course, you should be impeccably prepared (see Secret 87). If you've done the role many times, let your previous experience inform your participation in this production without any interference. If it's your first foray into a new role, jump feetfirst into the magical process of its debut. Be it your first Fricka or your thirteenth, take risks dramatically, albeit not vocally. Be ready to explore the emotional fabric of your character. As acclaimed director Frances Zambello shared: "You know what that's like in rehearsal, when someone is there and really prepared and brings something to offer to the process. It changes everything."
3. Take direction and run with it. Of course, write down all of your blocking and make clear acting choices as you work with your stage director (see Secret 84). Staying within the show's concept, follow your instinct and explore the trajectories outlined by the director. Directors love it when their actors' creative ideas inspire brilliant stage bits they may not have thought of themselves. If the bits work, they will embrace them, and if not, respect their decision to alter or omit in the best interest of the production.

Benefit

If you're in a university program, your opera director may be your stage director for a number of years. Getting along with him or her will help future casting opportunities and influence future letters of recommendation. If you are in the professional realm, word of mouth will circulate about whether you're a director's dream or nightmare. Getting along with directors can only encourage them to think of working with you again on future productions, and perhaps even help to establish a long-lasting, career-building creative collaboration.

SECRET 91: WATCH AND FOLLOW—GETTING ALONG WITH CONDUCTORS

Anna Netrebko once admitted, "I prefer it when the conductor follows me." Since a singer's breath is finite, indeed there are times when we really need the conductor to follow us. But singers need to have a greater grasp of what it takes to perform with a symphony or opera orchestra. The conductor may or may not have a long-standing relationship with the ensemble, depending on whether he or she is a resident or guest conductor. Help facilitate the process of interweaving your vocal line in the orchestral fabric, being acutely attuned to the conductor throughout rehearsals and performances.

Technique

1. Follow the conductor. You don't have to stare them down—that probably wouldn't please the director or your audience—but always have an awareness of the conductor and what he or she is trying to accomplish. Always know what is going on with the tactus and tempo. Definitely check in solidly at key musical transition points.
2. Be prepared and be professional (see Secret 87). Usually conductors will cue you before an important vocal entrance, but know your music so well that you don't even need to be cued. Of course, be early to rehearsal and show appreciation to your orchestral collaborators. Don't help to perpetuate the stigma of the "stupid singer." Be a strong musician, performing your part with precision in addition to passion. If you need to discuss a possible shift in tempo with the conductor, do so calmly and respectfully.
3. Be part of the orchestra. Yes, you may be the soloist, but don't be a diva (see Secret 86). Study the orchestral score, not just the piano reduction, so that you understand the instrumentation involved in what you're singing (see Secret 19). Have an understanding of the complex tasks facing the conductor, who has to coordinate numerous musicians into a unified and polished performance. Show empathy and esteem for this challenging musical mission.

Benefit

Performing with an orchestra is one of the most sublime experiences a singer can enjoy. But sometimes working with singers is not the most sublime experience. Composer Gioachino Rossini once stated, "Oh how wonderful, really wonderful opera would be if there were no singers!" As with the stage director, don't view the conductor as a despot. (Perhaps you should then avoid watching the 1985 *West Side Story* documentary revealing Leonard Bernstein's obvious disdain for tenor José Carreras!) It takes a lot of presence to command the respect of a large symphony orchestra, so let the conductor lead without resistance. You might forge a rewarding, enduring collaboration. Conductors such as Richard Bonynge (Joan Sutherland's husband) and James Levine certainly helped to nurture and build the careers of numerous successful singers. Of working with her husband, conductor Simon Rattle, mezzo-soprano Magdalena Kožená shared, "It's a relief knowing I don't have to be scared of the big maestro figure." But she also admits she eschews diva behavior, saying, "I know not to do that to him." Prove Rossini wrong and show the conductor how affable and astute singers can be.

SECRET 92: FIND YOUR (SHORT-TERM) FIT—AUDITIONING FOR SUMMER PROGRAMS

Summer programs can be a crucial part of your training and experience as a singer. As a career builder, attending summer programs is one of the most logical ways to transition from student to professional. You need to build your résumé so that it starts to develop past the collegiate realm. There are several different kinds of programs to consider. Exciting options include music festivals (Aspen or Brevard), opera company young artist programs (Chautauqua, Central City, or Glimmerglass), language-intensive workshops (Oberlin in Italy, Musiktheater Bavaria), and summer stock (nonunion or Actor's Equity Association). Some programs are "pay-to-sing," meaning you pay tuition to participate in the program. Others won't pay you but charge no tuition and may provide room and board (College Light Opera Company). Then there are the young artist programs sponsored by opera companies. Some of these YAPs, as they're called, have dual levels (student and apprentice divisions), and some are union (American Guild of Musical Artists). You'll probably start in a pay-to-sing program, then hopefully work your way swiftly into a scholarship somewhere and eventually a paid apprenticeship. Note that the union only allows you two American Guild of Musical Artists apprenticeships.

Technique

1. Figure out what program fits you best. Make sure that you don't apply for a high-level program (Santa Fe, Wolf Trap) before you're really ready. Discern whether you want or need a program that provides numerous private lessons (twice weekly at AIMS in Graz) or no voice lessons but intensive acting and scene work (Druid City Opera Workshop). Decide if you are primarily looking for training or for stage experience. You may need to build your skill set in opera scenes (Harrower Opera Workshop), or you may be looking to build your résumé with complete roles (Franco-American Vocal Academy). Decide between a summer program with a more tried-and-true traditional program (Des Moines Opera) or one with an innovative approach involving visualization and business (OperaWorks) as fits your comfort zone. Perhaps the program is your chance to travel to Europe and immerse yourself in foreign-language study (*Si parla, si canta!*). If an international endeavor is too intimidating or expensive, you might prefer an American program in a beautiful location that hopefully doesn't distract you from practicing (Hawaii Performing Arts Festival or Emerald City Opera Institute)! Instead of opera, you may want to focus on *Lieder* or other art song repertoire (SongFest).

2. Do your research. There are so many options and it can be overwhelming, but do careful research on your prospective programs. What are the real costs? If there is tuition, are there are any scholarship opportunities? What will it cost to travel to the program? What about room and board? What about free time? What will you be performing? Will you be chorus, understudy, principal, or soloist? What is the reputation of the program? Is it well established and well regarded, or is it the focus of numerous student complaints? Check out Opera America's career guide website page or *Classical Singer* magazine, which often highlights programs in its articles and directory. And you can also scour the Internet for information, checking out the program's website and Facebook page, not to mention its Twitter feed to see if a disgruntled singer created a hashtag to identify a bad experience.
3. Follow the application requirements. This is much easier to do these days thanks to YAP Tracker. You can register on one website and manage multiple applications and auditions. But be sure you're absolutely clear on each audition's deadline and requirements. Is there a live audition? Is a preliminary video submission required, or is a video all that is required? Do you need letters of recommendation? You'll also need to manage your finances since most programs have an application fee (see Secret 97). After deciding which applications/auditions to complete, follow through with promptness and professionalism, as it will impact your potential acceptance or rejection.

Benefit

Summer programs can give you indispensable experience and valuable instruction, as well as provide important credits and contacts to help shape your success as a singer. Investigate your options and put yourself out there so that you can sing, travel, train, and savor a summer of music making and career building.

SECRET 93: YES, YOU MAY NEED ANOTHER DEGREE—AUDITIONING FOR GRADUATE SCHOOL

At college graduations all across the country, new grads often trim the tops of their caps with the text "Hire Me!" Unfortunately, most aspiring classical singers can't expect to be hired right out of undergrad. At twenty-one, a classical singer is still emerging and maturing vocally. Your voice might not be fully mature until your late twenties, or early to midthirties if you're male. Thus many twenty-something (and early thirty-something) singers choose graduate school as a way to gain more preparation and practice on the path to becoming professionals.

Advice

1. Decide on a degree. If your focus is not on academics and you aren't planning on teaching in the future, then an artist diploma might be a possible choice. Taking one to two years to complete, artist diploma programs typically demand an incredibly high level of performance ability. For instance, the Peabody Conservatory describes its artist diploma as "a non-degree program reserved for exceptional and experienced performers, with emphasis on repertoire designed to meet the needs of performers who are preparing and qualified to embark upon a professional career." A master of music (MM) degree will also provide intensive and extensive performance training and experience in addition to academic coursework in music theory, musicology, and pedagogy. Some schools offer a master of fine arts (MFA) or master of arts (MA) in voice, opera, or musical theatre; an MA often takes two years to complete, while an MFA usually requires a three-year residency. The most involved vocal graduate degree is the doctor of musical arts (DMA). In addition to voice lessons and academic coursework, the DMA typically entails performing two to four full solo recitals, passing comprehensive exams, and writing a document or dissertation, all of which could take as little as three or as long as seven to ten years (a common time limit for the degree). DMAs are typically earned by artist-teachers who hope to teach at the college or university level.
2. Find the right school for you. Consider location. Do you want to be in a big city or a university town? Consider the type of school. Do you want a conservatory or a big state university? Does name recognition matter to you? Having a degree from Eastman, Juilliard, or Curtis on your curriculum vitae (CV) can certainly help open doors in academia, while an opera company won't care where you got your degree—just how well you sing. Consider what performing opportunities the school will provide you.

3. Find the right teacher for you. Some people think the right teacher is even more important than what graduate school you attend. You'll want to research teachers carefully, and hopefully you'll have the chance to observe their teaching or have sample lessons. Once you find the right teacher, make sure he or she has room in his or her studio for you. Reputation certainly matters, but the right personality "fit" might be even more important (see Secret 14).
4. Make sure you meet all the prerequisites for admission. Does the application require the GRE (Graduate Record Examination) or any other entrance exams? Do you meet the grade point average requirement? Does your previous degree meet the prerequisite (e.g., MM for a DMA degree)? Is there a foreign-language requirement?
5. Present yourself impeccably. When you audition for graduate school, you are most likely auditioning for an assistantship or fellowship, so look at it as both an audition and a job interview. Have both a performance résumé and a CV since you may want to be considered for teaching opportunities. Have a detailed repertoire list, and make sure it's free from error (see Secret 95). Prepare an audition package that showcases your greatest talents and none of your flaws. While schools may be somewhat forgiving when hearing a prospective freshman sing with less than perfect French, they will not be so forgiving when it comes to potential graduate students, who might end up being assigned to teach French diction to freshmen.
6. Plan financially for your education (see Secret 97). Grad school can be a huge financial investment. Apply for any financial aid, assistantships, and grants that you can. Crunch the numbers carefully so that you understand the true amount of student loan debt you might end up accruing or the true amount you'll need to earn in a part-time job to help pay for your schooling. Because of the implications on your finances, make sure that you can afford to complete your degree without negatively impacting your future credit. You don't want to go to grad school just to kill time and end up killing your credit rating.

Benefit

Graduate school can provide the training and seasoning you need to launch your career. A graduate degree can also give you the credentials you'll need to be considered for faculty positions at the collegiate level. Unless you're a huge international star, you'll need at least an MM to teach adjunct and probably a DMA to land a tenure-track slot.

SECRET 94: COMPETING WITHOUT DEFEATING YOURSELF—AUDITIONING FOR VOICE COMPETITIONS

Singing is not a sporting event—there is no vocal contest in the Olympics. But voice competitions have emerged as a way for singers to gain exposure and notoriety, not to mention prize money. At the same time, competitions can take a serious toll on the fragile singer's ego. Imagine this feedback from a judge: "We don't think you have anything to offer as an artist." That's the critique Joyce DiDonato received at a British voice competition before becoming an international opera star. So if you decide to enter the realm of voice competitions, here are some points to keep in mind.

Tips

1. Research the competition. Make sure it is appropriate for where you are in your development. Be sure to double-check the age limit (thirty or thirty-five for many opera competitions) as well as the entry fee (a hefty $120 for the MTNA Young Artist Competition). Make sure your repertoire fits the requirements as well, and then make sure it is polished so you are ready to sing your best possible performance. Besides prize money (which could be $30 at NATS chapter auditions or £15,000 for winning the BBC Cardiff Singer of the World competition), investigate the competition's other possible benefits. These could include management, performance opportunities, a record deal, travel, a spot in an apprentice program, a scholarship, and so on.
2. Use sports psychology. Some singers perform well but do not compete well because they aren't used to being ranked (and eliminated). The pressure of competition, and the thought of losing potential prize money, can cause some to "choke." For techniques on mastering the mental part of competition, check out the writings of W. Timothy Gallwey, ranging from *The Inner Game of Tennis* and *The Inner Game of Golf* to *The Inner Game of Music*. You can also use meditation to cultivate a positive mind-set so that you can compete under duress and avoid being overwhelmed by anxiety (see Secret 80).
3. Practice nonattachment. Try to detach yourself from the possible outcome. Instead of thinking about competing, invest in the performance as if you were portraying a role in a fully staged production or singing your own cabaret act. Yes, talent is a big part of voice competitions, but so is luck. As Effie Trinket from The Hunger Games series says, "May the odds be ever in your favor." Know that like a roll of the dice, there is an element of chance in any contest and thus the outcome will never be completely under your control.

4. Approach adjudication empirically. Don't take negative feedback personally. Be open to input, especially constructive criticism, but don't let your feelings be hurt. Judging is very subjective. Contradictory commentary is not uncommon: one adjudicator may say your voice is too bright while another may say it is too dark. Glean what you can from the critique to help improve for your next performance, but discard what you or your teacher feel doesn't serve you. If Fred Astaire had believed the person who wrote he "can't sing, can't act," then we never would have heard him sing "Pick Yourself Up" in *Swing Time*. So when it comes to harsh adjudication, as that Gershwin tune recommends, learn to "dust yourself off, and start all over again."

Note

Perhaps a necessary evil, voice competitions have become a potential path to a career as a professional singer. Many singers will start competing at their school talent show, a local NATS chapter's annual student auditions, or a collegiate concerto competition. At the highest levels, there are competitions for nearly every musical genre and vocal specialty: Placido Domingo's Operalia, the Lyndon Woodside Oratorio–Solo Vocal Competition, the Kurt Weill Foundation's Lotte Lenya Competition, the Sarah Vaughan International Jazz Vocal Competition, the NATS Hall Johnson Spirituals Competition, and of course televised talent competitions such as *America's Got Talent*. At every level, make sure you know the merit of the competition. For instance, after nine seasons, the popular show *The Voice* has yet to help launch one of its winners to fame, despite its high viewership. And remember, your career isn't over if you don't win first place. Miranda Lambert came in third on *Nashville Star* but went on to win two Grammy Awards; Jennifer Hudson won an Academy Award for *Dreamgirls* three years after she placed only seventh on *American Idol*. So whether you are entering your high school solo and ensemble festival or the Metropolitan Opera National Council (MONC) Auditions, try to enjoy the "game." Be it positive or negative, you shouldn't let the outcome define you.

SECRET 95: REPRESENT YOURSELF WELL ON PAPER—SPELLING AND SPACING MATTER

As the old adage says, you never get a second chance to make a first impression. As a singer, your first impression will probably still happen on paper, be it an audition panel perusing your résumé as you enter the room or a potential manager opening a PDF of the bio you've e-mailed. For better or worse, we make judgments about people based on how they present themselves on paper, whether it's actual paper or the digital version. You don't want to be discredited before they even hear you sing, or prevent yourself from gaining the opportunity to sing, because you don't look good on paper.

Technique

1. Be accurate. Proofread. Then proofread again. Unfortunately, if your appearance as Guglielmo in *Così fan tutte* is listed as Google elmo in *Cosi fan tutu*, we are likely to make a negative assumption about you, your linguistic facility, and your attention to detail. It can be so easy to make a mistake, especially since opera titles are often in foreign languages and spell-check will want to change *Suor Angelica* to *Sour Angelica*. So proofread your materials over and over. Have trusted friends and mentors proofread as well, because after a while we sometimes can't see our own obvious errors. Triple-check every opera title, each *accent aigu* and *accent grave*. Confirm the spelling of the names of the organizations with which you've performed (Was it Sarasota Opera or Opera Saratoga?), as well as the names of any teachers, conductors, directors, or clinicians you list so we won't wonder if you really worked with Keith Lockhard.
2. Be streamlined. Make sure your résumé is clean looking with symmetrical spacing and consistent font usage. Are you underlining or italicizing show titles? Are you capitalizing headers or using boldface? Just be consistent. And don't be too fussy. Keep your font choice sleek and readable, not like a fancy wedding invitation. Make sure all of your columns line up so that you present an organized image instead of a haphazard one.
3. Be up to date. Make sure you are always updating all the "paper" elements of your package: your résumé, CV, repertoire list, website, YouTube channel, and so forth. If your site lists upcoming engagements that were two years ago, it doesn't make you look like you're in high demand.
4. Be truthful. Don't lie on your résumé. You may be tempted, especially if you don't have many credits to include yet, but "padding" is risky, and you don't want to be caught in a lie. And while bios typically are prone to pandering and self-congratulatory effusion, don't make any statements that might seem doubtful or laughable.

5. Be tactful. Resist the urge to vent on social media since it has now become another part of your "paper" trail. If you slam LA Opera on your Instagram, that hashtag may come back to haunt you.

Benefit

With an organized and professional representation on paper, you can impress before you even start to sing!

SECRET 96: HAVE GOOD COMMUNICATION SKILLS—PROOFREADING AND PROFESSIONALISM

When you sing, you should communicate freely and expressively to your audience. But before you get the chance to sing, you'll most likely need to communicate well with people offstage: voice teachers, stage directors, stage managers, conductors, duet partners, casting personnel, audition coordinators, artist managers, and the list goes on. Developing good interpersonal skills is a key component of your package as a professional singer.

Technique

1. Write with a professional tone. Be polite and formal in e-mail correspondence with potential employers and collaborators. Follow appropriate form and etiquette. For guidelines on cover letters, check out career websites like The Muse and The Ladders. Today people often write e-mails on their smartphones, but remember that it is still professional communication. Therefore, don't write in the informal format of a text message—avoid emoticons and colloquial abbreviations (e.g., LOL, TTYS).
2. Proofread carefully. As with your résumé, make sure any written communication (cover letter, e-mail, application form) is error free so that you don't make a bad impression on paper (see Secret 95). I once received an e-mail that ended with "I look forward to seeing you aging," which was either a Freudian slip or a spell-check intervention.
3. Speak tactfully. Be direct in conversation without being blunt or rude. Be polite without being patronizing or artificial. Be yourself but the best version of yourself, without too many "likes" and "you knows." You want to be taken seriously not just as a singer but as a person.
4. Network sincerely. Yes, part of the business is making contacts, keeping contacts, and fostering continued interaction with your contacts for future gigs and potential opportunities. But you want to do so in a manner that isn't too pushy. People won't want to maintain contact, let alone work with you, if you seem like you're using them.
5. Communicate with confidence and positivity. Make your verbal and written communication a pleasant experience for its recipients. If they associate you with upbeat communication, people are more likely to respond in an affirmative way. Of course, you'll still receive some harsh rejection letters since that is an unavoidable part of what we do. But being optimistic and emanating positive energy can help buoy your spirit and attract like-minded positive people and projects your way.

Benefit

Communicating clearly and professionally can help facilitate your success as a singer. Managing the business of your career is absolutely necessary, especially before you have a manager or agent to help you with the process. Motivational speaker Jim Rohn advised, "Take advantage of every opportunity to practice your communication skills so that when important occasions arise, you will have the gift, the style, the clarity, and the emotions to affect other people."

SECRET 97: MANAGE YOUR FINANCES—HOW NOT TO BE A STARVING SINGER

If only singers were "discovered" like Lana Turner was! (She was simply sitting at a soda fountain counter.) As we've told our students, no one will knock on your practice room door and "discover" you; you have to put yourself out there and audition, perform, and compete. But training, auditioning, and promoting yourself can be an expensive endeavor. Expenses add up, including those for voice lessons, coachings, pianists, audition fees, summer programs, pay-to-sings, travel, sheet music, and so on. Most of us aren't independently wealthy or supported by a benevolent patron, so you will need to manage your finances carefully or—like Giacomo Puccini's (and Jonathan Larson's) bohemians—you may end up being late on your rent.

Approaches

1. Budget. Before you run up your credit card balance with charges you won't be able to pay, research and budget. At $35–$75 a pop ($150 for the Curtis Institute of Music), how many application fees for universities, conservatories, or apprentice programs can you truly afford? How many audition trips can you truly afford? Do you know what you're spending on a monthly basis for housing, transportation, food, clothing, entertainment? Track your spending via your bank's website, use Quicken software, make your own Excel spreadsheet, or try a money-managing site like Mint.com or a free financial app like Level Money.
2. Prioritize. Rank your potential expenses. Obviously, food, rent, utilities, and insurance should come first. But then go down the list and see where else your money is going. For instance, decide which is more essential, your YAP Tracker registration ($55/year), your Auditions Plus subscription ($24/year), your Netflix ($7.99/month), or your Starbucks habit (for many of us, more than we'd like to admit). Pick and pay your essential items, and don't feel bad about cutting out what you deem nonessential for now, be it cable television, manicures, or gym memberships.
3. Read your contracts. If you are fortunate enough to book a gig or obtain management, congratulations! Make sure you read your contract carefully so you know what is expected of you, what you're being paid, how you're being paid, and what percentage your management will be getting. And if you're lucky enough to become rich and famous, make sure you still monitor your finances. We've all heard the horror stories of stars being bilked by their financial managers (Billy Joel and the Backstreet Boys) or accused of tax evasion (Luciano Pavarotti and Montserrat Caballé).

4. Itemize. Keep your receipts so you can consider itemizing when tax time rolls around. Deductible expenses include travel to auditions and gigs (airfare, mileage, hotel, etc.). Be sure to check the current federal rate for mileage and per diem (irs.gov). Only 50 percent of meals is deductible. If you work with a tax professional, make sure they have experience with musicians. Ask about the IRS Qualified Performing Artist Deduction and see if you qualify. That subscription to *Opera News* ($25/year) or *Backstage* ($140/year) may also be deductible, but just be careful not to go overboard with itemizing home office expenses or you may end up with an audit.

5. Crowdfund with caution. The twenty-first century has ushered in the age of crowdsourcing or crowdfunding. Through websites such as Kickstarter, Indiegogo, GoFundMe, and YouCaring, people can ask others to help fund their indie film, medical costs for a traumatic injury, or tuition for a summer opera intensive in Italy. You need to be aware of what is now called "crowdfunding fatigue." These sites and people's requests for donations have become so prevalent that they can become overwhelming and off-putting to some weary donors. So don't be offended if friends or strangers can't or don't want to contribute—it doesn't necessarily mean they don't care. It's also hard to predict who may fund you and with how much. For instance, the New York City Opera's failed Kickstarter campaign could not save the company from closure in 2013, while the San Diego Opera's crowdfunding miraculously prevented its demise. Still, crowdfunding can be a powerful means of raising money, and the platform seems to be growing. As always, do your research so you know the parameters and possible success of your crowdfunding venture.

6. Make your own money. Yes, you may already have a full-time job, but there may be other small ways you can make some extra cash (that don't involve a Vegas blackjack table). Maybe you have some used books you could sell on Amazon Marketplace. Or perhaps you could trade in your old CDs and DVDs on Decluttr to make a few bucks and gain some more space in your home. Some singers do fund-raising recitals at local churches to help pay for travel to European summer programs. If you're crafty, your hobby could also turn into a small side business on Etsy. And, of course, you might do some private teaching or music directing or something related to singing that can enhance your experience and your budget (see Secrets 98 and 99).

7. Save. I know, it may not seem like any fun, but you should try to save your hard-earned money. Don't blithely spend the entire paycheck from your *Messiah* performance at Whole Foods (affectionately known as Whole Paycheck). You don't have to live on ramen noodles and PB&J, but saving money by comparing costs, shopping sale days or yard sales, using coupons

or promotion codes, or buying vintage makes sense for up-and-coming artists. Money-saving strategies can help you maximize what money you do have. No one likes a cheapskate, and dumpster diving can be dangerous, but frugal living is in because it's more sustainable, especially when you're trying to start your career as a singer.

Note

Lately there has been an active online debate about opera companies charging audition fees. Most of us expect entry fees for vocal competitions or college/grad school applications. But there is no fee to audition for professional theatrical productions or even Hollywood films, yet many or most opera companies charge singers a fee to audition for their young artist programs. In many cases, these nonrefundable audition fees apply even if you are not granted an audition with the opera company. It will be interesting to see if the groundswell around this issue causes any change in policy, but for now audition fees remain a substantial expense classical singers need to include in their budgeting.

SECRET 98: PROFESSIONAL CHORAL SINGING CAN BE REWARDING

Traditional curricula and university and conservatory voice programs primarily prepare young singers to be soloists in opera, concert, and recital work. This is never time wasted, and there are many great benefits to developing a solid classical technique. Many classical singers discover after they graduate, however, that the market is flooded and there are way too many wonderful singers for too few performance opportunities in the opera and art song world.

Some singers may find it worthwhile to consider choral opportunities to round out their schedules. These gigs—which often pay a modest honorarium—include church jobs, professional choral ensembles, symphony chorus work, and section leader positions in community choruses. Since choral singing tends to value a different kind of voice and skill set, some singers may even find their "niche" in this genre, with more career opportunities and artistic satisfaction than would have been possible with the traditional operatic track.

The choral culture of the United States is different than orchestral culture in that there are far fewer full-time positions as professional choristers. Notable exceptions include the all-male Chanticleer and Cantus, as well as the Washington, DC–based military choruses (such as the U.S. Army Chorus, Singing Sergeants, and Sea Chanters). While these can be wonderful gigs for the lucky few who land them, the opportunities described in this chapter represent more typical opportunities for part-time paid choral work.

How to Secure Choral Work

Like opera and oratorio, major metropolitan areas offer more paid choral opportunities than smaller cities and rural areas. While some professional choral ensembles (such as the Handel & Haydn Society and Boston Baroque) have annual auditions to hear new singers, many other groups schedule auditions by appointment. Securing church work almost always depends on personal contact (e-mail correspondence) directly with the organist or choirmaster. Sometimes conductors will not be willing to hear singers if they don't have an immediate opening, but more often than not they are happy to hear you in case a future opportunity arises. (Too many qualified singers on their extended roster is a good problem to have.)

At the audition, the singer will usually sing directly for the conductor or choirmaster. Auditions usually consist of singing a solo selection (accompanists are usually provided), sight-reading, and possibly ear-training/aural exercises. Conversation is also likely to take place. If a conductor is especially interested in hiring you, he or she may give a lot of details about the schedule and his or her expectations. How you respond could influence whether you are hired. (For example, if you are auditioning for a church job and you really want the job, don't bristle when the conductor tells you that singing on Christmas Eve is an expectation.)

Over the past several decades, a fair number of paid, all-professional choirs have emerged. These outstanding ensembles draw their rosters from all over the country. Usually, singers fly in for a week of rehearsals and performances and stay in hotels and with host families. Notable ensembles in this category include Conspirare, Seraphic Fire, the Spire Chamber Ensemble, and the Tucson Chamber Artists. There are also three high-profile, all-professional summer festival choral ensembles: Oregon Bach Festival, Carmel Bach Festival, and the Santa Fe Desert Chorale. Because of the international profile of these ensembles, getting selected for their rosters can be extremely competitive. There is very little turnover from year to year, with dozens of extremely qualified singers coveting the few spots available.

Secret 70 detailed the ways in which choral singing differs from solo singing, both technically and stylistically. The aspiring choral singer should carefully consider whether choral singing is a genre that feels right and suits his or her instrument and abilities. For one soprano, it might be easy to blend with her section above the staff; but for another, it could be stressful and fatiguing. Smaller voices and lower voice types tend to have less difficulty singing choral genres. Strong sight-reading skills, musicianship, dependability (see Secret 87), and willingness to control volume and vibrato so as to blend within your section are key attributes of the successful professional choral singer.

While some cities, such as Boston, Chicago, New York, and Washington, DC, are rife with opportunities for professional choral singers, others, such as Atlanta and Minneapolis, have more of a "volunteer chorister" culture. Oftentimes these nonpaying choirs sing every bit as well as paid choirs in other cities, but the singer must weigh carefully whether the artistic fulfillment of a volunteer position is worth the trade-off of not being paid.

Benefit

It's a job! While professional choral singers and church musicians will never get rich, it does provide some much-needed income during the financially lean student years and beyond. Many choral singers also find deep artistic fulfillment in choral singing. And the repertoire is wonderful! Professional choristers never get tired of singing Bach's *St. Matthew Passion*, Beethoven's *Missa solemnis*, or Britten's *War Requiem*.

SECRET 99: STAY IN TOUCH WITH YOUR ART FORM THROUGH TEACHING

Mounting a full-time career as a professional singer is extremely competitive. There simply are not enough jobs to accommodate all of the wonderful singers who audition for them, and the pay for many gigs is too modest to meet every expense of living in the cities that provide the opportunities. Many very fine singers—the vast majority, in fact—find that they must supplement their income with something besides singing. Some find secondary careers outside of music, but many others discover that teaching voice lessons can both be rewarding and pay some bills.

Teaching is, of course, a calling and should never be a "fallback" profession for the frustrated or short-on-work singer. Nurturing another person's voice is a great responsibility, and the last thing an aspiring student needs is a half-hearted teacher who is only there for the paycheck. Many singers, however, discover that they find teaching to be deeply fulfilling. Some may even discover that teaching is their true niche, and they are more at home teaching than performing.

Advice for New Teachers

1. Start small. Many voice teachers get their start as graduate students teaching voice class or lessons to nonmajors. After earning a master's degree, the world of adjunct teaching is also a possibility. Make contact with community colleges and university music departments in your area. (Or better yet, stop by and introduce yourself and your CV to the department chair.) If your life path has led you to settle in a small town, set up a shingle in your home. The world needs wonderful voice teachers who can offer quality lessons to junior high and high school students as well as adult avocational singers. The independent studio culture is extremely important to our profession.
2. Join the National Association of Teachers of Singing (NATS). This organization provides an international network for singing teachers, as well as resources such as the *Journal of Singing*, which is published five times per year and contains valuable articles related to voice pedagogy. NATS also offers regional events, a biennial national conference, monthly online NATS Chats, and annual student auditions. Getting involved in NATS is a surefire way to cultivate your skills and improve your pedagogical knowledge.
3. Seek out enrichment opportunities in voice pedagogy, both live and online. The New York Singing Teachers Association (NYSTA), for instance, offers a five-course "core curriculum" program in voice pedagogy entirely online in webinar format. And many weekend and summer workshops—too nu-

merous to list—are offered by numerous institutions and individuals. There have never been more opportunities to learn about voice pedagogy from top-flight professionals.

Benefit

The life of the artist-teacher can be deeply fulfilling. Many singers all over the world combine teaching with solo singing in opera, concert, and oratorio, as well as singing in choirs. This offers a vibrant, eclectic, variable, interesting, busy, scholarly, and profitable career. Helping students "discover" their voices and mature as singing artists can be just as fulfilling as the pleasures of performance. Both of us have dedicated our lives to this endeavor, and neither of us regret it for a second. As the movie title says, "It's a wonderful life!"

SECRET 100: BE RESOURCEFUL—USE EVERY TOOL AT YOUR DISPOSAL

This book—through its one hundred "secrets"—while not completely exhaustive, has reviewed many techniques and strategies that can help the advanced singer move his or her career forward. But the journey does not end here. In the twenty-first century, the resources available to singers are more bountiful than at any time before in the history of singing. The Internet alone has revolutionized the art form, and world-class performances and other pedagogical resources are at our fingertips twenty-four hours a day. Advanced students of singing should not take these opportunities for granted. Here are three final tips for being a lifelong learner in the vocal world.

Ways to Be Resourceful

1. Never stop networking. As the saying goes, "make new friends, but keep the old; one is silver and the other gold." Through your schooling and professional experiences, you have already made many contacts in the voice profession with people who can help you throughout your life. Treat them well and don't lose touch with them. Contact your former teachers and conductors regularly and let them know how you're doing. Cultivate genuine friendships and professional relationships—don't just call or e-mail when you need something. In addition, always make an effort to meet new people and form new relationships. This has never been easier than in this age of conferences and online forums.
2. Take advantage of technology. As an undergraduate student at Ithaca College in the 1990s, the only way I (Matthew) could listen to a top-flight artist sing a certain art song was to walk up the hill (in the snow) to the library, take the elevator to the top floor, look up a catalog number, check out an LP or CD (if it wasn't already borrowed), check out headphones, and hope that a listening console was open. How wonderful it is to be a student now in the age of YouTube and Spotify! Never take any of these resources for granted.
3. Join and become active in professional organizations. Secret 99 discussed the various benefits offered by NATS and NYSTA. But there are many other organizations that have much to offer the modern singer. Here is a brief list of some additional organizations:

    The Voice Foundation (TVF)
    Pan-American Vocology Association (PAVA)
    Music Teachers National Association (MTNA)
    American Choral Directors Association (ACDA)

National Opera Association (NOA)
Opera America (OA)
Early Music America (EMA)
American Guild of Musical Artists (AGMA)
Voice and Speech Trainers Association (VASTA)
International Voice Teachers of Mix (IVTOM)
Musical Theatre Educators Alliance (MTEA)
Southeastern Theatre Conference (SETC)
National Federation of Music Clubs (NFMC)
Actors' Equity Association (AEA)
Screen Actor's Guild–American Federation of Television and Radio Artists (SAG-AFTRA)

All of these organizations have websites, and most offer resources such as scholarly journals, conferences, and online networking opportunities.

Benefit

Serious students of singing will seek every way possible to improve themselves and their singing. Being resourceful and taking advantage of every opportunity over the course of your career will guarantee that you will never stop improving as a singer.

Epilogue

Knowing When to Shut Up (or Secret 101)

If you have made it this far, you have read a grand total of one hundred bits of advice intended to help you become a better, wiser, and more aware singer. No matter how hard you study and practice, however, there comes a time when silence is necessary. Sometimes after a long rehearsal or practice session, the best thing you can possibly do for your singing is shut your mouth and rest your body and voice.

Writers need to know when to stop too. As we were polishing the final draft of this manuscript, we had to hold ourselves back from the temptation to write one more secret or make one last point. All things must come to an end, including this book.

As a singer, however, you are never at the end of your yellow brick road. We hope that these brief pages will be a starting point for further vocal adventures and research. That is the ultimate secret: there are always opportunities to learn and grow . . . as long as you keep singing!

Anthologies

RECOMMENDED ANTHOLOGIES FOR VOICE TEACHERS

First Book and Second Book series
Edited by Joan Frey Boytim (b. 1934)
Published by Schirmer in 20 volumes

Affectionately known as "the Boytim Books," this colossal series gathers together a wealth of age-appropriate repertoire for the high school and first-year college student. Organized by voice type, the First Book series is published in three volumes for soprano, mezzo-soprano, tenor, and baritone, and the Second Book series in two volumes for the same four voice categories.

The Singer's Musical Theatre Anthology
Published by Hal Leonard in 27 volumes

The Singer's Musical Theatre Anthology is the industry standard for musical theatre performers and teachers. Six volumes are published for each of four voice categories: soprano, mezzo-soprano/belter, tenor, and baritone/bass, as well as three volumes of duets. All of the songs are published in their original keys, and the accompaniments are not simplified, appearing as they did in the original piano-vocal scores.

Singer's Library of Musical Theatre
Published by Alfred in 8 volumes

This additional eight volumes of musical theatre repertoire was introduced many years after Hal Leonard's *The Singer's Musical Theater Anthology* (*SMTA*) appeared, and while there are a few repeat selections, this series for the most part contains repertoire not found in *SMTA*. It is recommended that musical theatre singers and their teachers own both collections.

Canzone Scordate
Edited by Arne Dørumsgaard (1921–2006)
Published by Recital Publications in 22 volumes

   Arne Dørumsgaard's *Canzone Scordate* is a classic twenty-two-volume collection of art song arrangements of Renaissance, baroque, sacred, and folk songs in five languages: Italian, German, French, Spanish, and English.

Variazioni-Cadenze Tradizioni
Edited by Luigi Ricci (1893–1981)
Published by Ricordi in 2 volumes and 2 appendixes

   Luigi Ricci's vast collection of operatic cadenzas is a classic anthology and a must-own for serious students of opera. The collection is published in two volumes (for female voice and male voice) and two appendixes (a supplemental volume for all voice types and an all-Rossini collection).

La Flora
Edited by Knud Jeppesen (1892–1974)
Published by Wilhelm Hansen in 3 volumes

   Knud Jeppesen's *La Flora* is a pedagogical collection of Italian *arie antiche* by Renaissance and baroque composers. This collection is excellent for building technique and flexibility in young singers.

Great Opera Composers for Young Singers
Edited by Gabriella Ravazzi (b. 1942)
Published by Ricordi in 7 volumes

   Gabriella Ravazzi's collection gathers together age-appropriate arias for beginning singers. The collection serves as a pedagogical building block before singers advance to standard aria anthologies.

Pathways of Song
Edited by Frank LaForge (1879–1953) and Will Earhart (1871–1960)
Published by Alfred in 4 volumes and 2 keys

   A classic American collection of art songs, many of which are off the beaten path and seldom performed in the twenty-first century. *Pathways of Song* is a perfect collection for younger, less-experienced singers.

Resonance
Edited by the Royal Conservatory Music Development Program
Published by Frederick Harris in 12 volumes

   Resonance is a graded vocal method with level-appropriate songs. There are nine volumes of repertoire (beginning with a "preparatory volume" and then numbered one through eight) and three volumes of vocalises and recitatives, the final one published in two keys. The Royal Conservatory recently paired with the National Association of Teachers of Singing (NATS) to create the Achievement Program, a tiered curriculum for high school and avocational students of singing.

The New Millennium Series
Published by Conservatory Canada in 4 volumes

Conservatory Canada's New Millennium Series is a preconservatory, graded series designed for private studio use. Each book is paired with a syllabus and a guided rubric for assessment.

METHODOLOGIES AND TECHNIQUE BOOKS

While there are many technique books available for purchase, most methodologies used in North American voice studios are in the public domain and can therefore be downloaded free of charge from websites such as imslp.org. Another collection titled *Vocal Exercises: The Ultimate Collection* is available from CD Sheet Music, LLC. This volume includes all the major vocalise collections of Franz Abt (1819–1885), Pasquale Bona (1808–1878), Giovanni Marco Bordogni (1789–1856), Giuseppe Concone (1801–1861), Adolphe-Léopold Dannhauser (1835–1896), Louis Lablache (1794–1858), Francesco Lamperti (1811–1892), Giovanni Battista Lamperti (1839–1910), Bernard Lütgen (1835–1870), Mathilde Marchesi (1821–1913), Salvatore Marchesi (1822–1908), Henrich Panofka (1807–1887), Auguste Mathieu Panseron (1796–1859), Gioachino Rossini (1792–1868), Giovanni Battista Rubini (1794–1854), William Shakespeare (1849–1931), Ferdinand Sieber (1822–1895), Max Spicker (1858–1912), Nicola Vaccai (1790–1848), and Pauline Viardot (1821–1910).

Professional Organizations for Singers

The descriptions below have been adapted from each organization's website.

National Association of Teachers of Singing (NATS)

Founded in 1944, the National Association of Teachers of Singing, Inc. (NATS) is the largest professional association of teachers of singing in the world with more than seven thousand members in the United States, Canada, and over twenty-five other countries. NATS offers a variety of lifelong learning experiences to its members: workshops, intern programs, master classes, and conferences. NATS also annually provides chapter and regional auditions for students of singing, as well as artist-level competitions for classical and musical theatre performers. NATS Chats is a monthly web-based program enjoyed by voice professionals around the globe, and the *Journal of Singing* is regarded as the premier voice pedagogy journal in the world.

New York Singing Teachers Association (NYSTA)

The New York Singing Teachers Association (NYSTA) is the oldest professional association of singing teachers and voice professionals, founded in 1906, centered in New York, with local, national, and international members. NYSTA is dedicated to inspiring and educating those who work with the singing voice across all musical genres and around the globe. NYSTA is a leader in online education, offering professional development courses online through the Oren Lathrop Brown Professional Development Program. Voice professionals who complete the program earn NYSTA's Distinguished Voice Professional (DVP) certificate. NYSTA also publishes a professional journal, *VOICEPrints*, five times annually.

The Voice Foundation (TVF)

The mission of the Voice Foundation is to enhance knowledge, care, and training of the voice through educational programs and publications for voice-care professionals, the public, and professional voice users, and through supporting and funding research. Founded in 1969, the Voice Foundation brings together physicians, scientists, speech-language pathologists, performers, and teachers to share their knowledge and expertise in the care of the professional voice user. Since 1989, the Voice Foundation has been led by Robert Thayer Sataloff, MD, DMA, FACS, an internationally renowned otolaryngologist who is also a professional singer and conductor and author of more than six hundred publications, including more than thirty-six textbooks.

Music Teachers National Association (MTNA)

Founded in 1876, the Music Teachers National Association (MTNA) is a nonprofit organization of independent and collegiate music teachers committed to furthering the art of music through teaching, performance, composition, and scholarly research. MTNA also hosts an annual national convention that is linked to the prestigious national MTNA Young Artist Competition. MTNA publishes *American Music Teacher* bimonthly and offers a national certification program through which members can become nationally certified teachers of music (NCTM).

American Choral Directors Association (ACDA)

Founded in 1959, the American Choral Directors Association (ACDA) is a nonprofit music-education organization whose central purpose is to promote excellence in choral music through performance, composition, publication, research, and teaching. In addition, ACDA strives through arts advocacy to elevate choral music's position in American society. ACDA is particularly known for its national and regional conferences, as well as for its monthly publication, the *Choral Journal*.

Early Music America (EMA)

Early Music America (EMA) is a nonprofit service organization devoted to early music. Founded in 1985, EMA expands awareness of and interest in the music of the medieval, Renaissance, baroque, and classical periods performed on period instruments using historically informed performance practice. EMA's members receive a quarterly magazine, an annual directory, and a wide array of benefits. With its broad membership, including professional performers, ensembles, presenters, instrument makers, amateur musicians, and audience members, EMA serves as an advocate for the field throughout North America.

American Guild of Musical Artists (AGMA)

The American Guild of Musical Artists (AGMA) is the official American labor union for opera singers. AGMA represents approximately eight thousand current and retired opera singers, as well as ballet and other dancers, opera directors, backstage production personnel at opera and dance companies, and figure skaters.

AGMA claims exclusive jurisdiction over all aspects of the work of its members and shares some Broadway jurisdiction with its sister union, the Actors' Equity Association. Any artist who performs at principal American opera or dance companies works under AGMA contracts. The organization was founded in 1936 in an effort to eliminate exploitation of opera singers who were being forced into oppressive contracts without benefits or protections. Over the years, the Guild expanded its jurisdiction to include dancers (including athletes who dance on ice) and production personnel.

Opera America (OA)

Opera America is a service organization based in North America promoting the creation, presentation, and enjoyment of opera. Almost all professional opera companies and some semiprofessional companies in the United States are members of Opera America, including such opera companies as the Metropolitan Opera, San Francisco Opera, Lyric Opera of Chicago, and Dallas Opera. Opera America also includes international affiliated opera companies such as the Canadian Opera Company and Opera Australia, businesses, educational institutions, libraries, foundations, guilds, and opera artists such as singers and composers.

National Opera Association (NOA)

NOA is a national organization founded in 1955 that seeks to promote a greater appreciation of opera and musical theatre and encourages opera education programs in the United States. The National Opera Association (NOA) hosts annual competitions in singing and for collegiate opera scenes and publishes an academic journal entitled the *Opera Journal*. NOA membership includes professionals from the United States, Canada, Europe, Asia, and Australia.

Voice and Speech Trainers Association (VASTA)

VASTA is a nonprofit organization founded, grown, and guided by volunteers in the profession that services the needs of voice and speech professionals all over the world. VASTA is the only organization in the United States dedicated to fostering excellence in the field of voice and speech training. VASTA's current membership includes approximately five hundred members from around the globe, including professors, performers, voice, speech, text, and dialect coaches, speech/language pathologists, otolaryngologists, coaches in private practice, acting, movement, and singing specialists who are seeking to integrate disciplines, and others interested in the art and science of the human voice.

Musical Theatre Educators Alliance (MTEA)

MTEA is a forum for discussion of all matters relating to the recruitment, training, and placement of professionally bound college- and conservatory-affiliated music theatre students. It was formed to serve the following purposes: to facilitate the conversation among the diverse teaching populations who are involved in the practical training of music theatre students; to promote high standards; to share solutions; to broaden visibility; to strengthen credibility within the larger academic community and the profession; and to exchange curricular, production, and professional ideas and information.

Southeastern Theatre Conference (SETC)

SETC is a dynamic membership organization, serving a diverse constituency and reaching out across ten states in the southeast region of the United States and beyond. SETC is the strongest and broadest network of theatre practitioners in the United States. We provide extensive resources and year-round opportunities for our constituents. Our services, publications, and products contribute significantly to the careers of emerging artists, seasoned professionals and academicians. SETC energizes the practical, intellectual and creative profile of theatre in America.

National Federation of Music Clubs (NFMC)

Since its founding in 1898, the National Federation of Music Clubs (NFMC) has grown into one of the world's largest music organizations with club and individual members of all ages. The NFMC is chartered by the Congress of the United States, and is the only music organization member of the United Nations. NFMC provides both local events and national competitions for its members.

International Voice Teachers of Mix (IVTOM)

Founded in 2010, the International Voice Teachers of Mix (IVTOM) is an organization that provides education, accreditation, interaction, and community for teachers of "mix," a vocal technique that teaches singers to move smoothly through the bridges or "breaks" in the voice. In response to a high demand for training new teachers, IVTOM launched a teacher accreditation program in 2014. All members, both highly experienced and inexperienced, have access to ongoing education, a mentor program, student teacher training, regional workshops, and international conferences that provide unparalleled access to medical and scientific professionals who specialize in the human voice.

Actors' Equity Association (AEA)

The Actors' Equity Association—also known as "Equity"—is a United States labor union that represents more than fifty thousand actors and stage managers. Founded in 1913, Equity seeks to foster the art of live theatre as an essential component of society and advances the careers of its members by negotiating wages, working conditions, and providing a wide range of benefits, including health and pension plans. The AEA is a member of the AFL-CIO and is affiliated with FIA, an international organization of performing arts unions.

Screen Actors Guild–American Federation of Television and Radio Artists (SAG-AFTRA)

SAG-AFTRA brings together two great American labor unions: the Screen Actors Guild (SAG) and the American Federation of Television and Radio Artists (AFTRA). SAG-AFTRA represents approximately 160,000 actors, announcers, broadcast journalists, dancers, DJs, news writers, news editors, program hosts, puppeteers, recording artists, singers, stunt performers, voiceover artists, and other media professionals. SAG-AFTRA members are the faces and voices that entertain and inform America and the world. With national offices in Los Angeles and New York, and local offices nationwide, SAG-AFTRA members work together to secure the strongest protections for media artists into the twenty-first century and beyond.

Bibliography

Note: In some instances, a book falls into more than one category and is listed in two different locations. This is deliberate and intended for the convenience of the reader, who it is assumed is consulting the bibliography to research a particular topic.

CONTENTS

Singing (General)	221
Voice Pedagogy	221
Historical Pedagogy	222
Vocology and Voice Science	223
Voice Health	223
Diction	224
General	224
Pronunciation Dictionaries	225
German	225
French	225
Italian	226
English	226
Latin	226
Spanish	226
Russian	226
Scandinavian/Nordic Languages	227
Other Languages	227
IPA Transcriptions and Translations	227
General	227
Opera Libretti	227
German *Lieder*	229
French *Mélodies*	230
Italian Art Song	230
Russian Art Song	230

Scandinavian/Nordic Art Song	230
Other Art Song Languages	231
Translations (without IPA transcriptions)	231
General	231
German *Lieder*	231
French *Mélodies*	232
Italian Art Song	232
Spanish Art Song	232
Russian Art Song	232
Art Song	232
General	232
German *Lieder*	233
French *Mélodies*	233
English Art Song	234
American Art Song	234
Spanish and Latin American Art Song	234
Individual Composers	234
Repertoire	235
Collaboration	236
Opera	236
Opera Directing	236
Light Opera	237
Choral Music and Ensemble Singing	237
Class Voice	238
Performance Practice	238
New Music	239
Chamber Music	239
Church Music	239
Music Psychology	239
Inspiration	240
The Business	241
Great Singers	241
Music History	242
General	242
Medieval	242
Renaissance	243
Baroque	243
Classical	243
Romantic	243
Modern	244
Music Theory and Sight-Singing	244
CCM Pedagogy	245
Musical Theatre	246
Other Styles	247

American and Roots Genres	247
Rock Genres	248
Jazz	248
World Music	248
Bodywork	249
General	249
Alexander Technique	249
Feldenkrais	250
Yoga	250
Acting	250

SINGING (GENERAL)

Jander, Owen, Ellen T. Harris, David Fallows, and John Potter. "Singing." In *Grove Music Online*, edited by Deane Root. Accessed May 1, 2013. www.oxfordmusiconline.com.

Potter, John, ed. *The Cambridge Companion to Singing*. New York: Cambridge University Press, 2000.

Potter, John, and Neil Sorrell. *A History of Singing*. New York: Cambridge University Press, 2012.

VOICE PEDAGOGY

Alderson, Richard. *The Complete Handbook of Voice Training*. Mira Loma, CA: Parker, 1979.

Appelman, D. Ralph. *The Science of Vocal Pedagogy: Theory and Application*. Bloomington: Indiana University Press, 1986.

Blades-Zeller, Elizabeth. *A Spectrum of Voices: Prominent American Voice Teachers Discuss the Teaching of Singing*. Lanham, MD: Scarecrow Press, 2002.

Boytim, Joan Frey. *The Private Studio Handbook: A Practical Guide to All Aspects of Teaching*. New York: Hal Leonard, 2003.

Brown, Oren L. *Discover Your Voice: How to Develop Healthy Voice Habits*. San Diego, CA: Singular, 1996.

Bybee, Ariel, and James E. Ford. *The Modern Singing Master: Essays in Honor of Cornelius L. Reid*. Lanham, MD: Scarecrow Press, 2004.

Caldwell, Robert, and Joan Wall. *Excellence in Singing: Multilevel Teaching and Multilevel Learning*. 5 vols. Redmond, WA: Caldwell, 2001.

Chapman, Janice. *Singing and Teaching Singing: A Holistic Approach to Classical Voice*. 2nd ed. San Diego, CA: Plural, 2011.

Coffin, Berton. *Overtones of Bel Canto: Phonetic Basis of Artistic Singing with 100 Chromatic Vowel-Chart Exercises*. Lanham, MD: Scarecrow Press, 1980.

———. *Sounds of Singing: Principles and Applications of Vocal Technique with Chromatic Vowel Chart*. Revised and enlarged 2nd ed. Lanham, MD: Scarecrow Press, 1987.

David, Marilee. *The New Voice Pedagogy*. 2nd ed. Lanham, MD: Scarecrow Press, 2008.

Davids, Julia, and Stephen LaTour. *Vocal Technique: A Guide for Conductors, Teachers, and Singers*. Long Grove, IL: Waveland Press, 2012.

Dayme, Maribeth. *Dynamics of the Singing Voice*. 5th ed. New York: Springer, 2009.

Doscher, Barbara. *The Functional Unity of the Singing Voice*. 2nd ed. Lanham, MD: Scarecrow Press, 1994.

Hines, Jerome. *The Four Voices of Man*. Milwaukee, WI: Limelight Editions, 2004.

Kagen, Sergius. *On Studying Singing*. New York: Dover, 1950.

McCoy, Scott. *Your Voice: An Inside View*. 2nd ed. Columbus, OH: Inside View Press, 2012.

McKinney, James C. *The Diagnosis and Correction of Vocal Faults: A Manual for Teachers of Singing and Choir Directors*. Long Grove, IL: Waveland Press, 2005.

Miller, Richard. *English, French, German, and Italian Techniques of Singing: A Study in National Tonal Preferences and How They Relate to Functional Efficiency*. Lanham, MD: Scarecrow Press, 1977.

———. *National Schools of Singing: English, French, German, and Italian Techniques of Singing Revisited*. Lanham, MD: Scarecrow Press, 1997.

———. *On the Art of Singing*. New York: Oxford University Press, 1996.

———. *Securing Baritone, Bass-Baritone, and Bass Voices*. New York: Oxford University Press, 2008.

———. *Solutions for Singers: Tools for Every Performer and Teacher*. New York: Oxford University Press, 2004.

———. *The Structure of Singing*. New York: Schirmer Books, 1986.

———. *Training Soprano Voices*. New York: Oxford University Press, 2000.

———. *Training Tenor Voices*. New York: Schirmer Books, 1993.

Reid, Cornelius. *Bel Canto: Principles and Practices*. Reprint ed. New York: Joseph Patelson, 1975.

———. *A Dictionary of Vocal Terminology*. Huntsville, TX: Recital, 1983.

———. *Essays on the Nature of Singing*. Huntsville, TX: Recital, 1992.

———. *The Free Voice*. Reprint ed. New York: Joseph Patelson, 1975.

———. *Voice: Psyche and Soma*. Reprint ed. New York: Joseph Patelson, 1975.

Sell, Karen. *The Disciplines of Vocal Pedagogy: Towards an Holistic Approach*. Farnham, UK: Ashgate, 2005.

Smith, W. Stephen, with Michael Chipman. *The Naked Voice: A Wholistic Approach to Singing*. New York: Oxford University Press, 2007.

Vennard, William. *Singing: The Mechanism and the Technic*. Rev. ed., greatly enlarged. New York: Carl Fisher, 1967.

Ware, Clifton. *Basics of Vocal Pedagogy*. New York: McGraw-Hill, 1997.

HISTORICAL PEDAGOGY

Coffin, Berton. *Historical Vocal Pedagogy Classics*. Lanham, MD: Scarecrow Press, 1989.

Duey, Philip A. *Bel Canto in Its Golden Age: A Study of Its Teaching Concepts*. New York: Columbia University Press, 1951.

García, Manuel. *Hints on Singing*. London: Lowe & Brydone, 1894.

Lamperti, Giovanni Battista. *Vocal Wisdom: Maxims of Giovanni Battista Lamperti.* Enlarged ed. Transcribed by William Earl Brown. New York: Taplinger, 1931.
Manén, Lucie. *Bel Canto: The Teaching of the Classical Italian Song-Schools, Its Decline and Restoration.* New York: Oxford University Press, 1987.
Miller, Richard. "Historical Overview of Vocal Pedagogy." *Vocal Health and Pedagogy.* Vol. 2, *Advanced Assessment and Treatment.* 2nd ed. San Diego, CA: Plural, 2006.
Stark, James. *Bel Canto: A History of Vocal Pedagogy.* Toronto: University of Toronto Press, 1999.
Toft, Robert. *Bel Canto: A Performer's Guide.* New York: Oxford University Press, 2013.

VOCOLOGY AND VOICE SCIENCE

Bozeman, Kenneth W. *Practical Vocal Acoustics: Pedagogic Applications for Teachers and Singers.* Hillsdale, NY: Pendragon Press, 2013.
McCoy, Scott. *Your Voice: An Inside View.* 2nd ed. Columbus, OH: Inside View Press, 2012.
Peterson, Gorden E., and Harold L. Barney. "Control Methods Used in a Study of the Vowels." *Journal of the Acoustical Society of America* 24, no. 2 (March 1952): 175–184.
Sataloff, Robert Thayer. *Voice Science.* San Diego, CA: Plural, 2005.
Sundberg, Johann. *The Science of the Singing Voice.* DeKalb: Northern Illinois University Press, 1989.
Sundberg, Johann, Edward C. Carterette, and Morton P. Friedman. *The Science of Musical Sounds.* Waltham, MA: Academic Press, 1991.
Titze, Ingo. *Fascinations with the Human Voice.* Salt Lake City: National Center for Voice and Speech, 2010.
———. *The Myoelastic Aerodynamic Theory of Phonation.* Salt Lake City: National Center for Voice and Speech, 2006.
———. *Principles of Voice Production.* Salt Lake City: National Center for Voice and Speech, 2000.
Titze, Ingo, and Katherine Verdolini Abbott. *Vocology: The Science and Practice of Voice Habilitation.* Salt Lake City: National Center for Voice and Speech, 2012.
Tomatis, Alfred A. *The Ear and the Voice.* Lanham, MD: Scarecrow Press, 2005.

VOICE HEALTH

Baken, Ronald J., and Robert F. Orlikoff. *Clinical Measurement of Speech and Voice.* San Diego, CA: Singular, 1999.
Colton, Raymond H., Janina K. Casper, and Rebecca Leonard. *Understanding Voice Problems: A Physiological Perspective for Diagnosis and Treatment.* 4th ed. Baltimore: Lippincott, Williams & Wilkins, 2011.
DeVore, Kate, and Starr Cookman. *The Voice Book: Caring For, Protecting, and Improving Your Voice.* Chicago: Chicago Review Press, 2009.

Hixon, Thomas J. *Respiratory Function in Singing: A Primer for Singers and Singing Teachers*. San Diego, CA: Plural, 2007.
Leborgne, Wendy D., and Marci Rosenberg. *The Vocal Athlete*. San Diego, CA: Plural, 2014.
Lessac, Arthur. *The Use and Training of the Human Voice: A Bio-dynamic Approach to Vocal Life*. 3rd ed. New York: McGraw-Hill, 1997.
Linklater, Kristin. *Freeing the Natural Voice*. Hollywood, CA: Drama Publishers, 1976.
McClosky, David Blair, and Members of the McClosky Institute of Voice. *Your Voice at Its Best: Enhancement of the Healthy Voice, Help for the Troubled Voice*. Long Grove, IL: Waveland Press, 2011.
Rosenberg, Marci, and Wendy D. Leborgne. *The Vocal Athlete: Application and Technique for the Hybrid Singer*. San Diego, CA: Plural, 2014.
Rubin, John S., Robert Thayer Sataloff, and Gwen S. Korovin. *Diagnosis and Treatment of Voice Disorders*. 3rd ed. San Diego, CA: Plural, 2005.
Sataloff, Robert Thayer. *Professional Voice: The Science and Art of Clinical Care*. 4th ed. San Diego, CA: Plural, 2016.
———. *Vocal Health and Pedagogy*, vol. 1, *Science and Assessment*. 2nd ed. San Diego, CA: Plural, 2006.
———. *Vocal Health and Pedagogy*, vol. 2, *Advanced Assessment and Treatment*. 2nd ed. San Diego, CA: Plural, 2006.
Wicklund, Karen. *Singing Voice Rehabilitation: A Guide for the Voice Teacher and Speech-Language Pathologist*. Clifton Park, NY: Cengage Learning, 2010.

DICTION

General

Adams, David. *A Handbook of Diction for Singers: Italian, German, French*. 2nd ed. New York: Oxford University Press, 2008.
International Phonetic Association. *Handbook of the International Phonetic Association: A Guide to the Use of the International Phonetic Alphabet*. New York: Cambridge University Press, 1999.
Karna, Duane Richard, ed. *The Use of the International Phonetic Alphabet in the Choral Rehearsal*. Lanham, MD: Scarecrow Press, 2012.
Montgomery, Cheri. *IPA Handbook for Singers*. Nashville, TN: STM Publishers, 2015.
———. *Phonetic Readings for Lyric Diction*. 3rd ed. Nashville, TN: STM Publishers, 2015.
Moriarty, John. *Diction: Italian, Latin, French, German . . . the Sounds and 81 Exercises for Singing Them*. New York: Schirmer Books, 1975.
Pullum, Geoffrey K., and William A. Laduslaw. *Phonetic Symbol Guide*. 2nd ed. Chicago: University of Chicago Press, 1996.
Stapp, Marcie. *The Singer's Guide to Languages*. San Francisco: Teddy's Music Press, 1987.

Wall, Joan. *Diction for Singers*. 2nd ed. Redmond, WA: Caldwell, 2009.
———. *International Phonetic Alphabet for Singers: A Manual for English and Foreign Language Diction*. Redmond, WA: Pst., 1989.

Pronunciation Dictionaries

de Boor, Helmuth, Hugo Moser, and Christian Winkler. *Siebs Deutsche Aussprache: Reine und Gemässigte Hochlautung mit Aussprachewörterbuch*. Berlin: Walter de Gruyter, 1969.
Garzanti Linguistica Staff, eds. *Grande Dizionario Garzanti in Italiano*. New York: French and European Publications, 2012.
Jones, Daniel. *Cambridge English Pronouncing Dictionary*. 18th ed. Edited by Peter Roach, Jane Setter, and John Esling. Cambridge and New York: Cambridge University Press, 2011.
Kenyon, John Samuel, and Thomas Albert Knott. *A Pronouncing Dictionary of American English*. 2nd ed. Springfield, MA: Merriam-Webster, 1953.
Mangold, Max. *Duden's Das Aussprachewörterbuch*. 6th ed. Evanston, IL: Adler's Foreign Books, 2006.
Upton, Clive, William Kretzmar Jr., and Rafal Konopka. *Oxford Dictionary of Pronunciation for Current English*. Oxford: Oxford University Press, 2003.
Warnant, Leon. *Dictionnaire de la prononciation française dans sa norme actuelle*. Paris: Duculot, 1987.

German

Johnston, Amanda. *English and German Diction for Singers: A Comparative Approach*. Lanham, MD: Scarecrow Press, 2011.
Montgomery, Cheri. *German Lyric Diction Workbook*. 5th ed. Nashville, TN: STM Publishers, 2015.
Odom, William. *German for Singers: A Textbook of Diction and Phonetics*. 2nd ed. New York: Schirmer, 1997.

French

Bernac, Pierre. *The Interpretation of French Song*. New York: Norton, 1970.
Davis, Eileen. *Sing French: Diction for Singers*. Columbus, OH: Éclairé Press, 2010.
Grubb, Thomas. *Singing in French: A Manual of French Diction and French Vocal Repertoire*. New York: Schirmer Books; London: Collier Macmillan, 1979.
Hunter, David. *Understanding French Verse: A Guide for Singers*. New York: Oxford University Press, 2005.
Montgomery, Cheri. *Advanced French Lyric Diction Workbook*. Nashville, TN: STM Publishers, 2015.
———. *French Lyric Diction Workbook*. 4th ed. Nashville, TN: STM Publishers, 2015.

Italian

Colorni, Evelina. *Singer's Italian: A Manual of Diction and Phonetics*. New York: Schirmer Books, 1995.

Montgomery, Cheri. *Italian Lyric Diction Workbook*. 3rd ed. Nashville, TN: STM Publishers, 2015.

English

Blizzard, John. *Singing American English: Textbook for Diction for Singers*. Raleigh, NC: Lulu Press, 2002.

Forward, Geoffery G. *American Diction for Singers*. Van Nuys, CA: Alfred, 2001.

Johnston, Amanda. *English and German Diction for Singers: A Comparative Approach*. Lanham, MD: Scarecrow Press, 2011.

LaBouff, Kathryn. *Singing and Communicating in English: A Singer's Guide to English Diction*. New York: Oxford University Press, 2007.

Marshall, Madeleine. *The Singer's Manual of English Diction*. New York: Schirmer Books, 1953.

Montgomery, Cheri. *English Lyric Diction Workbook*. Rev. 3rd ed. Nashville, TN: STM Publishers, 2006.

Latin

Hines, Robert S. *Singer's Manual of Latin Diction and Phonetics*. New York: Schirmer Books, 1975.

Jeffers, Ron. *Translations and Annotations of Choral Repertoire*, vol. 1, *Sacred Latin Texts*. Corvallis, OR: Earthsongs, 1988.

Montgomery, Cheri, and Matthew Hoch. *Latin Lyric Diction Workbook*. Nashville, TN: STM Publishers, 2016.

Spanish

Castel, Nico. *A Singer's Manual of Spanish Lyric Diction*. New York: Excalibur, 1994.

Draayer, Suzanne. Pronunciation guides found in *Canciones de España: Songs of Nineteenth-Century Spain*. 6 vols. Lanham, MD: Scarecrow Press, 2005.

Russian

Belov, Anton. "The Sounds of Russian." *Twenty Arias for Baritone*. Geneseo, NY: Leyerle, 2005.

Olin, Emily. *Singing in Russian: A Guide to Language and Performance*. Lanham, MD: Scarecrow Press, 2011.

Piatak, Jean, and Regina Avrashov. *Russian Songs and Arias: Phonetic Readings, Word-by-Word Translations, and a Concise Guide to Russian Diction*. Dallas, TX: Pst., 1991.

Scandinavian/Nordic Languages

Ellingboe, Bradley. *Forty-Five Songs of Edvard Grieg*. Corrected ed. Geneseo, NY: Leyerle, 1988.
Hersey, Anna. *Scandinavian Song: A Guide to Swedish, Norwegian, and Danish Repertoire and Diction*. Lanham, MD: Rowman & Littlefield, 2016.
Holman, Eugene, with Gustav Djuosjöbacka and Donald Adamson. *Singing in Finnish: A Manual for Singers and Vocal Coaches*. Helsinki: Academy of Finnish Art Song, 2005.
Johansson, Annette. *Thirty Songs of Wilhelm Stenhammar*. Geneseo, NY: Leyerle, 1999.
Rosenberg-Wolff, Carita, with Gustav Djuosjöbacka. *Singing in Swedish: A Manual for Singers and Vocal Coaches*. Helsinki: Academy of Finnish Art Song, 2011.

Other Languages

Boire, Paula. *Romanian Art Songs*. 2 vols. Geneseo, NY: Leyerle, 2004.
Cheek, Timothy. *Singing in Czech*. Lanham, MD: Scarecrow Press, 2001.
Dechario, Joseph. *Timeless Jewish Songs: Hebrew, Yiddish, and Ladino Texts with IPA Transcriptions*. 2 vols. Geneseo, NY: Leyerle, 1994.
Schultz, Benjamin. *Singing in Polish: A Guide to Polish Lyric Diction and Vocal Repertoire*. Lanham, MD: Rowman & Littlefield, 2015.
Zervanos, Lydía. *Singing in Greek: A Guide to Greek Lyric Diction and Vocal Repertoire*. Lanham, MD: Rowman & Littlefield, 2015.
Zhong, Mei. *Newly Arranged Chinese Folk Songs*. Geneseo, NY: Leyerle, 2005.
———. *Traditional and Modern Chinese Art Songs*. Geneseo, NY: Leyerle, 2009.
Leslie de'Ath's regular column in the *Journal of Singing* is frequently devoted to languages that are off the beaten path.

IPA TRANSCRIPTIONS AND TRANSLATIONS

General

Retzlaff, Jonathan, and Cheri Montgomery. *Exploring Art Song Lyrics: Translation and Pronunciation of the Italian, German, and French Repertoire*. New York: Oxford University Press, 2012.

Opera Libretti

Belov, Anton. *Libretti of Russian Operas: "Ruslan and Ludmila" (Glinka); "Boris Godunov" (Mussorgsky); "Eugene Onegin" and "The Queen of Spades" (Tchaikovsky); "Aleko" (Rachmaninoff); and "The Golden Cockerel" (Rimsky-Korsakov)*. Geneseo, NY: Leyerle, 2004.
Castel, Nico. *The Complete Puccini Libretti*. Vol. 1, *"La bohème," "Edgar," "La fanciulla del West," "Madama Butterly," and "Manon Lescaut."* Edited by Marcie Stapp. Geneseo, NY: Leyerle, 1994.

———. *The Complete Puccini Libretti*. Vol. 2, *"La rondine," "Tosca," "Il trittico" ("Il tabarro," "Suor Angelica," and "Gianni Schicchi"), and "Le villi."* Edited by Marcie Stapp. Geneseo, NY: Leyerle, 1994.

———. *The Complete Verdi Libretti*. Vol. 1, *"Aida," "Alzira," "Aroldo," "Attila," "Un ballo in maschera," "La battaglia di Legnano," and "Il corsaro."* Geneseo, NY: Leyerle, 1996.

———. *The Complete Verdi Libretti*. Vol. 2, *"Don Carlo," "I due Foscari," "Ernani," "Falstaff," "La forza del destino," "Giovanna d'Arco," and "Un giorno di regno."* Geneseo, NY: Leyerle, 1996.

———. *The Complete Verdi Libretti*. Vol. 3, *"I Lombardi"; "Luisa Miller"; "Macbeth"; "I masnadieri"; "Nabucco"; "Oberto, Conte di San Bonifacio"; and "Otello."* Geneseo, NY: Leyerle, 1996.

———. *The Complete Verdi Libretti*. Vol. 4, *"Rigoletto," "Simon Boccanegra," "Stiffelio," "La traviata," "Il trovatore," and "I vespri siciliani."* Geneseo, NY: Leyerle, 1996.

———. *Four Strauss Opera Libretti: "Der Rosenkavalier," "Elektra," "Salome," and "Ariadne auf Naxos."* Edited by Marcie Stapp. Geneseo, NY: Leyerle, 2002.

———. *French Opera Libretti*. Vol. 1, *"Werther and Chérubin" (Massenet); "Carmen" (Bizet); "Samson et Dalila" (Saint-Saëns); "Lakmé" (Delibes); "Pelléas et Mélisande" (Debussy); "Don Carlos" (Verdi); and "Les contes d'Hoffman" (Offenbach)*. Edited by Marcie Stapp. Geneseo, NY: Leyerle, 1999.

———. *French Opera Libretti*. Vol. 2, *"Faust" and "Roméo et Juliette" (Gounod); "La Juive" (Halévy); "Mignon" and "Hamlet" (Thomas); "Thaïs" and "Manon" (Massenet); and "Les pêcheurs de Perles" (Bizet)*. Edited by Marcie Stapp. Geneseo, NY: Leyerle, 1999.

———. *French Opera Libretti*. Vol. 3, *"Le prophète" and "Les Huguenots" (Meyerbeer); "Cendrillon" and "Don Quichotte" (Massenet); "Louise" (Charpentier); and "Les Troyens" (Berlioz)*. Edited by Marcie Stapp. Geneseo, NY: Leyerle, 1999.

———. *German Miscellaneous Opera Libretti: "Tannhäuser," "Lohengrin," and "Der fliegende Holländer" (Wagner); "Die lustigen Weiber von Windsor" (Nicolai); "Hänsel und Gretel" (Humperdinck); "Fidelio" (Beethoven); and "Der Freischütz" (Weber)*. Edited by Marcie Stapp. Geneseo, NY: Leyerle, 2005.

———. *Gluck and Monteverdi Opera Libretti: "Orfeo ed Euridice," "Alceste," "Iphigénie en Aulide," and "Iphigénie en Tauride" (Gluck); "L'Orfeo," "Il ritorno d'Ulisse in Patria," and "L'incoronazione di Poppea" (Monteverdi)*. Edited by Marcie Stapp. Geneseo, NY: Leyerle, 2008.

———. *Handel Opera Libretti*. Vol. 1, *"Rodelinda," "Alcina," "Agrippina," "Giulio Cesare," "Rinaldo," and "Ottone."* Edited by Hemdi Kfir. Geneseo, NY: Leyerle, 2005.

———. *Handel Opera Libretti*. Vol. 2, *"Ariodante," "Serse," "Orlando," "Partenope," "Tamerlano," "Radamisto," and "Lotario."* Edited by Marcie Stapp. Geneseo, NY: Leyerle, 2005.

———. *Italian Belcanto Opera Libretti*. Vol. 1, *"Il barbiere di Siviglia" and "Il turco in Italia" (Rossini); "Lucia di Lammermoor," "L'elisir d'amore," and "Lucrezia Borgia"*

(Donizetti); and "Norma" and "I Capuleti e I Montecchi" (Bellini). Edited by Scott Jackson Wiley. Geneseo, NY: Leyerle, 2000.

———. *Italian Belcanto Opera Libretti*. Vol. 2, *"La Centerentola" and "L'italiana in Algeri" (Rossini); "La sonnambula" and "I puritani" (Bellini); "Anna Bolena," "Maria Stuarda," "Roberto Devereux," and "Don Pasquale" (Donizetti)*. Edited by Marcie Stapp. Geneseo, NY: Leyerle, 2000.

———. *Italian/French Belcanto Opera Libretti*. Vol. 3, *"Il viaggio a Reims," "Semiramide," and "Otello" (Rossini); "Beatrice di Tenda" (Bellini); "La fille du régiment" and "La favorite" (Donizetti); "Le comte Ory" and "Guillaume Tell" (Rossini)*. Edited by Marcie Stapp. Geneseo, NY: Leyerle, 2000.

———. *The Libretti of Mozart's Completed Operas*. Vol. 1, *"Bastien und Bastienne," "La clemenza di Tito," "Così fan tutte," "Don Giovanni," "Die Entführung aus dem Serail," "La finta giardiniera," and "La finta semplice."* Geneseo, NY: Leyerle, 1998.

———. *The Libretti of Mozart's Completed Operas*. Vol. 2, *"Idomeneo", "Lucio Silla", "Mitridate, re die Ponto", "Le nozze di Figaro", "Il re pastore", "Der Schauspieldirektor", and "Die Zauberflöte."* Geneseo, NY: Leyerle, 1998.

———. *"Der Ring des Nibelungen": "Das Rheingold," "Die Walküre," "Siegfried," and "Götterdämmerung."* Edited by Marcie Stapp. Geneseo, NY: Leyerle, 2003.

———. *Three Wagner Opera Libretti: "Die Meistersinger von Nürnberg," "Tristan und Isolde," and "Parsifal."* Edited by Marcie Stapp. Geneseo, NY: Leyerle, 2006.

———. *Verismo Opera Libretti: "Andrea Chénier" and "Fedora" (Giordano); "Adriana Lecouvreur" (Cilea); "La bohème" and "Pagliacci" (Leoncavallo); "Mefistofele" (Boito); "Cavalleria rusticana" and "L'amico Fritz" (Mascagni); and "La gioconda" (Ponchielli)*. Edited by Scott Jackson Wiley. Geneseo, NY: Leyerle, 2000.

———. *Viennese Operetta Libretti: Franz Lehár's "Die lustige Witwe" (The Merry Widow)*. Edited by Marcie Stapp. Geneseo, NY: Leyerle, 2006.

———. *Viennese Operetta Libretti: Johann Strauss's "Die Fledermaus" (The Bat)*. Edited by Marcie Stapp. Geneseo, NY: Leyerle, 2006.

German *Lieder*

Glass, Beaumont. *Brahms' Complete Song Texts*. Geneseo, NY: Leyerle, 1999.

———. *Hugo Wolf's Complete Song Texts*. Geneseo, NY: Leyerle, 2000.

———. *Richard Strauss' Complete Song Texts*. Mt. Morris, NY: Leyerle, 2004.

———. *Schubert's Complete Song Texts*. Vol. 1. Geneseo, NY: Leyerle, 1996.

———. *Schubert's Complete Song Texts*. Vol. 2. Geneseo, NY: Leyerle, 1996.

———. *Schumann's Complete Song Texts*. Geneseo, NY: Leyerle, 2002.

———. *Selected Song Texts of Great German Lieder*. Geneseo, NY: Leyerle, 2004.

Magner, Candace A. *Phonetic Readings of Brahms Lieder*. Lanham, MD: Scarecrow Press, 1995.

———. *Phonetic Readings of Schubert Lieder*. Lanham, MD: Scarecrow Press, 1994.

Reinhard, Thilo. *The Singer's Schumann*. New York: Rosen, 1989.

French *Mélodies*

Bathori, Jane. *On the Interpretation of the Melodies of Claude Debussy*. Hillsdale, NY: Pendragon Press, 1998.
Dibbern, Mary, Carol Kimball, and Patrick Choukroun. *The Songs of Jacques Leguerney: A Guide for Study and Performance*. Hillsdale, NY: Pendragon Press, 2002.
Gartside, Robert. *Interpreting the Songs of Gabriel Fauré*. Geneseo, NY: Leyerle, 1996.
———. *Interpreting the Songs of Maurice Ravel*. Geneseo, NY: Leyerle, 1992.
Néron, Martin. *Francis Poulenc: Selected Song Texts*. Geneseo, NY: Leyerle, 2010.
Rohinsky, Marie-Claire. *The Singer's Debussy*. New York: Rosen, 1987.

Italian Art Song

Gerhart, Martha. *Italian Song Texts from the Seventeenth through the Twentieth Centuries*. Vol. 1. Geneseo, NY: Leyerle, 2002.
———. *Italian Song Texts from the Seventeenth through the Twentieth Centuries*. Vol. 2. Geneseo, NY: Leyerle, 2002.
——— *Italian Song Texts from the Seventeenth through the Twentieth Centuries*. Vol. 3. Geneseo, NY: Leyerle, 2014.

Russian Art Song

Challis, Natalia. *The Singer's Rachmaninoff*. New York: Rosen, 1989.
Piatak, Jean, and Regina Avrashov. *Russian Songs and Arias: Phonetic Readings, Word-by-Word Translations, and a Concise Guide to Russian Diction*. Dallas, TX: Pst., 1991.
Richter, Laurence R. *Mussorgsky's Complete Song Texts*. Geneseo, NY: Leyerle, 2002.
———. *Prokofiev's Complete Song Texts*. Geneseo, NY: Leyerle, 2008.
———. *Rachmaninov's Complete Song Texts*. Geneseo, NY: Leyerle, 2000.
———. *Selected Nineteenth Century Russian Song Texts*. Geneseo, NY: Leyerle, 2005.
———. *Shostakovich's Complete Song Texts*. Geneseo, NY: Leyerle, 2007.
———. *Tchaikovsky's Complete Song Texts*. Geneseo, NY: Leyerle, 1999.

Scandinavian/Nordic Art Song

Ellingboe, Bradley. *Forty-Five Songs of Edvard Grieg*. Corrected ed. Geneseo, NY: Leyerle, 1988.
Holman, Eugene, with Gustav Djuosjöbacka and Donald Adamson. *Singing in Finnish: A Manual for Singers and Vocal Coaches*. Helsinki: Academy of Finnish Art Song, 2005.
Johansson, Annette. *Thirty Songs of Wilhelm Stenhammar*. Geneseo, NY: Leyerle, 1999.

Rosenberg-Wolff, Carita, with Gustav Djuosjöbacka. *Singing in Swedish: A Manual for Singers and Vocal Coaches*. Helsinki: Academy of Finnish Art Song, 2011.

Other Art Song Languages

Adams, David. *The Song and Duet Texts of Antonín Dvořák*. Geneseo, NY: Leyerle, 2003.
Boire, Paula. *Romanian Art Songs*. 2 vols. Geneseo, NY: Leyerle, 2004.
Cheek, Timothy. *Singing in Czech*. Lanham, MD: Scarecrow Press, 2001.
Dechario, Joseph. *Timeless Jewish Songs: Hebrew, Yiddish, and Ladino Texts with IPA Transcriptions*. 2 vols. Geneseo, NY: Leyerle, 1994.
Schultz, Benjamin. *Singing in Polish: A Guide to Polish Lyric Diction and Vocal Repertoire*. Lanham, MD: Rowman & Littlefield, 2015.
Sobrer, Josep Miquel. *The Singer's Anthology of Twentieth Century Spanish Song*. Edited by Edmon Colomer. Buffalo, NY: Rosen, 1987.
Wilson, Kathleen. *The Art Song in Latin America: Selected Works by Twentieth-Century Composers*. Hillsdale, NY: Pendragon Press, 1998.
Zervanos, Lydía. *Singing in Greek: A Guide to Greek Lyric Diction and Vocal Repertoire*. Lanham, MD: Rowman & Littlefield, 2015.
Zhong, Mei. *Newly Arranged Chinese Folk Songs*. Geneseo, NY: Leyerle, 2005.
———. *Traditional and Modern Chinese Art Songs*. Geneseo, NY: Leyerle, 2009.
Leslie de'Ath's regular column in the *Journal of Singing* is frequently devoted to languages that are off the beaten path.

TRANSLATIONS (WITHOUT IPA TRANSCRIPTIONS)

General

Miller, Philip L. *The Ring of Words: An Anthology of Song Texts*. New York: Norton, 1973.

German *Lieder*

Fischer-Dieskau, Dietrich. *The Fischer-Dieskau Book of Lieder*. Translations by George Bird and Richard Stokes. Milwaukee, WI: Limelight Publications, 1977.
Mercier, Richard. *The Songs of Hans Pfitzner: A Guide and Study*. Westport, CT: Greenwood Press, 1998.
———. *The Songs of Max Reger: A Guide and Study*. Lanham, MD: Scarecrow Press, 2008.
Sams, Eric. *The Songs of Hugo Wolf*. London: Faber Finds, 2008.
———. *The Songs of Johannes Brahms*. New Haven, CT: Yale University Press, 2000.
———. *The Songs of Robert Schumann*. London: Faber Finds, 2008.

Stokes, Richard. *The Book of Lieder: The Original Texts of Over 1000 Songs*. London: Faber & Faber, 2005.

Wigmore, Richard. *Schubert: The Complete Song Texts*. New York: Schirmer Books, 1988.

French *Mélodies*

Bernac, Pierre. *Francis Poulenc: The Man and His Songs*. London: Kahn & Averill, 2002.

———. *The Interpretation of French Song*. London: Kahn & Averill, 2002.

Johnson, Graham. *Gabriel Fauré: The Songs and Their Poets*. Translations by Richard Stokes. Farnham, UK: Ashgate, 2011.

Johnson, Graham, and Richard Stokes. *A French Song Companion*. New York: Oxford University Press, 2002.

Italian Art Song

Lakeway, Ruth C., and Robert C. White Jr. *Italian Art Song*. Bloomington: Indiana University Press, 1989.

Spanish Art Song

Cockburn, Jacqueline, and Richard Stokes. *The Spanish Song Companion*. Lanham, MD: Scarecrow Press, 2006.

Draayer, Suzanne. *A Singer's Guide to the Songs of Joaquín Rodrigo*. Lanham, MD: Scarecrow Press, 2003.

Russian Art Song

Sylvester, Richard D. *Tchaikovsky's Complete Songs: A Companion with Texts and Translations*. Bloomington: Indiana University Press, 2004.

ART SONG

General

Banfield, Stephen. *Sensibility and English Song: Critical Studies of the Early Twentieth Century*. New York: Cambridge University Press, 1989.

Dunsby, Jonathan. *Making Words Sing: Nineteenth- and Twentieth-Century Song*. New York: Cambridge University Press, 2004.

Emmons, Shirlee, and Stanley Sonntag. *The Art of the Song Recital*. Long Grove, IL: Waveland Press, 2001.

Emmons, Shirlee, and Wilbur Watkins Lewis. *Researching the Song: A Lexicon*. New York: Oxford University Press, 2006.
Goleeke, Thomas. *Literature for Voice: An Index of Songs in Collections and Source Book for Teachers of Singing*. Lanham, MD: Scarecrow Press, 1994.
Hall, James Husst. *The Art Song*. Norman: University of Oklahoma Press, 1953.
Kimball, Carol. *Art Song: Linking Poetry and Music*. Milwaukee, WI: Hal Leonard, 2013.
——. *Song: A Guide to Art Song Style and Literature*. Rev. ed. Milwaukee, WI: Hal Leonard, 2006.
Stevens, Denis, ed. *A History of Song*. New York: Norton, 1961.
Turnbridge, Laura. *The Song Cycle*. New York: Cambridge University Press, 2010.

German *Lieder*

Gorrell, Lorraine. *The Nineteenth-Century German Lied*. Portland, OR: Amadeus Press, 1993.
Hallmark, Rufus. *German Lieder in the Nineteenth Century*. 2nd ed. New York: Routledge, 2009.
Kramer, Lawrence. *Franz Schubert: Sexuality, Subjectivity, Song*. New York: Cambridge University Press, 2003.
Kravitt, Edward F. *The Lied: Mirror of Late Romanticism*. New Haven, CT: Yale University Press, 1996.
Malin, Yonatin. *Songs in Motion: Rhythm and Meter in the German Lied*. New York: Oxford University Press, 2010.
Parsons, James, ed. *The Cambridge Companion to the Lied*. New York: Cambridge University Press, 2004.
Stein, Deborah, and Robert Spillman. *Poetry into Song: Performance and Analysis of Lieder*. New York: Oxford University Press, 1996.
Youens, Susan. *Heinrich Heine and the Lied*. New York: Cambridge University Press, 2011.

French *Mélodies*

Barzun, Jacques. *An Essay on French Verse for Readers of English Poetry*. New York: New Directions, 1990.
Daykin, Frank. *Encyclopedia of French Art Song: Fauré, Debussy, Ravel, Poulenc*. Hillsdale, NY: Pendragon Press, 2013.
Hunter, David. *Understanding French Verse: A Guide for Singers*. New York: Oxford University Press, 2005.
Meister, Barbara. *Nineteenth-Century French Song: Fauré, Chausson, Duparc, and Debussy*. Bloomington: Indiana University Press, 1998.
Noske, Fritz. *French Song from Berlioz to Duparc*. 2nd ed. Mineola, NY: Dover Publications, 2012.

English Art Song

Pilkington, Michael. *English Solo Song: A Guide for Singers, Teachers, Librarians, and the Music Trade of Songs Currently Available*. London: Thames, 1997.

American Art Song

Carman, Judith E., William K. Gaeddert, and Rita M. Resch. *Art Song in the United States, 1759–2011: An Annotated Bibliography*. 4th ed. Lanham, MD: Scarecrow Press, 2013.
Clifton, Keith E. *Recent American Art Song*. Lanham, MD: Scarecrow Press, 2008.
Friedberg, Ruth, and Robin Fisher. *American Art Song and American Poetry*. 2nd ed. Lanham, MD: Scarecrow Press, 2012.
Villamil, Victoria Etnier. *A Singer's Guide to the American Art Song: 1870–1980*. Lanham, MD: Scarecrow Press, 2004.

Spanish and Latin American Art Song

Draayer, Suzanne. *Art Song Composers of Spain: An Encyclopedia*. Lanham, MD: Scarecrow Press, 2009.
Hoover, Maya, ed. *A Guide to the Latin American Art Song Repertoire*. Bloomington: Indiana University Press, 2010.

Individual Composers

Fischer-Dieskau, Dietrich. *Robert Schumann: Words and Music*. Translated by Reinhard G. Pauly. Portland, OR: Amadeus Press, 2003.
———. *Schubert's Songs: A Biographical Study*. Translated by Kenneth S. Whitton. Milwaukee, WI: Limelight Editions, 1984.
Foster, Beryl. *The Songs of Edvard Grieg*. Rev. ed. Rochester, NY: Boydell Press, 2007.
Miller, Richard. *Singing Schumann: An Interpretive Guide for Performers*. New York: Oxford University Press, 2005.
Moore, Gerald. *Poet's Love: The Songs and Cycles of Schumann*. London: Hamish Hamilton, 1981.
———. *The Schubert Song Cycles: With Thoughts on Performance*. London: Hamish Hamilton, 1975.
Pilkington, Michael. *Campion, Dowland, and the Lutenist Songwriters*. Bloomington: Indiana University Press, 1989.
———. *Delius, Bridge, and Somervell*. London: Thames, 1993.
———. *Gurney, Ireland, Quilter, and Warlock*. Bloomington: Indiana University Press, 1989.
———. *Purcell*. London: Thames, 1994.
Poulenc, Francis. *Diary of My Songs*. Translated by Winifred Radford. London: Kahn & Averill, 2007.

Reed, John. *The Schubert Song Companion*. London: Mandolin, 1997.

Stark, Lucien. *A Guide to the Solo Songs of Johannes Brahms*. Bloomington: Indiana University Press, 1995.

Suurpää, Lauri. *Death in "Winterreise": Musico-Poetic Associations in Schubert's Song Cycle*. Bloomington: Indiana University Press, 2013.

Wood, Vivian Lee Poates. *Poulenc's Songs: An Analysis of Style*. Oxford: University Press of Mississippi, 1979.

Youens, Susan. *Hugo Wolf: The Vocal Music*. Princeton, NJ: Princeton University Press, 1992.

——. *Hugo Wolf and His Mörike Songs*. New York: Cambridge University Press, 2006.

——. *Retracing a Winter's Journey: Schubert's "Winterreise."* Ithaca, NY: Cornell University Press, 1991.

——. *Schubert, Müller, and "Die schöne Müllerin."* New York: Cambridge University Press, 1997.

——. *Schubert's Late Lieder: Beyond the Song-Cycles*. New York: Cambridge University Press, 2002.

——. *Schubert's Poets and the Making of Lieder*. New York: Cambridge University Press, 1999.

REPERTOIRE

Boldrey, Richard. *Guide to Operatic Duets*. Redmond, WA: Caldwell, 1994.

——. *Guide to Operatic Roles and Arias*. Redmond, WA: Caldwell, 1994.

Clark, Mark Ross. *Guide to the Aria Repertoire*. Bloomington: Indiana University Press, 2007.

Coffin, Berton. *The Singer's Repertoire: Complete Edition*. Whitefish, MT: Literary Licensing, 2012.

DeVenney, David P. *The New Broadway Song Companion: An Annotated Guide to Musical Theatre Literature by Voice Type and Song Style*. 2nd ed. Lanham, MD: Scarecrow Press, 2009.

Doscher, Barbara M. *From Studio to Stage: Repertoire for the Voice*. Edited by John Nix. Lanham, MD: Scarecrow Press, 2002.

Hopkin, J. Arden. *Songs for Young Singers: An Annotated List for Developing Voices*. Lanham, MD: Scarecrow Press, 2002.

Kimball, Carol. *Art Song: Linking Poetry and Music*. Milwaukee, WI: Hal Leonard, 2013.

——. *Song: A Guide to Art Song Style and Literature*. Rev. ed. Milwaukee, WI: Hal Leonard, 2006.

Ord, Alan J. *Songs for Bass Voice: An Annotated Guide to Works for Bass Voice*. Lanham, MD: Scarecrow Press, 1994.

Singher, Martial. *An Interpretive Guide to Operatic Arias: A Handbook for Singers, Coaches, Teachers, and Students*. State College: Penn State University Press, 2003.

COLLABORATION

Katz, Martin. *The Complete Collaborator: The Pianist as Partner.* New York: Oxford University Press, 2009.

Moore, Gerald. *Am I Too Loud? Memoirs of an Accompanist.* London: Hamish Hamilton, 1962.

———. *Singer and Accompanist: The Performance of Fifty Songs.* Waterville, ME: Thorndike Press, 2008. Reprint of 1953 publication.

———. *The Unashamed Accompanist.* 2nd ed. London: Julia MacRae Books, 1990.

OPERA

Abbate, Carolyn. *In Search of Opera.* Princeton, NJ: Princeton University Press, 2003.

Abbate, Carolyn, and Roger Parker. *A History of Opera.* New York: Norton, 2012.

Batta, Andras. *Opera: Composers, Works, Performers.* Potsdam, Germany: H. F. Ullman, 2012.

Charlton, David, ed. *The Cambridge Companion to Grand Opera.* New York: Cambridge University Press, 2003.

Clark, Mark Ross. *Singing, Acting, and Moving in Opera: A Guide to Singer-getics.* Bloomington: Indiana University Press, 2009.

Cooke, Mervyn, ed. *The Cambridge Companion to Twentieth-Century Opera.* New York: Cambridge University Press, 2006.

DelDonna, Anthony R., and Pierpaolo Polzonetti, eds. *The Cambridge Companion to Eighteenth-Century Opera.* New York: Cambridge University Press, 2009.

Grout, Donald J., and Hermine Weigel Williams. *A Short History of Opera.* 4th ed. New York: Columbia University Press, 2003.

Helgot, Daniel. *The Third Line: The Opera Performer as Interpreter.* New York: Schirmer Books, 1993.

Kloiber, Rudolf, Wulf Konold, and Robert Maschka. *Handbuch der Oper.* Munich: Bärenreiter-Verlag Kassel, 1985.

Macy, Laura. *The Grove Book of Opera Singers.* New York: Oxford University Press, 2008.

Sadie, Stanley, and Laura Macy. *The Grove Book of Operas.* New York: Oxford University Press, 2009.

Simon, Henry W. *100 Great Operas and Their Stories: Act-by-Act Synopses.* New York: Anchor Books, 1989.

Stanislavski, Constantin. *Stanislavski on Opera.* New York: Theatre Arts Books, 1975.

Till, Nicholas, ed. *The Cambridge Companion to Opera Studies.* New York: Cambridge University Press, 2012.

OPERA DIRECTING

Cathcart, Kathryn, and Willene Gunn. *Teaching Opera: The Role of the Opera Workshop with Scene Catalog.* Geneseo, NY: Leyerle, 2008.

Eaton, Quaintance. *Opera Production: A Handbook*. Minneapolis: University of Minnesota Press, 1961.

Eaton, Quaintance, and Randolph Mickelson. *Opera Production II: A Handbook*. Minneapolis: University of Minnesota Press, 1974.

Gerbrandt, Carl. *Sacred Music Drama: The Producer's Guide*. 2nd ed. Bloomington, IN: AuthorHouse, 2006.

Goldovsky, Boris. *Bringing Opera to Life: Operatic Acting and Stage Direction*. Upper Saddle River, NJ: Pearson-Prentice Hall, 1968.

Goldovsky, Boris, and Arthur Schoep. *Bringing Soprano Arias to Life*. Lanham, MD: Scarecrow Press, 1990.

Summers, Franklin W. *Operas in One Act: A Production Guide*. Lanham, MD: Scarecrow Press, 1996.

LIGHT OPERA

Bordman, Gerald. *American Operetta: From "HMS Pinafore" to "Sweeney Todd."* New York: Oxford University Press, 1981.

Bradley, Ian. *The Complete Annotated Gilbert and Sullivan*. New York: Oxford University Press, 1996.

———. *O Joy! O Rapture! The Enduring Phenomenon of Gilbert and Sullivan*. New York: Oxford University Press, 2005.

Eden, David, and Meinhard Saremba, eds. *The Cambridge Companion to Gilbert and Sullivan*. New York: Cambridge University Press, 2009.

Traubner, Richard. *Operetta: A Theatrical Study*. New York: Routledge, 2003.

Williams, Carolyn. *Gilbert and Sullivan: Gender, Genre, Parody*. New York: Columbia University Press, 2011.

Wren, Gayden. *A Most Ingenious Paradox: The Art of Gilbert and Sullivan*. New York: Oxford University Press, 2001.

CHORAL MUSIC AND ENSEMBLE SINGING

Blocker, Robert, ed. *The Robert Shaw Reader*. New Haven, CT: Yale University Press, 2004.

Dürr, Alfred. *The Cantatas of J. S. Bach: With Their Librettos in German-English Parallel Text*. Translations by Richard D. P. Jones. New York: Oxford University Press, 2006.

Emmons, Shirlee, and Constance Chase. *Prescriptions for Choral Excellence*. New York: Oxford University Press, 1996.

Garretson, Robert L. *Choral Music: History, Style, and Performance Practice*. Upper Saddle River, NJ: Pearson-Prentice Hall, 1993.

Green, Jonathan D. *A Guide to the Choral-Orchestral Works of Johann Sebastian Bach*. Lanham, MD: Scarecrow Press, 2000.

Jeffers, Ron. *Translations and Annotations of Choral Repertoire*. Vol. 1, *Sacred Latin Texts*. Corvallis, OR: Earthsongs, 1988.

Jeffers, Ron, and Gordon Paine. *Translations and Annotations of Choral Repertoire*. Vol. 2, *German Texts*. Corvallis, OR: Earthsongs, 2000.

Jordan, James, and Matthew Mehaffey. *Choral Ensemble Intonation*. Chicago: GIA Publications, 2001.

Mussulman, Joseph A. *Dear People . . . Robert Shaw*. 2nd ed. Chapel Hill, NC: Hinshaw Music, 1996.

Nash, Ethan, and Joshua Jacobson. *Translations and Annotations of Choral Repertoire*. Vol. 4, *Hebrew Texts*. Corvallis, OR: Earthsongs, 2009.

Paine, Gordon. *Translations and Annotations of Choral Repertoire*. Vol. 3, *French and Italian Texts*. Corvallis, OR: Earthsongs, 2007.

Quadros, André de, ed. *The Cambridge Companion to Choral Music*. New York: Cambridge University Press, 2012.

Robinson, Ray, ed. *Choral Music: A Norton Historical Anthology*. New York: Norton, 1978.

Shrock, Dennis. *Choral Repertoire*. New York: Oxford University Press, 2009.

Steinberg, Michael. *Choral Masterworks: A Listener's Guide*. New York: Oxford University Press, 2005.

Strimple, Nick. *Choral Music in the Nineteenth Century*. Portland, OR: Amadeus Press, 2008.

———. *Choral Music in the Twentieth Century*. Portland, OR: Amadeus Press, 2002.

CLASS VOICE

Christy, Van Ambrose, and John Glenn Paton. *Foundations in Singing: A Basic Textbook in Vocal Technique and Song Interpretation*. 5th ed. New York: William C. Brown, 1990.

Dayme, Maribeth, and Cynthia Vaughn. *The Singing Book*. 3rd ed. New York: Norton, 2014.

Schmidt, Jan, and Heidi Counsell Schmidt. *Basics of Singing*. 6th ed. Clifton Park, NY: Cengage Learning, 2007.

Ware, Clifton. *Adventures in Singing: A Process for Exploring, Discovering, and Developing Vocal Potential*. 4th ed. New York: McGraw-Hill, 2007.

PERFORMANCE PRACTICE

Donington, Robert. *Baroque Music: Style and Performance: A Handbook*. New York: Norton, 1982.

———. *The Interpretation of Early Music*. New rev. ed. New York: Norton, 2008.

Duffin, Ross W. *How Equal Temperament Ruined Harmony (and Why You Should Care)*. New York: Norton, 2008.

Elliott, Martha. *Singing in Style: A Guide to Vocal Performance Practices*. New Haven, CT: Yale University Press, 2006.

McGee, Timothy J., A. G. Rigg, and David N. Klausner. *Singing Early Music: The Pronunciation of European Languages in the Late Middle Ages and the Renaissance*. Bloomington: Indiana University Press, 1996.

Neumann, Frederick. *Ornamentation in Baroque and Post-baroque Music*. Princeton, NJ: Princeton University Press, 1983.

NEW MUSIC

Mabry, Sharon. *Exploring Twentieth-Century Vocal Music: A Practical Guide to Innovations in Performance and Repertoire*. New York: Oxford University Press, 2002.

Manning, Jane. *New Vocal Repertory: An Introduction*. New York: Oxford University Press, 1994.

———. *New Vocal Repertory*. Vol. 2. New York: Oxford University Press, 1999.

CHAMBER MUSIC

Klaus, Kenneth S. *Chamber Music for Solo Voice and Instruments, 1960–1989: An Annotated Guide*. Berkeley, CA: Fallen Leaf Press, 1994.

Winchester, Barbara, and Kay Dunlap. *Vocal Chamber Music: A Performer's Guide*. 2nd ed. New York: Routledge, 2008.

CHURCH MUSIC

Daw, Carl P., Jr., and Thomas Pavlechko. *Liturgical Music for the Revised Common Lectionary: Year A*. New York: Church Publishing, 2009.

———. *Liturgical Music for the Revised Common Lectionary: Year B*. New York: Church Publishing, 2009.

———. *Liturgical Music for the Revised Common Lectionary: Year C*. New York: Church Publishing, 2009.

Laster, James. *Catalogue of Choral Music Arranged in Biblical Order*. 2nd ed. Lanham, MD: Scarecrow Press, 1996.

———. *Catalogue of Choral Music Arranged in Biblical Order: Supplement*. Lanham, MD: Scarecrow Press, 2002.

MUSIC PSYCHOLOGY

Green, Barry, with W. Timothy Gallwey. *The Inner Game of Music*. New York: Doubleday, 1986.

Hallam, Susan, Ian Cross, and Michael Thaut, eds. *The Oxford Handbook of Music Psychology*. New York: Oxford University Press, 2009.

Hemsley, Thomas. *Singing and Imagination: A Human Approach to a Great Musical Tradition.* New York: Oxford University Press, 1998.

Honing, Henkjan. *Musical Cognition: A Science of Listening.* Newark, NJ: Transaction Publishers, 2011.

Huron, David. *Sweet Anticipation: The Music and the Psychology of Expectation.* Cambridge, MA: MIT Press, 2008.

Jourdain, Robert. *Music, the Brain, and Ecstasy: How Music Captures Our Imagination.* New York: William Morrow, 2008.

Levitan, Daniel J. *This Is Your Brain on Music: The Science of a Human Obsession.* New York: Plume, 2007.

———. *The World in Six Songs: How the Musical Brain Created Human Nature.* New York: Plume, 2009.

Meyer, Leonard B. *Emotion and Meaning in Music.* Chicago: University of Chicago Press, 1961.

Parncutt, Richard, and Gary E. McPherson. *The Science and Psychology of Music Performance.* New York: Oxford University Press, 2002.

Patel, Aniruddh D. *Music, Language, and the Brain.* New York: Oxford University Press, 2010.

Sacks, Oliver. *Musicophilia: Tales of Music and the Brain.* Revised and expanded ed. New York: Vintage Books, 2008.

Storr, Anthony. *Music and the Mind.* New York: Ballantine Books, 1993.

Thompson, William Forde. *Music, Thought, and Feeling: Understanding the Psychology of Music.* New York: Oxford University Press, 2008.

Williamson, Aaron. *Musical Excellence: Strategies and Techniques to Enhance Performance.* New York: Oxford University Press, 2004.

Zbikowski, Lawrence M. *Conceptualizing Music: Cognitive Structure, Theory, and Analysis.* New York: Oxford University Press, 2005.

INSPIRATION

Cameron, Julia. *The Artist's Way.* New York: G. P. Putnam's Sons, 1992.

Dayme, Meribeth Bunch. *The Performer's Voice: Realizing Your Vocal Potential.* New York: Norton, 2005.

Edwards, Betty. *Drawing on the Right Side of the Brian.* 4th ed. New York: Tarcher, 2012.

Emmons, Shirlee, and Alma Thomas. *Power Performance for Singers: Transcending the Barriers.* New York: Oxford University Press, 1998.

Eustis, Lynn. *The Singer's Ego: Finding a Balance between Life and Music.* Chicago: GIA Publications, 2005.

———. *The Teacher's Ego: When Singers Become Voice Teachers.* Chicago: GIA Publications, 2012.

Fleming, Renée. *The Inner Voice: The Making of a Singer.* London: Penguin Books, 2005.

Gawain, Shakti. *Creative Visualization: Use the Power of Your Imagination to Create What You Want in Your Life.* 25th anniversary ed. San Francisco: New World Library, 2002.

———. *Creative Visualization Workbook.* 2nd ed. San Francisco: New World Library, 1995.
Herrigel, Eugen. *Zen in the Art of Archery.* New York: Random House, 1953/1981.
Jordan, James. *The Musician's Soul.* Chicago: GIA Publications, 1999.
———. *The Musician's Spirit: Connecting to Others through Story.* Chicago: GIA Publications, 2002.
———. *The Musician's Walk: An Ethical Labyrinth.* Chicago: GIA Publications, 2005.
Jordan, James, Mark Moliterno, and Nova Thomas. *The Musician's Breath: The Role of Breathing in Human Expression.* Chicago: GIA Publications, 2011.
Jordan, James, Nova Thomas, and James Conlon. *The Art of Being for Musicians, Actors, Dancers, and Teachers.* Chicago: GIA Publications, 2010.
Langer, Ellen J. *On Becoming an Artist: Reinventing Yourself through Mindful Creativity.* New York: Ballantine Books, 2005.
Mabry, Sharon. *The Performing Life: A Singer's Guide to Survival.* Lanham, MD: Scarecrow Press, 2012.
Norman, Jessye. *Stand Up Straight and Sing!* Boston: Houghton Mifflin, 2014.
Ristad, Eloise. *A Soprano on Her Head: Right-Side-Up Reflections on Life and Other Performances.* Moab, UT: Real People Press, 1982.
Ware, Clifton. *The Singer's Life: Goals and Roles.* St. Paul, MN: Birch Grove, 2005.

THE BUSINESS

Beeching, Angela Myles. *Beyond Talent: Creating a Successful Career in Music.* 2nd ed. New York: Oxford University Press, 2010.
Dornemann, Joan, and Maria Ciaccia. *Complete Preparation: A Guide to Auditioning for Opera.* Tucson, AZ: Excalibur, 1992.
Legge, Anthony, and Trevor Ford. *The Art of Auditioning: A Handbook for Singers, Accompanists, and Coaches.* London: Rhinegold, 1988.
Lenson, Benny, Dorothy Maddison, and Gail Sullivan. *Kein' Angst, Baby! A Singer's Guide to German Auditions in the 1990s.* London: Rhinegold, 1994.
Mabry, Sharon. *The Performing Life: A Singer's Guide to Survival.* Lanham, MD: Scarecrow Press, 2012.
Shepard, Philip, and Sarah Kristine Schäfer. *What the Fach?! The Definitive Guide for Opera Singers Auditioning and Working in Germany, Austria and Switzerland.* 2nd ed. Seattle, WA: CreateSpace Independent Publishing Platform, 2010.
Tindall, Blair. *"Mozart in the Jungle": Sex, Drugs, and Classical Music.* New York: Grove Press, 2006.
Williams, Janet. *Nail Your Next Audition: The Ultimate 30-Day Guide for Singers.* New York: Performance Enhancement by Design, 2006.

GREAT SINGERS

Blyth, Alan. *Song on Record.* Vol. 1. New York: Cambridge University Press, 1986.
———. *Song on Record.* Vol. 2. New York: Cambridge University Press, 1988.

Hines, Jerome. *Great Singers on Great Singing*. 7th ed. Milwaukee, WI: Limelight Editions, 2004.
Matheolpoulos, Helena. *Diva: Great Sopranos and Mezzos Discuss Their Art*. Boston: Northeastern University Press, 1992.
——. *Divo: Great Tenors, Baritones, and Basses Discuss Their Roles*. New York: Harper Collins, 1986.
Pleasants, Henry. *The Great American Popular Singers: Their Lives, Careers, and Art*. Rev. ed. New York: Simon & Schuster, 1985.
——. *The Great Singers: From Jenny Lind and Caruso to Callas and Pavarotti*. Rev. ed. Minnetonka, MN: Olympic Marketing Corporation, 1985.
Steane, J. B. *The Grand Tradition: Seventy Years of Singing on Record*. 2nd ed. Portland, OR: Amadeus Press, 1993.
——. *Singers of the Century*. Vol. 1. Portland, OR: Amadeus Press, 1996.
——. *Singers of the Century*. Vol. 2. Portland, OR: Amadeus Press, 2003.
——. *Singers of the Century*. Vol. 3. Portland, OR: Amadeus Press, 2003.
——. *Voices, Singers, and Critics*. Portland, OR: Amadeus Press, 2002.
Villamil, Victoria Etnier. *From Johnson's Kids to Lemonade Opera: The American Classical Singer Comes of Age*. Boston: Northeastern University Press, 2004.

MUSIC HISTORY

General

Burkholder, J. Peter, Donald J. Grout, Claude V. Palisca. *A History of Western Music*. Eighth Edition. New York: Norton, 2009.
Burkholder, J. Peter, and Claude V. Palisca. *Norton Anthology of Western Music*. Vol. 1, *Ancient to Baroque*. 6th ed. New York: Norton, 2009.
——. *Norton Anthology of Western Music*. Vol. 2, *Classic to Romantic*. 6th ed. New York: Norton, 2009.
——. *Norton Anthology of Western Music*. Vol. 3, *Twentieth Century*. 6th ed. New York: Norton, 2009.
Taruskin, Richard. *The Oxford History of Western Music*. Vol. 1, *Music from the Earliest Notations to the Sixteenth Century*. New York: Oxford University Press, 2005.
——. *The Oxford History of Western Music*. Vol. 2, *Music in the Seventeenth and Eighteenth Centuries*. New York: Oxford University Press, 2005.
——. *The Oxford History of Western Music*. Vol. 3, *Music in the Nineteenth Century*. New York: Oxford University Press, 2005.
——. *The Oxford History of Western Music*. Vol. 4, *Music in the Early Twentieth Century*. New York: Oxford University Press, 2005.
——. *The Oxford History of Western Music*. Vol. 5, *Music in the Late Twentieth Century*. New York: Oxford University Press, 2005.

Medieval

Everist, Mark. *The Cambridge Companion to Medieval Music*. New York: Cambridge University Press, 2011.

Fassler, Margot. *Anthology for Music in the Medieval West*. New York: Norton, 2013.
———. *Music in the Medieval West*. New York: Norton, 2013.
Haines, John. *Medieval Song in Romance Languages*. New York: Cambridge University Press, 2010.
Hoppin, Richard H. *Anthology of Medieval Music*. New York: Norton, 1978.
———. *Medieval Music*. New York: Norton, 1978.
Yudkin, Jeremy. *Music in Medieval Europe*. Upper Saddle River, NJ: Pearson-Prentice Hall, 1989.

Renaissance

Atlas, Allan W. *Anthology of Renaissance Music: Music in Western Europe, 1400–1600*. New York: Norton, 1998.
———. *Renaissance Music: Music in Western Europe, 1400–1600*. New York: Norton, 1998.
Brown, Howard M. *Music in the Renaissance*. Upper Saddle River, NJ: Pearson-Prentice Hall, 1976.
Freedman, Richard. *Anthology for Music in the Renaissance*. New York: Norton, 2013.
———. *Music in the Renaissance*. New York: Norton, 2013.

Baroque

Heller, Wendy. *Anthology for Music in the Baroque*. New York: Norton, 2013.
———. *Music in the Baroque*. New York: Norton, 2013.
Hill, John Walter. *Anthology of Baroque Music*. New York: Norton, 2005.
———. *Baroque Music: Music in Western Europe, 1580–1750*. New York: Norton, 2005.

Classical

Downs, Philip G. *Anthology of Classical Music*. New York: Norton, 1992.
———. *Classical Music: The Era of Haydn, Mozart, and Beethoven*. New York: Norton, 1992.
Pauly, Reinhard G. *Music in the Classic Period*. Upper Saddle River, NJ: Pearson-Prentice Hall, 1973.
Ratner, Leonard G. *Classic Music: Expression, Form, and Style*. New York: Schirmer Books, 1985.
Rice, John A. *Anthology for Music in the Eighteenth Century*. New York: Norton, 2012.
———. *Music in the Eighteenth Century*. New York: Norton, 2012.
Till, Nicholas. *Mozart and the Enlightenment: Truth, Virtue, and Beauty in Mozart's Operas*. New York: Norton, 1996.

Romantic

Frisch, Walter. *Anthology for Music in the Nineteenth Century*. New York: Norton, 2012.
———. *Music in the Nineteenth Century*. New York: Norton, 2012.

Longyear, Rey M. *Nineteenth-Century Romanticism in Music*. Upper Saddle River, NJ: Pearson-Prentice Hall, 1988.

Plantinga, Leon. *Anthology of Romantic Music*. New York: Norton, 1985.

———. *Romantic Music*. New York: Norton, 1985.

Modern

Auner, Joseph. *Anthology for Music in the Twentieth and Twenty-First Centuries*. New York: Norton, 2013.

———. *Music in the Twentieth and Twenty-First Centuries*. New York: Norton, 2013.

Morgan, Robert P. *Anthology of Twentieth-Century Music*. New York: Norton, 1991.

———. *Twentieth-Century Music*. New York: Norton, 1991.

Ross, Alex. *Listen to This*. New York: Farrar, Straus and Giroux, 2010.

———. *The Rest Is Noise: Listening to the Twentieth Century*. New York: Picador Books, 2008.

Salzman, Eric. *Twentieth-Century Music: An Introduction*. Upper Saddle River, NJ: Pearson-Prentice Hall, 2001.

MUSIC THEORY AND SIGHT-SINGING

Aldwell, Edward, Carl Schachter, and Allen Cadwallader. *Harmony and Voice Leading*. 4th ed. Clifton Park, NY: Cengage Learning, 2010.

Bell, John, and Steven R. Chicurel. *Music Theory for Musical Theatre*. Lanham, MD: Scarecrow Press, 2008.

Cadwallader, Allen, and David Gagné. *Analysis of Tonal Music: A Schenkerian Approach*. 3rd ed. New York: Oxford University Press, 2010.

Chafe, Eric. *Analyzing Bach Cantatas*. New York: Oxford University Press, 2003.

Christensen, Thomas, ed. *The Cambridge History of Western Music Theory*. New York: Cambridge University Press, 2002.

Clendinning, Jane Piper, and Elizabeth West Marvin. *The Musician's Guide to Theory and Analysis*. 2nd ed. New York: Norton, 2010.

Edlund, Lars. *Modus Novus: Studies in Reading Atonal Melodies*. Wappingers Falls, NY: Beekman Books, 1964.

———. *Modus Vetus: Sight Singing and Ear-Training in Major/Minor Tonality*. Wappingers Falls, NY: Beekman Books, 1963.

Gauldin, Robert. *A Practical Approach to Eighteenth-Century Counterpoint*. Long Grove, IL: Waveland Press, 1995.

———. *A Practical Approach to Sixteenth-Century Counterpoint*. Long Grove, IL: Waveland Press, 1995.

Hindemith, Paul. *Elementary Training for Musicians*. 2nd ed. Mainz, Germany: B. Schott's, 1984.

Kennan, Kent. *Counterpoint*. 4th ed. Upper Saddle River, NJ: Pearson-Prentice Hall, 1998.

Laitz, Steven G. *The Complete Musician: An Integrated Approach to Tonal Theory, Analysis, and Listening*. 3rd ed. New York: Oxford University Press, 2011.

Manoff, Tom. *The Music Kit*. 4th ed. New York: Norton, 2001.

Ottman, Robert W., and Nancy Rogers. *Music for Sight Singing*. 8th ed. Upper Saddle River, NJ: Pearson-Prentice Hall, 2010.

Salzer, Felix, and Carl Schachter. *Counterpoint in Composition: The Study of Voice Leading*. New York: Columbia University Press, 1989.

Stein, Deborah, ed. *Engaging Music: Essays in Music Analysis*. New York: Oxford University Press, 2004.

Stein, Deborah, and Robert Spillman. *Poetry into Song: Performance and Analysis of Lieder*. New York: Oxford University Press, 1996.

Straus, Joseph N. *Introduction to Post-tonal Theory*. 3rd ed. Upper Saddle River, NJ: Pearson-Prentice Hall, 2004.

Temperley, David. *The Cognition of Basic Musical Structures*. Cambridge, MA: MIT Press, 2004.

——. *Music and Probability*. Cambridge, MA: MIT Press, 2010.

CCM PEDAGOGY

Borch Zangger, Daniel. *Ultimate Vocal Voyage*. New York: Hal Leonard, 2008.

Edwards, Matthew. *So You Want to Sing Rock 'n' Roll: A Guide for Professionals*. Lanham, MD: Rowman & Littlefield, 2014.

Edwin, Robert. "Apples and Oranges: Belting Revisited." *Journal of Singing* 57, no. 2 (November 2000): 43–44.

——. "Belting 101." *Journal of Singing* 55, no. 1 (September 1998): 53–55.

——. "Belt Yourself." *Journal of Singing* 60, no. 3 (January 2004): 285–88.

——. "A Broader Broadway." *Journal of Singing* 59, no. 5 (May 2003): 431–32.

LeBorgne, Wendy Lynn DeLeo. "Defining the Belt Voice: Perceptual Judgments and Objective Measures." PhD diss., University of Cincinnati, 2001.

LoVetri, Jeannette. "Contemporary Commercial Music: More than One Way to Use the Vocal Tract." *Journal of Singing* 58, no. 3 (January 2002): 249–52.

——. "Female Chest Voice." *Journal of Singing* 60, no. 2 (November 2003): 161–64.

——. "Who's Minding the Store?" *Journal of Singing* 59, no. 4 (March 2003): 345–46.

McCoy, Scott. "A Classical Pedagogue Explores Belting." *Journal of Singing* 63, no. 5 (May 2007): 545–49.

Nix, John. "Criteria for Selecting Repertoire." *Journal of Singing* 58, no. 3 (January 2002): 217–221.

Popeil, Lisa. "Comparing Belt and Classical Techniques Using MRU and Video-Fluoroscopy." *Journal of Singing* 56, no. 2 (November 1999): 27–29.

——. "The Multiplicity of Belting." *Journal of Singing* 64, no. 1 (September 2007): 77–80.

Titze, Ingo. "Belting and a High Larynx Position." *Journal of Singing* 63, no. 5 (May 2007): 557–58.

MUSICAL THEATRE

Alper, Steven M. *Next! Auditioning for Musical Theatre*. Portsmouth, NH: Heinemann, 1995.

Bell, Jeffrey E. "American Musical Theatre Songs in the Undergraduate Vocal Studio: A Survey of Current Practice, Guidelines for Repertoire Selection, and Pedagogical Analysis of Selected Songs." DMA diss., Ball State University, 1996.

Bloom, Ken. *The Routledge Guide to Broadway*. New York: Routledge, 2006.

Blumenfield, Robert. *Blumenfield's Dictionary of Musical Theater*. Milwaukee, WI: Limelight Editions, 2010.

Bordman, Gerald. *American Musical Comedy: From "Adonis" to "Dreamgirls."* New York: Oxford University Press, 1982.

———. *American Musical Revue: From "The Passing Show" to "Sugar Babies."* New York: Oxford University Press, 1985.

Burdick, Barbara. "Vocal Techniques for Music Theater: The High School and Undergraduate Singer." *Journal of Singing* 61, no. 3 (January 2005): 261–268.

DeVenney, David P. *The New Broadway Song Companion: An Annotated Guide to Musical Theatre Literature by Voice Type and Song Style*. 2nd ed. Lanham, MD: Scarecrow Press, 2009.

Edwin, Robert. "Contemporary Music Theater: Louder than Words." *Journal of Singing* 61, no. 3 (January 2005): 291.

Everett, William A., and Paul R. Laird. *Historical Dictionary of the Broadway Musical*. Lanham, MD: Scarecrow Press, 2008.

Forte, Allen. *The American Popular Ballad of the Golden Era: 1925–1950*. Princeton, NJ: Princeton University Press, 1995.

———. *Listening to Classic American Popular Songs*. New Haven, CT: Yale University Press, 2001.

Green, Stanley. *Broadway Musicals Show by Show*. 7th ed. Revised and updated by Cary Ginell. New York: Applause, 2011.

Hall, Karen. *So You Want to Sing Music Theater: A Guide for Professionals*. Lanham, MD: Rowman & Littlefield, 2014.

Hischak, Thomas S. *Off-Broadway Musicals since 1919: From "Greenwich Village Follies" to "The Toxic Avenger."* Lanham, MD: Scarecrow Press, 2011.

———. *The Oxford Companion to the American Musical: Theatre, Film, and Television*. New York: Oxford University Press, 2008.

Melton, Joan. *Singing in Musical Theatre: The Training of Singers and Actors*. New York: Allworth Press, 2007.

Miller, D. A. *Place for Us: Essay on the Broadway Musical*. Cambridge, MA: Harvard University Press, 1998.

Mordden, Ethan. *Beautiful Mornin': The Broadway Musical of the 1940s*. New York: Oxford University Press, 1999.

———. *Coming Up Roses: The Broadway Musical of the 1950s*. New York: Oxford University Press, 2000.

———. *The Happiest Corpse I've Ever Seen: The Last Twenty-Five Years of the Broadway Musical*. New York: Palgrave Macmillan, 2004.
———. *Make Believe: The Broadway Musical of the 1920s*. New York: Oxford University Press, 1997.
———. *One More Kiss: The Broadway Musical of the 1970s*. New York: Palgrave Macmillan, 2004.
———. *Open a New Window: The Broadway Musical of the 1960s*. New York: Palgrave Macmillan, 2002.
———. *Sing for Your Supper: The Broadway Musical of the 1930s*. New York: Palgrave Macmillan, 2005.
Sondheim, Stephen. *Finishing the Hat: Collected Lyrics (1954–1981) with Attendant Comments, Principles, Heresies, Grudges, Whines, and Anecdotes*. New York: Alfred A. Knopf, 2010.
———. *Look, I Made a Hat: Collected Lyrics (1981–2011) with Attendant Comments, Amplifications, Dogmas, Harangues, Digressions, Anecdotes, and Miscellany*. New York: Alfred A. Knopf, 2011.
Spivey, Norman. "Music Theatre Singing . . . Let's Talk. Part 1: On the Relationship of Speech and Singing." *Journal of Singing* 64, no. 4 (March 2008): 483–489.
———. "Music Theater Singing . . . Let's Talk. Part 2: Examining the Debate on Belting." *Journal of Singing* 64, no. 5 (May 2008): 607–11.
Stempel, Larry. *Showtime: A History of the Broadway Musical Theater*. New York: Norton, 2010.
Wolf, Stacy. *A Problem like Maria: Gender and Sexuality in the American Musical*. Ann Arbor: University of Michigan Press, 2002.

OTHER STYLES

American and Roots Genres

Averill, Gage. *Four Parts, No Waiting: A Social History of American Barbershop Harmony*. New York: Oxford University Press, 2003.
Cohen, Norm. *Ethnic and Border Music: A Regional Exploration*. Westport, CT: Greenwood Press, 2007.
———. *Folk Music: A Regional Exploration*. Westport, CT: Greenwood Press, 2005.
Cohen, Ronald. *Folk Music: The Basics*. New York: Routledge, 2006.
Crawford, Richard, and Larry Hamberlin. *An Introduction to America's Music*. 2nd ed. New York: Norton, 2012.
LeBlanc, Eric. *Blues: A Regional Exploration*. Westport, CT: Greenwood Press, 2013.
Malone, Bill C., and Jocelyn R. Neal. *Country Music, USA*. 3rd ed. Austin: University of Texas Press, 2010.
Tribe, Evan. *Country: A Regional Exploration*. Westport, CT: Greenwood Press, 2006.
Wiessman, Dick. *Blues: The Basics*. New York: Routledge, 2004.

Rock Genres

Campbell, Michael. *Popular Music in America: The Beat Goes On*. 3rd ed. Clifton Park, NY: Cengage Learning, 2008.

Campbell, Michael, and James Brody. *Rock and Roll: An Introduction*. 2nd ed. Clifton Park, NY: Cengage Learning, 2007.

Charlton, Katherine. *Rock Music Styles: A History*. 6th ed. New York: McGraw-Hill, 2010.

Covach, John, and Andrew Flory. *What's That Sound? An Introduction to Rock and Its History*. 3rd ed. New York: Norton, 2012.

Jones, Timothy, and James McIntosh. *Rock 'n' Roll: Origins and Innovators*. Dubuque, IA: Kendall Hunt, 2009.

Robins, Wayne. *A Brief History of Rock, Off the Record*. New York: Routledge, 2007.

Stuessy, Joe, and Scott D. Lipscomb. *Rock and Roll: Its History and Development*. 6th ed. Upper Saddle River, NJ: Pearson-Prentice Hall, 2008.

Walser, Robert. *Running with the Devil: Power, Gender, and Madness in Heavy Metal Music*. Middletown, CT: Wesleyan University Press, 1993.

Jazz

Gioia, Ted. *The History of Jazz*. 2nd ed. New York: Oxford University Press, 2011.

———. *The Jazz Standards: A Guide to the Repertoire*. New York: Oxford University Press, 2012.

Gridley, Mark C. *Jazz Styles: History and Analysis*. 10th ed. Upper Saddle River, NJ: Pearson-Prentice Hall, 2008.

Meeder, Christopher. *Jazz: The Basics*. New York: Routledge, 2007.

Megill, Donald D., and Richard S. Demory. *Introduction to Jazz History*. 6th ed. Upper Saddle River, NJ: Pearson-Prentice Hall, 2003.

Shapiro, Jan. *So You Want to Sing Jazz: A Guide for Professionals*. Lanham, MD: Rowman & Littlefield, 2015.

Walser, Robert. *Keeping Time: Readings in Jazz History*. New York: Oxford University Press, 1998.

Whitehead, Kevin. *Why Jazz? A Concise Guide*. New York: Oxford University Press, 2011.

Yanow, Scott. *Jazz: A Regional Exploration*. Westport, CT: Greenwood Press, 2005.

World Music

Alves, William. *Music of the Peoples of the World*. 2nd ed. Clifton Park, NY: Cengage Learning, 2008.

Bakan, Michael. *World Music: Traditions and Transformations*. New York: McGraw-Hill, 2011.

Miller, Terry E., and Andrew Shahriari. *World Music: A Global Journey*. 3rd ed. New York: Routledge, 2012.

Nettl, Bruno, Thomas Turino, Isabel K. F. Won, and Charles Capwell. *Excursions in World Music*. 5th ed. Upper Saddle River, NJ: Pearson-Prentice Hall, 2007.

Nidel, Richard O. *World Music: The Basics*. New York: Routledge, 2005.

Titon, Jeff Todd, ed. *Worlds of Music: An Introduction to the Music of the World's Peoples*. Clifton Park, NY: Cengage Learning, 2008.

Wald, Elijah. *Global Minstrels: Voices of World Music*. New ed. New York: Routledge, 2006.

BODYWORK

General

Conable, Barbara. *The Structures and Movement of Breathing: A Primer for Choirs and Choruses*. Chicago: GIA Publications, 2000.

Dimon, Theodore. *Your Body, Your Voice: The Key to Natural Singing and Speaking*. Berkeley, CA: North Atlantic Books, 2011.

Malde, Melissa, Mary Jean Allen, and Kurt-Alexander Zeller. *What Every Singer Needs to Know About the Body*. 2nd ed. San Diego, CA: Plural, 2012.

Alexander Technique

Alcantara, Pedro de. *The Alexander Technique: A Skill for Life*. Marlborough, UK: Crowood, 1999.

——. *Indirect Procedures: A Musician's Guide to the Alexander Technique*. Oxford: Clarendon, 1997.

Alexander, F. Matthias, and Edward Maisel. *The Alexander Technique: The Essential Writings of F. Matthias Alexander*. London: Thames and Hudson, 1990.

Conable, Barbara, and William Conable. *How to Learn the Alexander Technique: A Manual for Students*. Columbus, OH: Andover, 1995.

Gelb, Michael. *Body Learning: An Introduction to the Alexander Technique*. New York: Holt, 1995.

Harer, John B., and Sharon Munden. *The Alexander Technique Resource Book*. Lanham, MD: Scarecrow Press, 2008.

Heirich, Jane Ruby. *Voice and the Alexander Technique*. 2nd ed. Berkeley, CA: Mornum Time Press, 2011.

Jones, Frank Pierce. *Freedom to Change: The Development and Science of the Alexander Technique*. London: Mouritz, 1997.

Jones, Frank Pierce, Theodore Dimon, and Richard A. Brown. *Frank Pierce Jones: Collected Writings on the Alexander Technique*. Cambridge, MA: Alexander Technique Archives, 1998.

McEvenue, Kelly, and Patsy Rodenburg. *The Actor and the Alexander Technique*. New York: Palgrave Macmillan, 2006.

Nettl-Fiol, Rebecca, and Luc Vanier. *Dance and the Alexander Technique: Exploring the Missing Link.* Urbana: University of Illinois Press, 2011.

Vineyard, Missy. *How You Stand, How You Move, How You Live: Learning the Alexander Technique to Explore Your Mind-Body Connection and Achieve Self-Mastery.* New York: Marlowe & Sons, 2007.

Feldenkrais

Feldenkrais, Moshé. *Awareness through Movement: Easy-to-Do Health Exercises to Improve Your Posture, Vision, Imagination, and Personal Awareness.* New York: HarperOne, 2009.

———. *Body Awareness as Healing Therapy: The Case of Nora.* 2nd ed. Berkeley, CA: Frog Books, 1993.

———. *The Elusive Obvious; or, Basic Feldenkrais.* Soquel, CA: Meta Publications, 1981.

———. *Embodied Wisdom: The Collected Papers of Moshé Feldenkrais.* Edited by Elizabeth Beringer. Berkeley, CA: North Atlantic Books, 2010.

———. *The Potent Self: A Study of Spontaneity and Compulsion.* Berkeley, CA: Frog Books, 2002.

Nelson, Samuel H., and Elizabeth Blades-Zeller. *Singing with Your Whole Self: The Feldenkrais Method and Voice.* Lanham, MD: Scarecrow Press, 2002.

Yoga

Carman, Judith E. *Yoga for Singing: A Developmental Tool for Technique and Performance.* New York: Oxford University Press, 2012.

Lister, Linda. *Yoga for Singers: Freeing Your Voice and Spirit through Yoga.* Raleigh, NC: Lulu Press, 2011.

ACTING

Adler, Stella. *The Art of Acting.* New York: Applause Books, 2000.

Bogart, Anne. *And Then, You Act: Making Art in an Unpredictable World.* New ed. New York: Routledge, 2007.

———. *Conversations with Anne.* New York: Theatre Communications Group, 2012.

———. *A Director Prepares: Seven Essays on Art and Theatre.* New York: Routledge, 2001.

———. *The Viewpoints Book: A Practical Guide to Viewpoints and Composition.* New York: Theatre Communications Group, 2004.

Brunetti, David. *Acting the Song.* Seattle, WA: BookSurge, 2006.

Chekhov, Michael. *On the Technique of Acting.* New York: Harper Perennial, 1993.

Cohen, Robert. *Acting Power.* Palo Alto, CA: Mayfield, 1998.

Hagen, Uta. *A Challenge for the Actor.* 10th ed. New York: Scribner, 1991.

———. *Respect for Acting*. 2nd ed. New York: Wiley, 2008.

Mamet, David. *True and False: Heresy and Common Sense for the Actor*. New York: Vintage Books, 1999.

Meisner, Sanford, and Dennis Longwell. *Sanford Meisner on Acting*. New York: Vintage Books, 1987.

Moore, Tracey, and Allison Bergman. *Acting the Song: Performance Skills for Musical Theatre*. New York: Allworth Press, 2008.

Ostwald, David F. *Acting for Singers: Creating Believable Singing Characters*. New York: Oxford University Press, 2005.

Spolin, Viola. *Improvisation for the Theater: A Handbook of Teaching and Directing Techniques*. 3rd ed. Evanston, IL: Northwestern University Press, 1999.

Stanislavski, Constantin. *An Actor Prepares*. Translated by Elizabeth Reynolds Hapgood. New York: Routledge, 1989.

———. *Becoming a Character*. Translated by Elizabeth Reynolds Hapgood. New York: Routledge, 1989.

———. *Creating a Role*. Translated by Elizabeth Reynolds Hapgood. New York: Routledge, 1989.

Strasberg, Lee. *A Dream of Passion: The Development of the Method*. New York: Plume, 1988.

Index

abdominal muscles, 5, 52, 61, 84
absurdity, 135
abuse, 53
a cappella, 159–60
accents, 97, 98, 116n1, 134
accompaniment: orchestration, 40–41; piano, 38–39, 123, 181–82
acid reflux, 51, 57–58
acting, 130–31, 143, 148, 169–70, 183
Adams, Yolanda, 151
admissions, 190
aerobic exercise, 10–11
aesthetic, tonal, 145
affirmations, 164
agility exercise, *10*
alcohol, 57, 58
allergies, 56
alto clefs, 40
Amazon Marketplace, 198
American art songs, 119–20
American diction, 97
American Idol, 192
American operetta, 133–34
America's Got Talent, 192
antibiotics, 59
antidepressants, 60
anxiety, 55, 60, 163–64, 191
appearance, 149
apples, 51
appoggio, 5–6, 22
apprenticeships, 187

arie antiche, 117–18
arrival rituals, 177
articulators, 64, 74
artistic fulfillment, 201
artists diplomas, 189–90
The Artist's Way (Cameron), 165
art songs, 116n3, 117–18; American, 119–20; British, 119–20; French, 123–24; German, 121–22; Nordic, 126; Russian, 125; Spanish, 125
Asanas, 61–62, 165. *See also* yoga
Astaire, Fred, 192
attire, 146, 155
auditions, 90, 178, 181; book, 148; choral singing, 200–201; fees, 199; graduate school, 190; MONC, 192; package, 190; for summer programs, 187–88
audits, 198
authentic performance. *See* historically informed performance
autistic spectrum, 169
avant-garde music, 140–41

Bach, Johann Sebastian, 127
backstage demands, 175
ballet, 147
bananas, 51
barbershop singing, 159–60
baroque, 10; *arie antiche* and, 117, 118; opera, 129; oratorio experiments in, 127–28; tuning, 138; vibrato, 26

Bartoli, Cecilia, 170
Barzun, Jacques, 123
bass clef, 40
Battle, Kathleen, 175
Beethoven, Ludwig Van, 129
bel canto tradition, 16, 27, 130
belting, 13, 147–48
belt-mix, 13, 148
biographies, 193
blocking, 52, 128, 131, 171–72, 183–84
blood pressure, 55
body: alignment, 1, *2–3*, 4, 73; Body Mapping, 61; mind and, 84–85; posture, 1, *2–3*, 4; spirit and, 95; type, 147; work, 61–62. *See also* breath; yoga
Boot Camp, 94
braces, 63–64
breath: *appoggio*, 5–6; clavicular, 73; connection with, 27; control, 5, 163; double kala technique, 5–6; exhalation, 5, 6; flow, 48; inhalation, 5, 22; *kala*, 5–6, 61, 163; management, 4, 5–7, 16, 25, 47, 52, 149, 152, 163; Pranayama, 61–62, 80, 163; recordings and, 87; *Shitali*, 61; *Ujjayi*, 55, 61, 163. *See also* yoga
Breath of Fire, 61
British art songs, 119–20
British diction, 97
Broadway, 147, 156
buccal speech, 140
budgeting, 197, 198, 199
business. *See* professionalism

Callas, Maria, 45, 165
camel pose, *166*
Cameron, Julia, 165
cantatas, 127
cardiovascular exercise, 52
Carey, Mariah, 15, 175
Cash, Johnny, 155
casting, 183–84
Catholic Church, 107
CCM. *See* contemporary commercial music

chamber music, 136–37
characterization, 171–72, 183
cheering, 53
chemistry, 173
Chenoweth, Kristin, 84, 179
chest voice, 12, 47, 152; chest-dominant, 148; female, 13
chiaroscuro, 8–9
choral conductors, 142–44
choral culture, 200
choral music, 142–44
choral singing, 200–201
chords, 36–37
choreography, 52, 134, 148, 171
Classical Singer, 188
classical singing, 65, 68
clavicular breathing, 73
clefs, 40
collaboration, 79, 181–84
collaborative pianists, 181–82
college degrees, 189–90
coloratura, 10–11
comic opera, 133
communication: collaboration and, 79; e-mail correspondence, 195, 200; of emotions, 165; facial expressions, 73, 168, 169, *170*; gestures, 152, 167–68, 169–70; skills, 195–96
compassion, 180
competitions, 90, 191
composers: genres of, 116nn2–3; intentions of, 31–32, 38–39, 116; rhythm and, 33
concentration, 179
conductors, 204; choral, 142–44; following, 185; frustration of, 40; job complexity of, 185; relationships with, 185–86; tempo and, 185
confidence, 164, 195
connection, 40
consonants, 16, 64, 67; of Finnish language, 113; of French language, 105–6; of German language, 104; of Hawaiian language, 113; IPA and, 99,

100; of Latin language, 107; legato and, 68; rhythm of, 68; of Russian language, *111*, 112; of Spanish language, 109; style and, 69; types of, 68
constructive criticism, 192
contacts, 195
contemporary commercial music (CCM), 20, 43, 65, 68, 145–46
contracts, 197
country music, 155–56
cover letters, 195
creativity, 177, 181
credit cards, 197
credit rating, 190
critique, 179–80
crowdfunding, 198
cultural context, 42–43
Cyrillic alphabet, *111*, 112
Czech language, 114

dairy products, 51
dance, 134, 148. *See also* choreography
d'Arezzo, Guido, 35–36
Da Vinci, Leonardo, *2*, *167*
debt, 190
debut, 183
degrees, 189–90, 202
dehydration, 45–46
dialects, 97, 98, 116n1
dialogue, 134
diaphragm, 5, 22
diction, 74, 97–98, 99
DiDonato, Joyce, 178, 191
diet, 51, 56, 57–58
digestion, 51, 57
diphthongs, 104
diplomas, 189–90
direction, 171–72, 175, 183–84
discipline, 42
discographies, 87
distractions, 20
diva/divo behavior, 173, 175–76
double kala technique, 5–6
Dreamgirls, 192

ear, nose, and throat doctors (ENTs), 49, 56
early music, 138–39
ear plugs, 53
ear-training, 40
education, 115, 161–62; finances, 190; masters degrees, 189–90, 202; student loans, 190
EGG. *See* electroglottograph
ego, 175–76
electroglottograph (EGG), 92, *93*
electronic devices, 80
Elliott, Martha, 43
Ellis, 165
e-mail correspondence, 195, 200
emoticons, 195
emotions, 165, 169–70
empathy, 185
employment opportunities, 161
energy, 46, 51, 149
English comic opera, 133
enrichment opportunities, 202
ENTs. *See* ear, nose, and throat doctors
environment, 53–54, 181
esophagus, 57
An Essay on French Verse: For Readers of English Poetry (Barzun), 123
ethnomusicology, 157
Etsy, 198
exercise, 52, 149
exhalation, 5, 6
expenses, 197–98
exploration, 172, 178
expression, 169–70
eyebrow acting, 169
eyes, 169

Fach system, 23–24, 143
facial expressions, 73, 168, 169, *170*
fact-based pedagogy, 22–23, 27
failure, 192
falsetto, 13–14, 149
fashion, 63
fatigue management, 20, 27, 201

feedback: constructive criticism, 192; objective, 76; recording, 76; video, 73, 168
feeling, 76–77, 84, 165, 169–70
festivals, 187, 201
fidgeting, 168
fight-or-flight response, 163, 164
finances, 27; budgeting, 197, 198, 199; education, 190; management of, 197–98
Finnish language, 113
Fischer-Dieskau, Dietrich, 33
fitness. *See* exercise
Fitzgerald, Ella, 11, 153
flageolet register, 14–15
Fleming, Renée, *49*, 163
flexibility, 10–11
florid music, 10
flow, 70
fluid intake. *See* hydration
focus, yoga and, 80–81
food, 198–99. *See also* diet
foreign languages, 74, 75, 99, 115, 116n1, 177
formants, 92
forward bend, 1, *3*
Franklin, Aretha, 165
freedom, 95
French art songs, 123–24
French language: consonants in, 105–6; difference between singing and speaking in, 106; vowels of, 105–6
fricative vocalese, *8*

gastroesophageal reflux disease (GERD), 57–58
genres, 43; of composers, 116nn2–3; style and, 145–46
GERD. *See* gastroesophageal reflux disease
German art songs, 121–22
German language, 103–4, 132; consonants of, 104; diphthongs in, 104; exception words of, 103–4, 107; schwas in, 104; vowels of, 103–4

gestures, 152, 167–68, 169–70
Gheorghiu, Angela, 171, 172, 183
Gilbert and Sullivan, *133*, 134, 135
Glee!, 95
glottal cycle, 92
glottal fry, 14, 140
glottis, 7
goals, 180
God, 151–52
golden rule, 175
Gold Wave, 94
Gospel music, 151–52, 167
graduate degrees, 189–90, 202
Grand Ole Opry, 156
grants, 190
Great American Songbook, 159–60
greatness, 178
Greek language, 114
Gregorian chant, 107
growling, 140
Guidonian Hand, *36*

Hampson, Thomas, 52
Handel, George Frideric, 127, 129–30
hands, 152, *167*, 168
hands-on practices, 84
handwritten repetition, 82
harmony, barbershop singing, 159–60
hashtags, 194
Hawaiian language, 113
Haydn, Franz Joseph, 127
head voice, 12, 13, 47
health, 131
hearing, 53
heart, 165
heart-openers, 165, *166*
herbal medication, 59
historically informed performance (HIP), 138–39
historical maxims, 22
holistic teachers, 28
honesty, 193
hormonal medication, 60
Houston, Whitney, 165

humidifiers, 56
humility, 176
humming, 8, 20, 49
Hunter, David, 123
Huxley, Aldous, 159
hydration, 21, 45–46, 51, 56, 71
hypermeter, 33–34

ibn Firnas, Abbas, 95n1
imagery, 22
improvisation, 83, 153
IMSLP. *See* International Music Score Library Project
industry facts, 161–62
inflammation, 56
inhalation, 5, 22
inhaled singing, 141
inspiration, 178
Instagram, 194
instruments, period, 138
intentions, 165
International Italian School, 20, 27, 102, 118
International Music Score Library Project (IMSLP), 31
International Phonetic Alphabet (IPA), 32, 65–66, 98, 99, *100*, 116n1
international programs, 187
Internet, 204
interpersonal skills, 195–96
interpretation, 31–32
intervals, 35–37
intonation, 76
IPA. *See* International Phonetic Alphabet
iPads, 94
iPhones, 94
Italian language, 102; *arie antiche*, 117–18; legato, 101; phonetics of, 101; vowels of, 101

Jackson, Mahalia, *151*, 152
Jackson, Phil, 180
jaw: alignment, 73; braces, 63–64; tension, 18–19, 51, 63; tongue and, 74; underbite, 64

jazz, 181; scatting, 11, 153–54; standards, 153–54; vibrato in, 153
"Johnny One Note," 75
Journal of Singing, 202
joy, 95

kala breath, 5–6, 61, 163
Karaoke, 150

Lamperti, Giovanni Battista, 1, 27
Lang, Jonny, *170*
language: accents, 97, 98, 116n1; Czech, 114; dialects, 97, 98, 116n1; English, 97–98; Finnish, 113; foreign, 74, 75, 99, 115, 116n1, 177; French, 105–6; German, 103–4, 107, 132; Greek, 114; Hawaiian, 113; Italian, 101–2, 117–18; Latin, 107–8; Nordic, 126; Polish, 114; Portuguese, 114; rhythm and, 33; Russian, *111*, 112; Scandinavian, 113; skills, 16; software, 115; Spanish, 109–10; translation of, 115–16. *See also* consonants; vowels
laryngopharyngeal reflux disease (LPRD), 57–58
larynx, 4, 12, 57
lateness, 177–78
Latin language, 108; consonants of, 107; vowels of, 107
learning styles, 28–29
legato, 16–17, 66, 75, 143; consonants and, 68; Italian language, 101
lessons, 28–29; plan, 70; preparation for, 70–71, 179; presence during, 179; recording, 70, 90. *See also* teachers
letters of recommendation, 184
liaison, 82
Lieder, 121–22
light opera, 132–35
lips: position, 72; trills, 20, 49; vowels and, 103
listening: active, 154; feeling and, 76–77; to recordings, 86–87; too much, 76–77
locust pose, *166*

Lombard effect, 53–54
long-term medication, 59–60
Lopez, Jennifer, 175
lotus pose, *164*
loud environments, 53–54
love, 95
LPRD. *See* laryngopharyngeal reflux disease
Lully, Jean-Baptiste, 129

Maelzel, Johann, 78
manners, 175
Marchesi vocal method, 10
marketplace, 161–62
masters degrees, 189–90, 202
meals, 198, 199
mechanistic teachers, 28
medication, 59
meditation, 163, *164*, 191
melismatic singing, 10–11
mélodies, 86, 105, 113, 123–24
memorization, 82–83, 115, 128
memory, yoga and, 83
mental health, 152
Merman, Ethel, 13, 147
metronomes, 32, 33, 78–79, 95n1
Metropolitan Opera National Council (MONC) Auditions, 192
microphones, 149
Miller, Donald, 92
Miller, Richard, 7
mind: body and, 84–85; presence of, 179
mindfulness, 80, 180
mirror, for practice, 72, 169
mission statement, 165
mix, 14
mixed register, 12–13
mobility, 84
modern science, 20, 22
MONC. *See* Metropolitan Opera National Council Auditions
Monteverdi, Claudio, 129
Moore, Gerald, 33
mountain pose, 1
movement, 131, 134

Mozart, Wolfgang Amadeus, 130, 132, 144n2
mucus production, 51, 56
multiphonics, 141
muscle control, 61
musical goals, 42–43
musical theatre, 20, 135, 147–48, 161
musical transition points, 185
musicianship, 32–33
musicology, 127, 144n3

nasal resonance, 50
Nashville, 156
Nashville Star, 192
National Association of Teachers of Singing (NATS), 202, 204
National Center for Voice and Speech (NCVS), 49
NATS. *See* National Association of Teachers of Singing
NCVS. *See* National Center for Voice and Speech
N'Dour, Youssou, 157
nervous tics, 168
Neti pot, 56
Netrebko, Anna, 185
networking, 195, 204–5
New York Singing Teachers Association (NYSTA), 202–3, 204
niche, 149
nonattachment, 191
non-legato, 143
nonsteroidal NSAIDs, 59
Nordic art songs, 126
NYSTA. *See* New York Singing Teachers Association

online resources, 31
onset and release, 7
openness, 172, 180
opera, 101–2, 130–31, 142; baroque, 129; direction, 183–84; English comic, 133; light, 132–35; scores, 32; *zarzuela*, 109–10, 132, 134
opéra bouffe, 132

operatic head voice, 13
operatic release, 7
operetta, 132–35
oral repetition, 82
oral tradition, 27
oratorio, 32, 127–28
orchestra, 185–86
orchestration, 40–41
organizations, 204–5
ornamentation, early music, 139
OTC. *See* over-the-counter
overhydration, 46
over-the-counter (OTC), 59
overtones, 141
overuse, 53

Parallels Desktop, 94
partnerships, 173–75
Parton, Dolly, 155
Passagio, 14
Pavarotti, Luciano, 51
performance: anxiety, 55, 60, 163–64, 191; energy and, 149; HIP, 138–39; interaction with performers during, 173–75; pre, 21; résumé, 190; rituals, 51, 55; safety and chemistry in, 173–74
period instruments, 138
period performance. *See* historically informed performance
Perry, Katy, *63*, 175
personality type, 23
Peters, Bernadette, *147*
Phlegm, 56
phonation, 7; straw, 20, *49*, 50; threshold, 50
phrasing, 153
physicality, 84–85
piano accompaniment, 38–39, 123, 181–82
Pilates, 61
pitch: contexts of, 35–37; range, optimal, 47–48
placing, 18–19
poetry: French, 123–24; German romantic, 121–22; Russian, 125
Polish language, 114

pop music, 149
Portuguese language, 114
positivity, 195
posture, 1, *2–3*, 4
practice, 42, 72, 115. *See also* rehearsals
Pranayama, 61–62, 80, 163. *See also* breath; yoga
preparation, 70–71, 177–78, 179, 183
presence of mind, 179
pressure, 163, 191
Price, Leontyne, 27
procrastination, 71
production, 183–84
productivity, 177
professionalism, 173–76; collaboration, 181–84; communication skills, 195–96; conductor relationships, 185–86; management of finances, 197–98; relationship with teachers, 179–80; résumé, 193–94; self-representation, 193–94
professional organizations, 204–5
projection, 8, 53
promotion, 197
pronunciation, 70, 97, 177. *See also* consonants; vowels
proofreading, 193, 195
punctuality, 177–78
Purcell, Henry, 129

Qualified Performing Artist Deduction, 198
quality. *See* timbre

rag doll pose, 1, *3*
Rameau, Jean-Philippe, 129
range, 23–24
reading music, 31–32
recitalists, 167
recitals, 137
recitation, 82
recitative, 127–28
recording industry, 86
recordings: of barbershop singing, 160; breath and, 87; discographies, 87;

feedback, 76; lessons, 70, 90; listening to, 86–87; scores and, 86; speaking voice, 47; style and, 87; yourself, 76, 90–91
Reeves, Dianne, 11, 153
regionalism, 97
registration, 12–15, 145
rehearsals, 40; attendance and punctuality at, 177–78; techniques for chamber music, 136
repertoire selection, 23–24
repetition, 82
resonance, 8–9, 17, 18, 48, 142, 145; early music, 139; formants and, 92; nasal, 50; opera and, 130; vowels and, 65–67
Resonance in Singing (Miller), 92
resourcefulness, 204–5
respect, 175–76, 180, 181
respiratory muscles, 50
rest, 53
résumé, 190, 193–94
rhythm, 32; composers and, 33; of consonants, 68; hypermeter, 33–34; integrity of, 34; internalization of, 33; language and, 33; macro aspects of, 33; micro aspects of, 33. *See also* metronomes
rib cage isolations, 74
riffs, 10–11
rituals, 51, 55
rock music, 149
role study, 177
romanticism, 121–22
romantic relationships, 173
Ronstadt, Linda, 174
Rossini, Gioachino, 185
runs, 10–11
Russian art songs, 125
Russian language: consonants of, *111*, 112; Cyrillic alphabet of, *111*, 112; vowels of, *111*, 112

sacred music, 116n2
safety, 173
saving money, 198

scale degrees, 35–37
Scandinavian languages, 113
scatting, 11, 153–54
Schoenberg, Arnold, 144n4
scholarships, 188
schwas, in German language, 104
scores, 31–32; orchestration, 40–41, 185; piano accompaniment, 38–39; preparation of, 37; recordings and, 86
screaming, 53, 141
self-reliance, 180
self-representation, 193
self-serving, 183
semi-occluded vocal tract (SOVT), 16, 20, 49–50
sensation, 18
service, 183–84
sheet music, 31–32
Shitali breath, 61
short-term medication, 59
should stand and plow pose, *83*
sight reading, 36, 201
Singing in Style: A Guide to Vocal Performance Practices (Elliott), 43
skill sets, 161
sleep deprivation, 71
Smith, Michael W., 23
smoke, 53
social media, 194
social responsibility, 158
soft palette, 22
software, language, 115
solfège system, 35–37
solo classical singing, 26
Somatic Voicework, 14
songs, 153–54. *See also* art songs
Sontag, Susan, 42
SoundCloud, 90
soundtracks, 95
SOVT. *See* semi-occluded vocal tract
Spanish art songs, 125
Spanish language, 110; consonants of, 109; vowels of, 109
speaking voice, 47–48
spectrographic analysis, 92, *93*, 94

Spectrum View, 94
speech-language pathologists, 50
spine, 1, *2*
spirit, body and, 95
sports psychology, 191
Spotify, 86, 204
Sprechstimme, 141, 144n4
stage crew, 176
stage direction, 171–72, 175, 183–84
stage fright, 163–64
stage presence, 131
staging, 171
stamina, 152
steroids, 59
stock gestures, 168
storytelling, 168
straight-tone singing, 26, 160
straining, 53
straw phonation, 20, *49*, 50
streamlining, 193
Streisand, Barbra, 163
stress, 52, 163, 201
structure, 153–54
The Structure of Singing (Miller), 7
student loans, 190
style, 26, 42–43; attire and, 146, 155; consonants and, 69; genres and, 145–46; niche, 149; recording and, 87; vowels and, 65–67
subdivisions, 78
success, 179, 180
summer programs, 187–88
support, 176
survival, 164
symphonies, 185–86

TA dominant, 148
talent, 176, 181
tardiness, 177–78
taxes, 197–98
teachers, 28–29, 43, 49, 70–71, 179–80, 190, 202, 204. *See also* lessons
technology, 80, 204
television shows, 192
tempo, 78, 185

tenor clefs, 40
tessitura, 23
text messages, 195
text painting, 121
texts, 33
thinking, 84–85
third eye, 22, 169
throat clearing, 55, 56
throat singing, 141
throat sprays, 59
thyroid, 60
timbre, 23, 47
Tin Pan Alley, 159–60
Titze, Ingo, *49*, 50
tonal aesthetic, 145
tone, 8–9
tongue, 64; jaw and, 74; position, 72; vowels and, 103
tongue tension, 18–19
tongue trills, 49
Tourette's syndrome, 169
touring, 149
traditions, 42–43, 113, 178
translations, 115–16, 177
transpositions, 181
traveling, 52, 198
treble clef, 40
tree pose, 80, *81*
tremolo, 25
truthfulness, 193
tuning, baroque, 138
Tuvan throat singing, 141
24 Italian Songs and Arias, 117–18

Ujjayi breathing, 55, 61, 163
ululation, 141
underbite, 64
Understanding French Verse: A Guide for Singers (Hunter), 123
unintentional movements, 168
upstaging, 173
"Ut Queant Laxis," *35*

Vaccai method, 101
vibration, 18

vibrato, 11, 25, 66, 145; in barbershop singing, 160; baroque, 26; in choral music, 143; control of, 148, 160; early music, 139; in jazz, 153
video feedback, 73, 168
Viennese operetta, 132–33
visualization, 82
vocal abuse, 53
vocal breaks, 53
vocal chamber music, 136
vocal cords, 55
vocalese, *8*, 20
vocal folds, 7, 18, 25, 45, 50, 57
vocal freedom, 74
vocal fry, 47
vocal-health professionals, 49, 50
vocal lines, 38–39
vocal parts, 177
vocal quality, 130
vocal tract, 25, 65, 92
Vocal Wisdom (Lamperti), 1, 27
VoceVista software, 92, *93*, 94
The Voice, 192
voice classification, 23
voice competition, 191
Voice Foundation, 49
voice production, 42
voice scientists, 49
vowels, 8, 16, 64; in choral music, 142; closed, 103; of Finnish language, 113; formation of, 65, *66*, 67; of French language, 105–6; of German language, 103–4; of Hawaiian language, 113; IPA and, 99, *100*; of Italian language, 101; of Latin language, 107; lips and, 103; mixed, 103; modification of, 18; naturalness of, 67; open, 103; purity of, 98; resonance and, 65–67; of Russian language, *111*, 112; of Spanish language, 109; style and, 65–67; tongue and, 103

warming up, 20–21, 50, 52
warrior pose, *62*
water. *See* hydration
water bottles, 45
websites, 88
wobble, 25
world music, 157–58

YAP Tracker, 188, 197
yodeling, 141
yoga, 56; Asanas, 61–62, 165; Bikram, 46; Breath of Fire, 61; camel pose, *166*; focus and, 80–81; forward bend, 1, *3*; heart-openers, 165, *166*; locust pose, *166*; lotus pose, *164*; memory and, 83; mountain pose, 1; Pranayama, 61–62, 80, 163; rag doll pose, 1, *3*; shoulder stand and plow pose, *83*; tree pose, 80, *81*; as warm-up, 52; warrior pose, *62*. *See also* breath
young artist programs, 187, 199
YouTube, 86, 88–89, 204

zarzuela, 109–10, 132, 134
Zeffirelli, Franco, 171, 172

About the Authors

Matthew Hoch is associate professor of voice and coordinator of the vocal studies at Auburn University, where he teaches applied voice, diction, and vocal literature courses. Prior to this position, he spent six years as assistant professor of voice at Shorter College, where he taught applied voice, vocal literature, and served as coordinator of vocal studies. Dr. Hoch's students have gone on to successful careers in both classical and musical theatre genres and have won awards from the Metropolitan Opera National Council, National Association of Teachers of Singing (NATS), Music Teachers National Association, American College Theater Festival, and others.

As a professional baritone, Dr. Hoch has appeared as a soloist with the Oregon Bach Festival, Atlanta Baroque Orchestra, Harmonie Universelle, Trinity Church Boston, Santa Fe Desert Chorale, and with the Hartford, Nashua, and Rome Symphony Orchestras. His first book, *A Dictionary for the Modern Singer*, was released by Rowman & Littlefield in 2014, and his second book, *Welcome to Church Music and the Hymnal 1982*, was released in 2015. His recent articles have appeared in the *Journal of Singing*, *Opera Journal*, the *Journal of the Association of Anglican Musicians*, and the *Chorister*. From 2008 to 2016, he served as editor in chief of *VOICEPrints: The Official Journal of NYSTA*. He has been the recipient of many awards, including the 2007 NATS Voice Pedagogy Award and the 2016 Van Lawrence Fellowship, given jointly by the Voice Foundation and NATS.

In addition, Dr. Hoch has presented his research at many national and international conferences, including the International Congress of Voice Teachers, Pan-European Voice Conference, Pan-American Vocology Association, National Association of Teachers of Singing, National Opera Association, National Association for Music Education, College Music Society, Hawaii International Conference on Arts and Humanities, International Horn Symposium, Hymn Society in the United States and Canada, Southeastern Theatre Conference, the

Voice Foundation Symposium in Philadelphia, and the International Symposium on Singing and Song in St. John's, Newfoundland and Labrador. He is a "double alumnus" of the NATS Intern Program, completing the program as an intern in 2006 and hosting the program at Shorter College in 2009.

Dr. Hoch earned the bachelor of music degree (summa cum laude) from Ithaca College with a triple major in vocal performance, music education, and music theory; the master of music degree from the Hartt School in vocal performance and music history; the doctor of musical arts degree from the New England Conservatory in vocal performance; and the certificate in vocology from the National Center for Voice and Speech. He has pursued additional studies in voice science and pedagogy with Scott McCoy, Johann Sundberg, and Ingo Titze and is a three-level graduate of Somatic VoiceWork™ with Jeannette LoVetri. In addition to his academic life, Dr. Hoch serves as choirmaster and minister of music at Holy Trinity Episcopal Church in Auburn, Alabama, where he lives with his wife, Theresa, and three children, Hannah, Sofie, and Zachary.

A Phi Beta Kappa graduate of Vassar College, **Linda Lister** received her master of music degree from the Eastman School of Music and her doctor of musical arts degree in voice performance from the University of North Carolina at Greensboro. The Durham *Herald-Sun* has described her singing as "gloriously refulgent, with a brightly etched sound that enchanted," while the *Buffalo News* praised her "strong, shimmering soprano."

Her solo credits include performances with the Washington Symphony Orchestra, Buffalo Philharmonic, Evansville Philharmonic, Las Vegas Philharmonic, Piedmont Opera Theatre, Opera Theatre of Rochester (NY), Long Leaf Opera, Greensboro Oratorio Society, Rome Bach Festival, Cambridge Gilbert and Sullivan Society, Clocktower Jazz, and Maine State Music Theatre. She created the role of Madge in the world premiere of Libby Larsen's opera *Picnic* (2009) and sang Savannah in the world premiere concert version of *The Prince of Tides* (2010) with the Carolina Master Chorale. Her favorite roles include Musetta in *La bohème*, Adina in *L'elisir d'amore*, Adele in *Die Fledermaus*, Maggie in *A Chorus Line*, and Woman 1 in *Songs for a New World*.

Her writings have been featured in the *Journal of Singing*, *American Music Teacher*, *Opera Journal*, *Classical Singer*, *VOICEPrints*, and *Popular Music and Society*. A certified CorePower Yoga teacher, she is the author of the books *Yoga for Singers: Freeing Your Voice and Spirit through Yoga* (2011) and *Red Rock Mantras* (2016). She has done presentations on yoga for musicians at the University of Evansville, Auburn University, University of Tennessee–Knoxville, University of Wisconsin–Stevens Point, University of Kentucky, Columbus State University, Clayton State University, Campbell University, Druid City Opera

Workshop, Taos Opera Institute, Big Yoga Houston, and Bija Yoga NYC, as well as at national conventions of the College Music Society, National Opera Association, and NATS; the Sixth International Conference on the Physiology and Acoustics of Singing; and the 2013 International Congress of Voice Teachers.

Winner of the 2014 American Prize in Directing, she directed UNLV Opera to two first-place awards in the 2015 National Opera Association Collegiate Opera Scenes Competition in both musical theatre and graduate opera divisions. She is the soprano soloist on the Centaur Records CD *Moments of Arrival* (2016) as well as the Albany Records releases *The American Soloist* and *Midnight Tolls* with the Dvořák Symphony Orchestra. Also a composer, she has written a number of vocal works, including *Pleas to Famous Fairies*, *Bring Me the Wine of Love*, *Flags: Summer of 2015*, and a chamber opera about the Brontë sisters titled *How Clear She Shines!* Dr. Lister is director of opera theater and associate professor of music at the University of Nevada, Las Vegas.